50 Hikes in Southern Virginia

50 *Hikes*

In Southern Virginia

From the Cumberland Gap to the Atlantic Ocean

LEONARD M. ADKINS

Second Edition

The Countryman Press
Woodstock, Vermont

Note: Many water sources are identified for hikers' convenience, but this is not an endorsement of their purity. All water should be treated before consuming.

With time, access points may change, and trails, signs, and landmarks referred to in this book may be altered. If you find that such changes have occurred on the trails described in this book, please let the author and the publisher know so that corrections may be made in future editions. The author and publisher also welcome other comments and suggestions. Address all correspondence to:

The Countryman Press
P.O. Box 748
Woodstock, VT 05091

ISBN 978-0-88150-728-7

Text and cover design by Glenn Suokko
Composition by Doug Porter, Desktop Services & Publishing, San Antonio, TX
Maps by Mapping Specialists Ltd., Madison, WI
Cover photograph of Cumberland Gap National Historical Park © Laurence Parent
All interior photographs by Leonard M. Adkins

Published by The Countryman Press, P.O. Box 748, Woodstock, Vermont 05091

Distributed by W.W. Norton & Company, Inc., 500 Fifth Avenue, New York, NY 10110

Printed in the United States of America

10 9 8 7 6 5 4 3 2 1

What joy awaits you,
when the breeze hath found you out among the trees,
and calls you forth again!
—*Wordsworth*

OTHER BOOKS BY LEONARD M. ADKINS

*50 Hikes in Northern Virginia: Walks, Hikes, and Backpacks
from the Allegheny Mountains to the Chesapeake Bay*

*50 Hikes in Maryland: Walks, Hikes, and Backpacks
from the Allegheny Plateau to the Atlantic Ocean*

*50 Hikes in West Virginia:
From the Allegheny Mountains to the Ohio River*

Maryland: An Explorer's Guide

The Appalachian Trail: A Visitor's Companion

Wildflowers of the Appalachian Trail
(with photographers Joe and Monica Cook)

Best of the Appalachian Trail: Day Hikes
(with Victoria and Frank Logue)

Best of the Appalachian Trail: Overnight Hikes
(with Victoria and Frank Logue)

Wildflowers of the Blue Ridge and Great Smoky Mountains
(with photographer Joe Cook)

West Virginia: An Explorer's Guide

Seashore State Park: A Walking Guide

*Walking the Blue Ridge:
A Guide to the Trails of the Blue Ridge Parkway*

Adventure Guide to Virginia

The Caribbean: A Walking and Hiking Guide

Dedicated to the memories of Michael J. Pauley, Chris Deffler, Leonard Wilson Adkins, Steve Shipe, Bill Foot, and Gary Close. All good trail companions now walking the pathways of a different place.

50 Hikes at a Glance

HIKE	REGION
1. First Landing State Park	Eastern Virginia
2. Back Bay and False Cape	Eastern Virginia
3. Northwest River	Eastern Virginia
4. Great Dismal Swamp	Eastern Virginia
5. Dismal Town Boardwalk	Eastern Virginia
6. Hog Island	Eastern Virginia
7. Petersburg National Battlefield	Central Virginia
8. Pocahontas State Park	Central Virginia
9. Amelia Wildlife Management Area	Central Virginia
10. Twin Lakes State Park	Central Virginia
11. Kerr Reservoir	Central Virginia
12. Occoneechee State Park	Central Virginia
13. Staunton River State Park	Central Virginia
14. Appomattox History Trail	Central Virginia
15. Blackwater Creek	Central Virginia
16. Fairy Stone State Park	Central Virginia
17. The Appalachian Trail and the Mount Rogers NRA	The Blue Ridge Region
18. Mount Rogers	The Blue Ridge Region
19. Buzzard Rock	The Blue Ridge Region
20. Virginia Creeper Trail	The Blue Ridge Region
21. Grayson Highlands	The Blue Ridge Region
22. Iron Mountain	The Blue Ridge Region
23. Comers Creek Falls	The Blue Ridge Region
24. Rowlands Creek Falls	The Blue Ridge Region
25. Hungry Mother State Park	The Blue Ridge Region

W=Water views
M=Mountain views
D=Developed camping available within the park
B=Backcountry camping
* =For kids with a bit of stamina

DISTANCE (in miles)	VIEWS	GOOD FOR KIDS	WATERFALLS	CAMPING	NOTES
11.4	W			D	Swamps, Spanish moss and cypress trees in VA Beach
23.7	W			B	Miles of Atlantic beaches untouched by development
4.5	W	★		D	Cypress knees and easy walking
9.0	W				One of only two natural lakes in Virginia
1.0		★			Easy introduction to Dismal Swamp
4.0	W	★			Refuge for tens of thousands of geese and ducks
6.7					Site of longest siege in U.S. military history
2.5	W	★		D	Wealth of birds, mammals and scenery near Richmond
7.75	W			B	Few marked trails; for the experienced hiker
4.9	W	★*		D	A circumambulation of two lakes
7.2	W				Most isolated hike in Central Virginia; lightly used
2.4		★		D	An exploration of Occoneechee Plantation and environs
7.5	W			D	A walk beside three different bodies of water
4.0					Retraces the final days of the Civil War
5.7		★*			A backcountry experience inside Lynchburg
6.4	W,M			D	A chance to hunt for fairy stones
17.1	M			B	Like being in Montana and Wyoming
19.2	M			B	A visit to the state's highest point
3.3	M	★		B	A naturally-occurring mountain bald
17.4	M		★	B	Virginia's most scenic rail-trail; totally downhill
8.3	M		★	D,B	Wild ponies, great views and waterfalls
14.1	M			D,B	Near Beartree Lake, a great spot for the entire family
8.9	M		★	D,B	Public outcry saved it from four-lane highway
11.8			★	B	Numerous 50–100-foot falls
5.9	W,M			D,B	One of Virginia's first state parks; lake & mountain views

50 Hikes at a Glance

HIKE	REGION
26. Burke's Garden and the Appalachian Trail	The Blue Ridge Region
27. Little Wolf Creek	The Blue Ridge Region
28. Dismal Creek and Sugar Run Mountain	The Blue Ridge Region
29. Huckleberry Ridge Loop	The Blue Ridge Region
30. Barneys Wall and The Cascades	The Blue Ridge Region
31. Mountain Lake	The Blue Ridge Region
32. Wind Rock	The Blue Ridge Region
33. Virginia's Triple Crown	The Blue Ridge Region
34. Potts Mountain	The Blue Ridge Region
35. Patterson and Price Mountains	The Blue Ridge Region
36. Lake Robertson	The Blue Ridge Region
37. House Mountain	The Blue Ridge Region
38. The Maury River	The Blue Ridge Region
39. Fallingwater Cascades	The Blue Ridge Region
40. Devil's Marbleyard	The Blue Ridge Region
41. Pinnacle Natural Area Preserve	Far Southwest Virginia
42. Natural Tunnel	Far Southwest Virginia
43. Breaks	Far Southwest Virginia
44. Red Fox Trail	Far Southwest Virginia
45. North Fork of Pound Reservoir	Far Southwest Virginia
46. Chief Benge Scout Trail	Far Southwest Virginia
47. Little Stony Creek	Far Southwest Virginia
48. Stone Mountain	Far Southwest Virginia
49. Cumberland Gap National Historical Park	Far Southwest Virginia
50. Cumberland Mountain	Far Southwest Virginia

DISTANCE (in miles)	VIEWS	GOOD FOR KIDS	WATERFALLS	CAMPING	NOTES
12.6	M			B	Spectacular views into "God's Thumbprint"
10.5	M			B	Two loops; could be done at different times
9.6	M		★	B	Has all the elements of a great day hike
9.0				B	Rugged hike; for those with route-finding experience
4.9	M		★	B	Outstanding view and waterfalls; very popular
6.4	W,M				One of Virginia's two natural lakes
0.6	M	★		B	Easiest hike in book, but one of most outstanding views
35.9	M			B	Considered by many to be Virginia's best three views
5.8	M			B	Outstanding vistas on a rarely-used trail
15.7	M			B	A hike upon two parallel ridges
5.1	W,M			D	With amenities like a commercial campground-resort
6.4	M	★*		B	Good introduction to hiking and backcountry camping
6.2	W	★*			Miles of level walking; easy for older kids
1.6	M	★	★	D	One of the most popular hikes on the Blue Ridge Parkway
8.2	M			B	One of the largest boulder fields in Southern Appalachians
4.6	M	★*	★		Wide waterfall, spectacular view, and rare species
4.3	M	★		D	850-foot long, 175-foot high, 100-foot wide natural tunnel
3.7	M	★		D	Largest canyon east of the Mississippi
2.3		★		B	Has many historical aspects
3.2	W			B	Possibly the least-visited designated campsite in Virginia
16.1	M			D,B	Downhill all the way, many wading pools
2.9		★	★	B	Three major falls & dozens of small cascades
14.2	M			B	Challenging hike on isolated terrain
10.8	M			D,B	A circuit hike from the lowlands to mountain crest
20.6	M			B	Reconstructed mountain community, views, possibly elk!

W=Water views
M=Mountain views
D=Developed camping available within the park
B=Backcountry camping
* =For kids with a bit of stamina

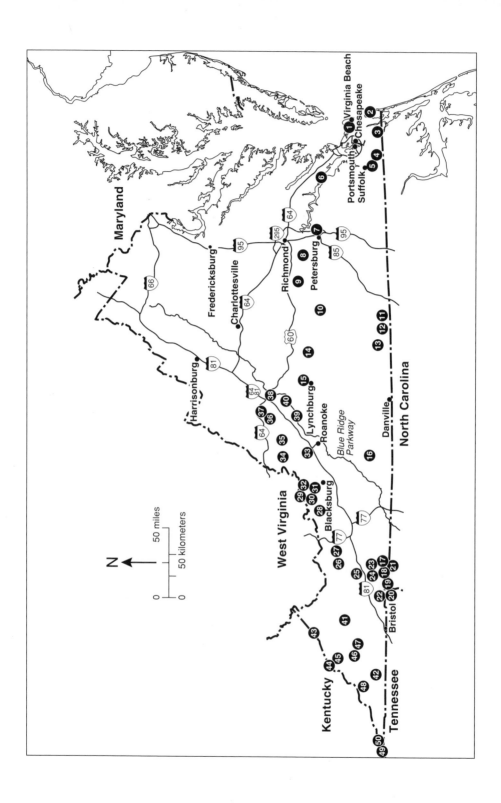

Contents

FAR SOUTHWEST VIRGINIA

Acknowledgments

I am always pleasantly surprised that so many people willingly give of their expertise, knowledge, and time to help me make a book as complete and accurate as possible. Without such unselfish aid, this book would have never have been written. Thank you for your guidance, assistance, and support:

Rick Bently, Pat Eagan, Jerry Jacobsen, Bob McKinney, and John Stollard with the U.S. Forest Service; Ann Blumenshine, Carol Borneman, Brian Eick, Reed Johnson, and Bobby D. Miller with the U.S. National Park Service; Lloyd Calp and Teresa M. Cherry with the U.S. Fish and Wildlife Service; Joseph Boswell and Edwin Iverson Ryland, Jr., with the U.S. Army Corps of Engineers; Paul Anderson, Kyle L. Barbour, Major Benton, Joshua Ellington, Fred Hazelwood, Marty McConnell, James P. Morgan, Ann L. Reeder, Craig Seaver, Scott Shanklin, Harvey Thompson, Theresa M. Tibbs, and Ann E. Zahn with the Virginia Department of Conservation and Recreation; Cale L. Godfrey with the Virginia Department of Game and Inland Fisheries; Claiborne A. Woodall with the Virginia Division of Natural Heritage; Wayne Nicely with Lake A. Willis Robertson; Jim Douglass with the City of Lynchburg Parks and Recreation Department; Lee Browder with the Petersburg Convention & Visitors Bureau; Jean Clark with Lexington Tourism Development; Becky Cutchims and Keith Toler with the Portsmouth Convention and Visitors Bureau; Karen Cox with Best Western, Marion; Lousie K. Dooley with the VMI Foundation, Inc.; Rosa Lee Jude with the Wytheville Convention and Visitor's Bureau; Royster Lyle, Jr., with the Rockbridge Area Conservation Council; Robin Magrisi with Barker, Campbell, Farley & Mansfield; Kathryn Mayer with Colonial Inn, Virginia Beach; Dave Deshler, Jason Nicolai and Buzz Scanland with Mountain Lake; Geneva O'Quinn with the Heart of Appalachia Tourism Authority; Bill Petree and Kevin S. Kaul with the City of Chesapeake; Beth and John Reese with the Apple Tree B&B, Damascus; Sherry Reeter and Kitty Ward with the Virginia Southwest Blue Ridge Highlands, Inc.; Katherine Wright with the Surry County Tourism Bureau; Roger and Janet Serens with The Inn at Union Run, Lexington; Blue Blaze Bike and Shuttle Service, Damascus; Dan Hall Mountain Resort; Meadows of Dan Campground; New River Inn and Bookstore; Surry House Restaurant and Country Inn.

Dr. Stephen Lewis, Caroline Charonko, Terry and Susie—it has been more than a decade now. Thank you.

Nancy Adkins and Kathleen, John, Tim and Jay Yelenic—a more supportive family would be impossible to find.

Laurie—You are the center of my universe.

Introduction

This book has been a long time coming. Upon completion of *50 Hikes in Northern Virginia* nearly a decade before, the plan had been to follow it immediately with a southern counterpart. However, life, as it is wont to do, took me upon many a divergent path. In addition to family happinesses and sorrows, opportunities to travel and hike in the American West, the Caribbean, Iceland, and a fourth complete traverse of the Appalachian Trail presented themselves and could not be ignored. The writing of various books based on those and other travels occupied several more years.

Through it all, though, the vision of *50 Hikes in Southern Virginia* remained, and finally it is here. What a joy it has been once again to turn my efforts to the area in which I make my home. Virginia is a beautiful state, full of cultural, topographic, floral, and faunal diversity, and it was a grand journey reacquainting myself with familiar places and discovering new delights.

This book will take you on your own travels from southern Virginia's lowest point on the Atlantic coast to its loftiest mountain more than 5,000 feet above sea level, and from its easternmost point to its very western tip—farther west than Columbus, Ohio. As I stated in the Northern Virginia book, only a person traveling by foot can truly see and appreciate all of the natural wonders to be found in Virginia.

In the eastern part of the state, you can walk for miles upon undeveloped, isolated sandy beaches, stroll beside tannin-stained swamps bordered by cypress trees festooned with luxuriant folds of Spanish moss, and hike out across Tidewater lands preserved as refuges for tens of thousands of migrating birds. Upon the rolling piedmont of central Virginia are historic sites from the days of the Civil War, hikes around lakes both large and small, open meadows and deep forestlands, and a backcountry experience within the center of one of the state's larger towns.

It may take a greater amount of physical energy to negotiate the ups and downs found within the Blue Ridge region, but the rewards more than compensate. Here your gaze extends for miles upon wave after wave of Southern Appalachian ridgelines, dozens of waterfalls rush down steep slopes, hundreds of miles of the Appalachian Trail course over the mountains and into lush hardwood coves, and the opportunities to backcountry camp well isolated from the modern world are limitless.

The pathways in far southwest Virginia can be even more rugged and remote, going over terrain that may rarely be walked upon by human feet. Hemlock-lined mountain streams, deep gorges, and an abundance of deer, black bears, coyotes, and other wildlife are the norm rather than the exception.

Although this book contains pages of interpretive information about the human and natural history you will experience, there is certainly much more to be learned than can be presented here. To help you gain an even greater awareness, enjoyment, and understanding of your surroundings, I urge you to read, and possibly carry, some additional books and field guides, and the "Suggested Readings and Field Guides" section near the end of this Introduction is a good place to start.

Like other guidebooks, this one will direct you to the most popular hikes to be found within a particular region, but it will also open up marvelous new areas that are too often overlooked. With descriptions of more than 400 miles of trails, this book offers hikes for every degree of physical stamina and every time constraint. Mirroring the bounty of outdoor opportunities in southern Virginia is the fact that, no matter where you happen to be at any given moment (south of US 60), you will never be more than a 30-minute drive from one of the hikes.

One of the Mid-Atlantic states, Virginia can experience a wide range of temperatures and weather conditions. Winters can be unpredictably cold or relatively mild, while summers can become hot and humid or may be rather temperate. Spring and autumn can be the most pleasant times of the year to be outdoors, as days warm up to a comfortable temperature, nights cool down for easy sleeping, and crowds are fewer. Snow is common in the mountains, moderate in the central regions, and quite infrequent in eastern Virginia. When heat and humidity take the joy and fun out of outdoor activities in the eastern portion of the state, the mountains beckon with temperatures that can be 10 or more degrees lower.

Be willing to visit an area more than once and do not limit your outings in southern Virginia to just one or two seasons. Outdoor adventuring here can be a year-round activity.

In putting this book together, it has been my desire that it will inspire you to visit, appreciate, and learn more about the best that the commonwealth has to offer. If you need an additional incentive to get you going, I offer one final bit of advice from the well-loved children's book *The Wind in the Willows:* "Take the adventure, heed the call, now, ere the irrevocable moment passes. 'Tis but a banging of the door behind you, a blithesome step forward, and you are out of the old life and into the new!"

HOW TO USE THIS BOOK

The outings in *50 Hikes in Southern Virginia* range from easy walks on level ground to ambitious, multi-day backpacking excursions over rugged terrain. No matter your level of fitness or outdoor experience, there are trips that will best fit your abilities, time constraints, or quest for adventure. The headings at the beginning of each hike provide a quick overview of what to expect.

The total distance was determined by walking each hike with a surveyor's measuring wheel. There may be some differences if you look to other sources—trail signs, brochures from the park or agency, or other books—for additional information. Many of these merely measure distance from the trailhead and do not take into account how far you must walk to reach it. To be as accurate as possible, I measured the hike from the point where you leave your automobile to where you return to it and I have included the distance of any side trails the hike description tells you to take.

A one-way hike ends at a different point from where you started, necessitating a car shuttle. A round trip is an out-and-back excursion following the same route in both directions. You will take a circular journey on a circuit hike, rewalking very little, if any, of the same trail or trails.

Keep in mind that the hiking time is the minimum amount of time it would take a person of average ability to do a trip at a leisurely pace. Some of you may go faster, some slower. When planning the hike,

The first falls of Little Stony Creek (Hike 47)

remember that the hiking time does not take into account rest breaks or time out for sightseeing and nature study.

The vertical rise provides the best indication of how strenuous a hike will be. It is the sum total of all the uphill hiking you will do, not just the difference in elevation between the lowest and highest points of a hike. This rise was determined by using information on United States Geological Survey (USGS) maps.

The specific USGS maps that contain the topographic features of the hike are included in the map heading. The hike route is traced on these maps and reproduced for you in this book. Of course, you are only getting a partial view; the entire map can help identify various features, such as nearby peaks or waterways, and can help you become proficient in orienteering. They may be obtained through outfitters or from the United States Geological Survey, Box 25286, Federal Center, Denver, CO 80225. You can also purchase the maps directly through the USGS Web site (www. usgs.gov). You may need several maps to complete just one hike, and the price of each is now in the multiple dollars range.

Most of the other maps identified can be obtained, often free of charge, at the appropriate contact stations, visitors centers, or agency offices.

If you are going to be hiking any of the Forest Service trails, I suggest you purchase the two inexpensive maps to the entire Jefferson National Forest—the Jefferson National Forest Map and the Clinch Ranger District Map. These maps will not only give you a broad overview of the areas in which you will be hiking, but since they show almost all of the national forest's trails, they can open up a whole new world of hiking options for you. The maps mark the trails with official Forest Service inventory num-

bers, and to help you orient yourself, I have included these numbers in brackets (e.g., {FS 621}) in the hike descriptions. Like the Forest Service, I have used FDR (Forest Development Road) to refer to Forest Service roads (which are usually unpaved). Be aware that trails in the national forest may not be as well maintained or marked as those in the national, state, or regional parks.

There are, of course, a number of different routes you could take to each hike's trailhead, but the ones described are designed to keep you on four-lane highways as much as possible and, hopefully, take the least amount of driving time.

Do not reject a hike or an area because the length, time, or vertical rise appear to be beyond your abilities. Because of my proclivity to want to experience the outdoors as much as possible, I often depict the most circuitous and longest possible hike in a particular area. Yet, many places have numerous side trails or alternate routes you could take to shorten a hike. A good example is the very first hike, First Landing State Park. I describe a trip of more than 11.0 miles, but there are so many interconnecting trails that you could take a rewarding circuit hike of only 1.0 or 2.0 miles with very little elevation change. Study maps and my descriptions and you will find that this is the case in many places.

You do not have to be in the best physical shape to enjoy a walk, but do take into account the difficulty of the terrain, the weather report, and your conditioning. Allow enough time to complete your outing before dark, and always let someone know where you are hiking.

Be aware that fees are charged for you to gain access to many of the hikes in this book. Since the imposition and amount of these fees seems to change constantly, they are not identified in the text of each individual hike. Just know that you will pay them at a large percentage of the state parks as well as some of the national parks.

ADVICE AND PRECAUTIONS

Water

If you are going to be hiking for more than an hour, take along some water. On overnight trips you are going to have to depend on a stream or spring, but the rise in the number of people visiting the natural areas of southern Virginia has brought about an increase in Giardia, a water-borne parasite. Water can also become tainted by viruses, bacteria, and pollutants.

Boiling could make stream or spring water potable, but a portable purifier is more convenient, and possibly more effective. Be aware that a "filter" removes only bacteria, while a "purifier" is also capable of eliminating viruses. Since they cost and weigh about the same, be sure to purchase a purifier.

Please note! For your convenience, water sources are identified in a number of the hike descriptions, but this is not an endorsement of their purity. Water from all sources should be treated before drinking!

Snakes

Only four snakes in southern Virginia are poisonous. The copperhead and timber rattlesnake are found throughout most of the region, while the cottonmouth (sometimes called water moccasin) inhabits eastern Virginia and a small part of central Virginia. The very easternmost part of the state is within the range of the canebrake rattlesnake (considered by many to be the same species as the timber rattler), but sightings have been almost nonexistent within the last few decades. It would be wise to learn how to identify all four of these pit vipers.

Do remember that the outdoors is a snake's natural habitat and that it has as much right, if not more, to be there as you do. Please refrain from killing any snake; just walk around it, giving it a wide berth, and continue on your way.

Important: All snakebites may contain bacteria, so seek medical attention as soon as possible for any bite.

Black Bears

Southern Virginia is home to well over 1,000 black bears. Although it is exceedingly rare for a black bear to attack a human, you must remember that they are wild animals and do not like to be approached at close range. Do not try to feed a bear. Not only does this endanger you, it also endangers the bear. Once a bear becomes used to close human contact, it may begin wandering into campsites or housing developments looking for handouts. This often results in the bear having to be destroyed by the authorities.

Insects

Warm weather brings no-see-ums, gnats, fleas, sand fleas, deerflies, mosquitoes, ticks, and more. Although the mountains have their fair share, the lowlands, marshes, and beaches of central and eastern Virginia can be nearly swarming with them at times. Bring lots of repellent on any hike from late spring to mid-autumn. (And remember that one of the pleasures of hiking during the colder months is the absence of insects.)

Recent years have seen a rise in the reported cases of Lyme disease, a bacterial infection transmitted by the bite of the deer tick. Check yourself for ticks after each outing, remembering that the thing you are looking for could be as small as the period at the end of this sentence.

Plants

Poison ivy is found just about everywhere in southern Virginia. Learn how to identify it, as it can grow in a number of forms. The most common is a woody shrub up to 2 feet high that grows in large patches, often lining or overtaking pathways. Just as likely, it will grow as a hairy, root-covered vine that clings to the trunk of a tree, climbing far up into the branches. All parts of the plant contain the poison and can give you an itchy rash; this is true even in winter, when it appears to be dead.

Not as prevalent, but certainly present, poison oak is most often found in sandy soil habitats. As its name suggests, its leaflets resemble the leaves of an oak tree, but they are fuzzy. Poison sumac is considered by some to be one of the most dangerous plants in the U.S.; it occurs most notably in the eastern part of Virginia. Unlike the low-standing poison ivy, poison sumac can grow to be 25 feet tall and has compound leaves with an odd number of leaflets. The upper side of the leaflets is shiny green, while the underside is lighter and has small hairs.

Trumpet creeper or vine is most often found in the lowlands. Also known as cow itch, it can cause contact dermatitis.

Stinging nettle will grow in large carpets and encroach upon pathways that are not well maintained. Brushing up against the plant may cause your skin to itch for the rest of the day.

Sun

The consensus in the medical community is that you should apply a high-strength sunblock whenever you will be outdoors for extended periods of time—any time of year.

Hunting

Due to the abundance of wildlife, hunting is extremely popular in southern Virginia, even in the more populated counties. Hunting seasons usually run from early fall into January, and again for part of the spring. Dates vary from year to year and place to place, so check with local authorities. During hunting season, it may be best to hike in a group; do not venture forth without wearing some kind of blaze-orange clothing. If you are hunting (or fishing), be sure to obtain the proper licenses and check into local regulations.

Unattended Vehicles

There is always the possibility of theft and vandalism to cars left unattended at trailheads, so it is wise to leave your valuables at home. Bring valuables with you when you go hiking, or stash them out of sight and lock the car. If you are going to leave a car overnight, be sure to give a ranger or the proper authority your vehicle's make and license number, the length of time you will be leaving it, and the name of each person in your party.

A way to avoid a car shuttle on a one-way hike as well as the problems associated with leaving an automobile overnight is to have someone drop you off at the trailhead and pick you up when you have finished.

Proper Clothing & Equipment

As with any outdoor pursuit, you need to be ready for abrupt fluctuations in the weather. Warm and sunny summer days may become cold and rainy within minutes. Also, do not be surprised if a pleasant spring or fall day changes to one with sleet or snow.

Because people are caught off guard on days such as this, when the temperature dips into the low 60s and 50s, hypothermia—one of the leading causes of hiker and camper deaths—may strike. Be prepared by carrying rain gear and an insulating layer of clothing, such as a wool sweater or synthetic jacket, in your day pack. Layering is a

McAfee Knob (Hike 33)

more effective means of keeping warm than wearing one thick garment, so carry several items of clothing for winter travel.

In addition to the above, your pack should include a first-aid kit, flashlight, knife, compass, toilet paper, and waterproof matches. Be prepared for possible cool nights even in the summer.

It is not necessary to subject your feet to the tortures of heavy-duty boots to enjoy hiking in southern Virginia. Unless you have ankle or foot problems, comfortable tennis, walking, or running shoes will probably suffice for most of the hikes—especially the shorter ones in the eastern half of the state. Lightweight hiking boots or shoes should be sufficient for journeys into the mountains and on overnight trips.

Applying moleskin (available at most pharmacies and outdoors outfitters) immediately at the first sign of a "hot spot" will help prevent blisters from developing.

These are just the basics you should know about foot travel in areas removed from the mainstream. Obviously it is not the intent of this guidebook to be a hiking or backpacking primer, so I suggest you solicit advice from backpacking acquaintances, trail-club members, and outdoors outfitters. I am a firm believer in supporting your neighborhood backpack shop instead of mail-order companies. Not only will the local folks help fit and adjust your equipment and be there if you have any questions, but many shops rent hiking and camping equipment, enabling you to try something before you decide to buy it.

A number of books are available if you feel the need for further information. Currently, two of the most complete books on the subject of outdoor travel are *Trailside Guide: Hiking and Backpacking* by Karen Berger and *Backpacking: Essential Skills to Advanced Techniques* by Victoria Logue.

Introduction

Beyond Backpacking: Ray
to Lightweight Backpack-
he debatable yet very inno-

Hiking and Camping Etiquette

Endorsed by almost every organization connected with the outdoors, the Leave No Trace principles below have been developed to protect a fragile natural world from increased usage. (Reprinted by permission of Leave No Trace, Inc., www.LNT.org, 1-800-332-4100.)

Plan Ahead and Prepare

- Know the regulations and special concerns for the area you'll visit.
- Prepare for extreme weather, hazards, and emergencies.
- Schedule your trip to avoid times of high use.
- Visit in small groups. Split larger parties into groups of 4–6.
- Repackage food to minimize waste.
- Use a map and compass to eliminate the use of marking paint, rock cairns, or flagging.

Travel and Camp on Durable Surfaces

- Durable surfaces include established trails and campsites, rock, gravel, dry grasses, or snow.
- Protect riparian areas by camping at least 200 feet from lakes and streams.
- Good campsites are found, not made. Altering a site is not necessary.

In popular areas:

- Concentrate use on existing trails and campsites.
- Walk single file in the middle of the trail, even when wet or muddy.
- Keep campsites small. Focus activity in areas where vegetation is absent.

In pristine areas:

- Disperse use to prevent the creation of campsites and trails.
- Avoid places where impacts are just beginning.

Dispose of Waste Properly

- Pack it in, pack it out. Inspect your campsite and rest areas for trash or spilled foods. Pack out all trash, leftover food, and litter.
- Deposit solid human waste in catholes dug 6 to 8 inches deep at least 200 feet from water, camp, and trails. Cover and disguise the cathole when finished.
- Pack out toilet paper and hygiene products.
- To wash yourself or your dishes, carry water 200 feet away from streams or lakes and use small amounts of biodegradable soap. Scatter strained dishwater.

Leave What You Find

- Preserve the past: examine, but do not touch, cultural or historic structures and artifacts.
- Leave rocks, plants, and other natural objects as you find them.
- Avoid introducing or transporting non-native species.
- Do not build structures, furniture, or dig trenches.

Minimize Campfire Impacts

- Campfires can cause lasting impacts to the backcountry. Use a lightweight stove for cooking and enjoy a candle lantern for light.
- Where fires are permitted, use established fire rings, fire pans, or mound fires.
- Keep fires small. Only use sticks from the ground that can be broken by hand.

A wild pony along the Appalachian Trail in the Crest Zone of Mount Rogers

- Burn all wood and coals to ash, put out campfires completely, then scatter cool ashes.

Respect Wildlife

- Observe wildlife from a distance. Do not follow or approach them.
- Never feed animals. Feeding wildlife damages their health, alters natural behaviors, and exposes them to predators and other dangers.
- Protect wildlife and your food by storing rations and trash securely.
- Control pets at all times, or leave them at home.
- Avoid wildlife during sensitive times: mating, nesting, raising young, or winter.

Be Considerate of Other Visitors

- Respect other visitors and protect the quality of their experience.
- Be courteous. Yield to other trail users.
- Step to the downhill side of the trail when encountering pack stock.
- Take breaks and camp away from trails and other visitors.
- Let nature's sounds prevail. Avoid loud voices and noises.

For further information, *Backwoods Ethics* by Laura and Guy Waterman is an excellent resource, not only providing details on the "how" of making little or no impact on the environment, but also the "why."

ıdings and Field Guides
ıd Marty Casstevens.
f the Southern
How to Photograph and
Identify Them. Winston-Salem, NC:
John F. Blair, Publisher, 1996.

Adkins, Leonard M. Adventure Guide to
Virginia. Edison Hill, N.J.: Hunter
Publishing, 2000.

___. The Appalachian Trail: A Visitor's
Companion. Birmingham, AL.:
Menasha Ridge Press, 2000.

___. 50 Hikes in Maryland: Walks, Hikes,
and Backpacks from the Allegheny
Plateau to the Atlantic Ocean.
Woodstock, VT: The Countryman Press,
2007.

___. 50 Hikes in Northern Virginia:
Walks, Hikes, and Backpacks from
the Allegheny Mountains to the
Chesapeake Bay. Woodstock, VT:
The Countryman Press, 2006.

___. 50 Hikes in West Virginia: From the
Allegheny Mountains to the Ohio River.
Woodstock, VT: The Countryman Press,
2005.

___. Seashore State Park: A Walking
Guide. Centreville, MD: Tidewater
Publishers, 1990.

___. Wildflowers of the Appalachian Trail.
Birmingham, AL: Menasha Ridge Press,
2006.

___. Wildflowers of the Blue Ridge and
Great Smoky Mountains. Birmingham,
AL: Menasha Ridge Press, 2005.

Brill, David. As Far as the Eye Can See:
Reflections of an Appalachian Trail
Hiker. Harpers Ferry, WV: Appalachian
Trail Conservancy, 2004.

Brooks, Maurice. The Appalachians.
Morgantown, WV: Seneca Books, 1995.

Burn, Barbara. North American Trees.
Avenel, NJ: Gramercy Books, 1992.

Burt, William Henry. A Field Guide to the
Mammals. Boston, MA: Houghton Mifflin,
1998.

Busch, Phyllis. Wildflowers and the Stories
Behind Their Names. New York:
Charles Scribner's Sons, 1977.

Byrd, Nathan, ed. A Forester's Guide to
Observing Animal Use of Forest Habitat
in the South. Atlanta, GA: U.S. Department of Agriculture, Forest Service,
1981.

Chambers, Kenneth A. A Country-Lover's
Guide to Wildlife: Mammals, Amphibians, and Reptiles of the Northeastern United States. Baltimore, MD:
Johns Hopkins University Press, 1979.

Dana, Mrs. William S. (Frances Theodora
Parsons) How to Know the Wildflowers.
Dover: Dover Publications, 1963. (out
of print)

Douglas, William O. My Wilderness: East
to Katahdin. San Francisco, CA: Com-
stock Editions, 1989.

Eastman, John. The Book of Forest and
Thicket: Trees, shrubs, and Wildflowers
of Eastern Nortash America. Mechanicsburg, PA: Stackpole Books, 1992.

Frye, Kenneth. Roadside Geology of
Virginia. Missoula, MT: Mountain Press
Publishing Company, 1986.

Grimm, William C. and John T. Kartesz.
The Illustrated Book of Trees: The
Comprehensive Field Guide to More
Than 250 Trees of Eastern North
America. Mechanicsburg, PA:
Stackpole Books, 2001.

___. The Illustrated Book of Wildflowers
and Shrubs: The Comprehensive Guide
to More Than 1,300 Plants of Eastern
North America. Mechanicsburg, PA:
Stackpole Books, 1993.

Gupton, Oscar W., and Fred C. Swope. *Wildflowers of the Shenandoah Valley and Blue Ridge Mountains.* Charlottesville, VA: University of Virginia Press, 2002.

Johnson, Hugh. *Hugh Johnson's Encyclopedia of Trees.* New York: Portland House, 1990.

Kephart, Horace. *Our Southern Highlanders.* Knoxville, TN: University of Tennessee Press, 1987.

Martof, Bernard, et al. *Amphibians and Reptiles of the Carolinas and Virginia.* Alexander, NC: Alexander Books, 2004.

Murie, Olaus J. *A Field Guide to Animal Tracks.* Boston, MA: Houghton Mifflin, 2005.

Peterson, Roger Torey. *A Field Guide to Birds of Eastern and Central North America.* Boston, MA: Houghton Mifflin, 2004.

Peterson, Roger T., and Margaret McKenny. *A Field Guide to Wildflowers: Northeastern and North-Central North America.* Boston, MA: Houghton Mifflin, 1998.

Petrides, George A. *A Field Guide to Trees and Shrubs.* Boston, MA: Houghton Mifflin, 1988.

Simpson, Marcus B., Jr. *Birds of the Blue Ridge Mountains: A Guide for the Blue Ridge Parkway, Great Smoky Mountains, Shenandoah National Park, and Neighboring Areas.* Chapel Hill, NC: University of North Carolina Press, 1992.

Slone, Harry. *Trout Streams of Virginia: An Angler's Guide to the Blue Ridge Watershed.* Woodstock, VT: The Countryman Press, 2006.

Stokes, Donald W. *The Natural History Wild Shrubs and Vines: Eastern and Central America.* New York: Harper and Row, 1981.

Webster, William D., et al. *Mammals of the Carolinas, Virginia, and Maryland.* Chapel Hill, NC: University of North Carolina Press, 1985.

White, Christopher P. *Chesapeake Bay: Nature of the Estuary, a Field Guide.* Centreville, MD: Tidewater Publishers, 1990.

___. *Appalachian Trail Guide to Central Virginia.* Harpers Ferry, WV: Appalachian Trail Conference, 2001.

___. *Appalachian Trail Guide to Southwest Virginia.* Harpers Ferry, WV: Appalachian Trail Conference, 1998.

ADDRESSES

Hike 1:
First Landing State Park
2500 Shore Drive
Virginia Beach, VA 23451
757-412-2300
www.state.va.us/dcr/parks/1stland.htm

Hike 2:
False Cape State Park
4001 Sandpiper Road
Virginia Beach, VA 23456
757-426-7128
www.state.va.us/dcr/parks/falscape.htm

Hike 3:
Northwest River Park
1733 Indian Creek Road
Chesapeake, VA 23322
757-421-3145
www.cityofchesapeake.net/services/
depart/park-rec/nwrp/index.shtml

amp National Wildlife

d

ᴊuffoik, VA 23434
757-986-3705
www.fws.gov/northeast/greatdismalswamp

Hike 6:
Hog Island Wildlife Management Area
7938 Hog Island Road
Surry, VA 23883
757-357-5224
www.dgif.state.va.us/hunting/WMA/hog_
island.html

Hike 7:
Petersburg National Battlefield
1539 Hickory Hill Road
Petersburg, VA 23804
804-732-3531
www.nps.gov/pete

Hike 8:
Pocahontas State Park
10301 State Park Road
Chesterfield, VA 23838
804-796-4255
www.state.va.us/dcr/parks/pocahont.htm

Hike 9:
Department of Game & Inland Fisheries
4010 West Broad Street
Richmond, VA 23230-1104
804-367-1000
www.dgif.state.va.us/hunting/wma/amelia.
html

Hike 10:
Twin Lakes State Park
788 Twin Lakes Road
Green Bay, VA 23942
434-392-3435
www.dcr.virginia.gov/parks/twinlake.htm

Hike 11:
John H. Kerr Reservoir
1930 Mays Chapel Road
Boydton, VA 23917
434-738-6143
www.saw.usace.army.mil/jhkerr/index.htm

Hike 12:
Occoneechee State Park
1192 Occoneechee Park Road
Clarksville, VA 23927
434-374-2210
www.state.va.us/dcr/parks/occoneec.htm

Hike 13:
Staunton River State Park
1170 Staunton Trail
Scottsburg, VA 24589
434-572-4623
www.state.va.us/dcr/parks/staunton.htm

Hike 14:
Appomattox Court House National
   Historical Park
P.O. Box 218
Appomattox, VA 24522
804-352-9887
www.nps.gov/apco

Hike 15:
Lynchburg Parks and Recreation
   Department
301 Grove Street
Lynchburg, VA 24501
434-847-1640
www.lynchburgva.gov/home/index.asp?
   page=86

Hike 16:
Fairy Stone State Park
967 Fairystone Lake Drive
Stuart, VA 24171
276-930-2424
www.state.va.us/dcr/parks/fairyst.htm

Hikes 17, 18, 19, 20, 22, 23, & 24:
Mount Rogers NRA
3714 Highway 16
Marion, VA 24354-4097
276-783-5196
www.fs.fed.us/r8/gwj/mr

Hike 21:
Grayson Highlands State Park
829 Grayson Highlands Lane
Mouth of Wilson, VA 24363
276-579-7092
www.state.va.us/dcr/parks/graysonh.htm

Hike 25:
Hungry Mother State Park
2854 Park Boulevard
Marion, VA 24354
276-781-7400
www.state.va.us/dcr/parks/hungrymo.htm

Hikes 26 & 27:
USFS New River Valley Ranger District
South Office
155 Sherwood Drive
Wytheville, VA 24382
276-228-5551
www.fs.fed.us/r8/gwj/nrv

Hikes 28, 29, 30, & 32:
USFS New River Valley Ranger District
North Office
Blacksburg, VA 24060
540-552-4641
www.fs.fed.us/r8/gwj/nrv

Hike 31:
Mountain Lake
115 Hotel Circle
Mountain Lake, VA 24136
540-626-7121
www.wcaml.org or
www.mountainlakehotel.com

Hikes 33, 34, & 35:
USFS New Castle Ranger District
P.O. Box 246
New Castle, VA 24127
540-864-5195
www.fs.fed.us/r8/gwj/newcastle

Hike 36:
Lake A. Willis Robertson
106 Lake Roberston Drive
Lexington, VA 24450
540-463-4164
www.co.rockbridge.va.us/departments/lake_
    robertson.htm

Hike 37:
Rockbridge Area Conservation Council
P.O. Box 564
Lexington, VA 24450
540-463-2330
http://organizations.rockbridge.net/racc

Hike 38:
Chessie Trail Committee
VMI Foundation, Inc.
Box 932
Lexington, VA 24450
540-464-7287
www.case.org/guide/vmi_foundation.html

Hike 39:
BRP Peaks of Otter Office
85919 Blue Ridge Parkway
Bedford, VA 24523
540-586-4257
www.nps.gov/blri

Hike 40:
USFS Glenwood/Pedlar Ranger District
P.O. Box 10
Natural Bridge Station, VA 24579
540-291-2188
www.fs.fed.us/r8/gwj/gp

Natural Heritage
n Office
itreet
..g....., vn 24210
276-676-5673
www.dcr.virginia.gov/dnh/pinnacle.htm

Hike 42:
Natural Tunnel State Park
Route 3, Box 250
Duffield, VA 24244
276-940-2674
www.state.va.us/dcr/parks/naturalt.htm

Hike 43:
Breaks Interstate Park
P.O. Box 100
Breaks, VA 24607
276-865-4413
www.breakspark.com

Hikes 44, 45, 46, 47, & 48:
USFS Clinch Ranger District
9416 Darden Drive
Wise, VA 24293
276-328-2913
www.fs.fed.us/r8/gwj/clinch

Hikes 49 & 50:
Cumberland Gap National Historical Park
Box 1848
Middlesboro, KY 40965
606-248-2817
www.nps.gov/cuga

Eastern Virgini

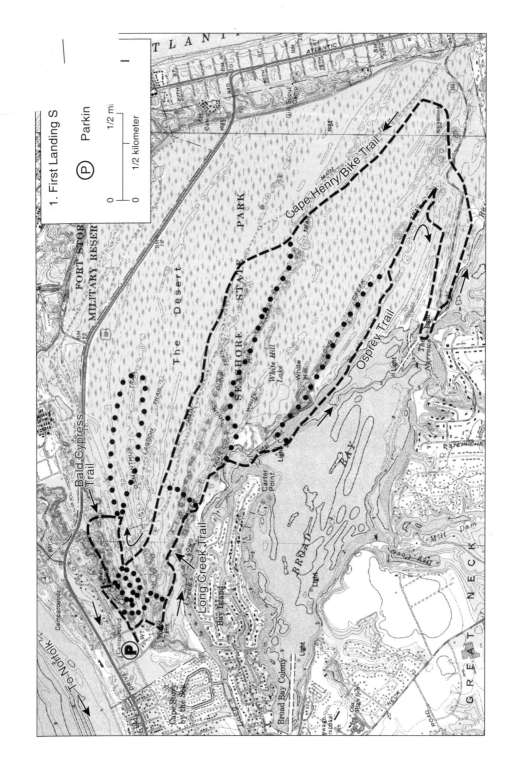

1. First Landing S

(P) Parkin

1

First Landing State Park

Total distance (circuit): 11.4 miles

Hiking time: 5 hours, 15 minutes

Vertical rise: 130 feet

Maps: USGS 7½' Cape Henry; park map

Spanish moss drips from the trees over-head, a five-lined skink scampers underfoot; off in the distance a pileated woodpecker laughs as it takes wing, while nearby a painted turtle silently slips into the caramel-colored water of a swamp crowded with bald cypress. This is not the Everglades in Florida nor even the Okeefenokee Swamp in Georgia, but First Landing State Park and Natural Area—nearly 3,000 acres of lush greenery tucked in amongst the high-rise condominiums and beachfront hotels of Virginia Beach.

The state park may be the best opportunity on all of the East Coast to explore myriad ecological zones while putting out very little effort to do so. (Look at how little elevation you will gain in a walk of more than 11.0 miles). Thousands of years of geological, biological, and botanical evolution, on a piece of land hemmed in by three bodies of water, have crowded much into this small area. During this hike you will walk over hickory- and pine-covered sand dunes, onto a secluded beach, into a salt marsh populated by fiddler crabs, through a lowland forest of sweet gum and red maple, and around freshwater swamps of cypress trees festooned with thick folds of Spanish moss.

The idea for a Virginia state park near the coast was originally advanced in 1929, and enough interest was sparked that the Virginia Seashore State Park Association was formed in 1931. With a gift (and a subsequent sale) of land from the Cape Henry Syndicate, Seashore State Park was dedicated on June 15, 1936 along with five other state parks. (Virginia was the first state to dedicate an entire state park system on the same day.) The Civilian Conservation Corps soon began development of the park by building trails, roadways, six cabins, maintenance work areas, and administrative offices. Many of these are still in use today.

Court litigation on the subject of integration led to the closure of the park from 1954 to 1961. In 1965, a portion of the park was declared a National Natural Landmark to reflect its significant position as the northernmost location where subtropical and temperate plants thrive side by side. The park's name was changed to First Landing in 1995 to commemorate the 1607 landfall of the first permanent English settlers in the New World at Cape Henry.

In addition to the trails, the park offers a beach on the Chesapeake Bay, a trail center, rental cabins, and more than 200 campsites. The varied interpretive programs include crabbing demonstrations, beach walks, sunset and night hikes, swamp strolls, and campfire presentations.

First Landing State Park may be reached from the intersection of US 13 and US 60 (near the Chesapeake Bay Bridge-Tunnel) in Virginia Beach by driving east on US 60 (Shore Drive) for 4.5 miles. Turn right into the park entrance (VA 343) and go just an additional few hundred yards before making another right to leave your car in the picnic area parking lot.

Begin the hike by turning right out of the parking area, walking along the main park road for 0.3 mile, and turning right onto the orange-blazed Long Creek Trail. The beginning of this pathway twists and winds through and along several dunes, which almost resemble miniature versions of the mountain ridges in western Virginia. Cross a dune at 0.5 mile, drop to a barricade, and

reach a wider trail. This portion of the route is used as an emergency access road. Come to cane for the first time on the hike. Dense stands of this plant make excellent shelter for many animals and, in earlier days, the shoots were an important livestock food.

Avoid the trail to the right at 0.6 mile, walking along a dune ridgeline with a salt marsh to your right. Sweet pepperbush and cane line both sides of the trail. Cross a small creek on a wooden bridge at 0.8 mile; you will soon come to open views to the north and south along Long Creek.

Amidst a wonderful display of Spanish moss, reach a junction with the yellow-blazed Fox Run Trail. (To the left it is 0.3 mile to the main park road.) Bear right (avoid the trail to the extreme right that dead-ends at the creek) and ascend a dune ridgeline to continue on the Long Creek Trail.

Spanish moss is reaching its northern limits in the park. Despite its name, it is not a moss but rather a member of the pineapple family. Being an epiphyte and not a parasite as many people think, the moss has no roots; therefore it does no harm to its host tree and receives all the nutrients it needs from the air and from rainwater running down the bark of its host.

There is a grand view at 1.2 miles that overlooks salt marshes, Long Creek, beaches, and the Narrows of Broad Bay—all things still to be experienced on this hike. It was near here that the Chesapeake Indians camped while on hunting parties.

(On April 26, 1997, the remains of 64 Chesapeake Indians were reinterred in a sacred burial site located in a sandy, wooded area near the park's trail center. Dating from 800 B.C. to A.D. 1600, the remains were unearthed in the 1970s and 1980s from the site of a former Indian village in what is now the city of Virginia Beach.)

Broad Bay

Enjoy pleasant views of a salt marsh and Broad Bay from the top of a dune at 1.6 miles and avoid the trail to the right.

Bypass the white-blazed Kingfisher Trail, which comes in from the left at 1.8 miles, ascend a low dune, and come into a salt marsh. As the park's marshes are flooded by saltwater tides twice each day, be sure to stay on the trail or face the consequences of sinking into soft mud and muck. This spot, however, is a great place to discover great blue herons, egrets, and fiddler crabs. The crab received its name from the early settlers, who observed the male of the species waving its larger claw back and forth like a fiddler would move a bow across violin strings. Like many other notable behaviors conducted by creatures throughout the natural world, this performance is done to attract females for mating.

The gold-blazed White Hill Lake Trail comes in from the left at 2.0 miles. Make a sharp right to cross an outlet stream and continue on the Long Creek Trail. Avoid a trail that ascends a dune to the right at 2.1 miles, bear left, skirt the edge of the marsh, and come to White Hill Lake, one of the quietest and most peaceful spots in the park and a place to possibly observe nesting ospreys. These majestic birds were once an endangered species, but they have made a remarkable comeback since the banning of the pesticide DDT. They are now a common sight, swooping out of the sky to crash onto the water and rise with a fish clutched in powerful claws.

Leave White Hill Lake at 2.3 miles and begin a long climb to the top of a dune where you will have grand views across Broad Bay. This might be a good place to learn how to identify and avoid the three-fingered leaves and the stems of tread-softly. This plant's pretty white flower, which blooms in July and August, is tempting to touch and examine closely. However, the points of its hollow thorns may break off, injecting a toxin that will continue to cause itching for quite some time afterward.

In an area thick with tread-softly and poison ivy at 2.5 miles, the Long Creek Trail bears off to the left. You want to keep to the right, now following the green-blazed Osprey Trail as it drops steeply on steps, crosses a wooden footbridge, and arrives at a small beach with a salt marsh to your left. Cross another footbridge at 2.8 miles and come to a larger beach. This may be the time to take a well-deserved break and refresh your feet in the cool waters of Broad Bay. (Swimming, though, is prohibited.)

Passing by a salt marsh to the right at 3.1 miles, the trail gives a final view of the bay, enters the forest, and becomes wider. The southern end of the Long Creek Trail comes in from the left at 3.7 miles; stay right. Early in the morning the dense forest at this spot makes it a good birdsong listening area. Avoid pathways that cross the trail at 3.9 miles, reach 64th Street at 4.2 miles, and turn right along the paved road.

Continue to follow the park road and make a left turn onto the dark-green-blazed Cape Henry/Bike Trail at 5.0 miles. (The parking area, water fountain, and rest rooms of the Narrows on Broad Bay—open year-round—are just a few hundred yards ahead along the roadway.)

Benches overlook the bay at 5.3 miles before you reenter the forest at 5.4 miles. Begin the traverse of a large salt marsh at 5.5 miles, where you may see numerous great blue herons trawling the shallow water in search of a meal.

Benches that overlook the marsh at 5.6 miles make for a warm place to observe nesting osprey and red-headed woodpeckers. This particular marsh was a freshwater swamp until the Ash Wednesday storm of 1962 breached its outer edge. Soon afterward, mosquito drainage ditches were dug, allowing more salt water into the area. Although these ditches are no longer maintained, rising sea levels continue to wash salt water over the land.

Leave the marsh at 5.7 miles, with tall grasses lining both sides of the trail. This spot, with its view of the man-made lake at 6.0 miles—the result of dredging done by the City of Virginia Beach to replace beach sand that was washed away by the tremendous Ash Wednesday storm of 1962—is another good place for a rest break. While the dredging certainly changed the face of the land, it also created this lovely scene.

Continue to follow the dark-green-blazed pathway to a boardwalk over a swamp at 6.4 miles. Much of the year this swamp may be dry, but it is still a place to enjoy a good display of Spanish moss draped over black gum trees growing out of the tannin-stained water.

Cross paved 64th Street at 6.5 miles (a water fountain—turned off in winter—and chemical toilets are available here) and continue along the Cape Henry/Bike Trail. Now walking upon the bed of an old country road—used by automobiles until the mid-1950s—you will pass by luxuriant canebrakes. With a large dune on the left, the cane begins to fade around 7.2 miles; avoid the well-used but unauthorized trail to the left.

Stay on the Cape Henry/Bike Trail when gold-blazed White Hill Lake Trail comes in from the left at 7.6 miles. If you are observant, you will notice that the land is gradually changing from dry, sandy soil to areas dotted with small, boggy, wet areas.

A bench beside the trail at 8.0 miles is about as far from any trailheads as you can get on the Cape Henry/Bike Trail. Therefore, it is a nice, quiet place to sit and enjoy the cool shade provided by the oak, loblolly pine, sweet gum, beech, and red maple trees. The red bay, which makes up much of the understory, has leaves that taste similar to those of the Mediterranean bay, which are used to flavor soups, stews, and spaghetti sauces. This bush's flowers are often overlooked in the spring, but its dark blue fruit is prominent later in the fall.

Bypass the white-blazed Kingfisher Trail as it comes in from the left at 8.6 miles and arrive at benches along the pathway at 9.1 miles. To the left is a small swamp that is a good spot to study the black gum and bald cypress trees. When in the water, the black gum trees—also commonly known as tupelo—develop a broad base, as do the bald cypress trees. A theory to explain this habit is that it better anchors them in the moist, swampy bottoms.

Be alert when you come to a four-way intersection at 9.75 miles. You will leave the Cape Henry/Bike Trail and turn right to follow the red-blazed Bald Cypress Trail to the very edge of a large cypress pool, a spot worthy of a few minutes of study.

Begin a gradual ascent up a dune ridgeline and avoid the unauthorized pathway to the right. On both sides of the trail are swamps in the low points between parallel dunes. Avoid the unauthorized trail that ascends to the right at 10.0 miles; bear left and descend into an area thick with sweet pepperbush. One of the most widespread plants in the park, the pepperbush's fragrant flowers blossom on spikes in midsummer.

Be alert at 10.1 miles! You want to follow the Bald Cypress Trail as it makes an abrupt hard turn to the left onto a wide, straight path. (The blue-blazed Osmanthus Trail goes off to the right.) At this junction is a good example of an osmanthus, or American olive tree. Also known as devilwood, it

reaches its very northern limit in the park. A member of the olive family, its green berries appear late in the summer and turn a dark purple in the fall. Early settlers gave it the devilwood name, claiming its grain made it a devil of a tree to split.

Keep to the left again at 10.2 miles, where another section of the Osmanthus Trail comes in from the right. Avoid a trail to the left at 10.3 miles and ascend and descend a couple of dunes. On top of one of them, the exposed roots of trees show just how shallow the layer of decaying matter and soil is in the park and how precariously the vegetation exists.

Soon, turn onto a boardwalk that goes out into a cypress pool and may afford a chance to watch turtles or snakes sunning themselves. Among the species of turtles living in the park are painted, spotted, box, snapping, and mud. The last prefers shallow water but is adept at moving about on land. As the swamps begin to dry up in late summer, mud turtles may be seen migrating to pools that still have a few inches of water remaining.

With more than 10 different species of snakes in the park, encountering one is a real possibility, but only the copperhead and the cottonmouth, or water moccasin, are poisonous. While the park is within the range of the poisonous canebrake rattler, none has been sighted in recent years.

Turn right at 10.4 miles (straight ahead 0.2 mile is the Cape Henry/Bike Trail), descend stairs, and cross a large cypress pool on a boardwalk. About midway in the pool is a cypress island so large that it has red maple, sweet gum, and Virginia willow growing on it. These islands are often created when cypress knees grow so closely together that decomposing material becomes caught on or between them. After many years, enough of this matter will build up to form a rich soil in which other vegetation begins to grow.

A second cypress pool is a good place to study the broad bases of the bald cypress and tupelo trees; Spanish moss drapes itself over the vegetation.

In a dry and sandy area, reach the trail center at 10.5 miles (worth a visit, if it is open), follow the main park road straight ahead through the parking lot, and turn right onto the upper portion of the Cape Henry/Bike Trail at 10.6 miles. Make a sharp left at 10.7 miles. To the right, behind a wooden fence, is the old route that at one time was the entrance road leading from Shore Drive to the trail center. Through the vegetation to the right at 11.0 miles are the rental cabins built by the CCC in the 1930s, located on one of the largest dunes in the park.

Cross a dirt service road at 11.2 miles; pass through loblolly pine, blueberry bushes, and greenbrier vines; and cross the paved park road. Walk onto the old bed of a railroad that brought tourists to Virginia Beach up until World War II. The picnic area, your car, and the end of the hike are to the right through a stand of loblollies at 11.4 miles.

2

Back Bay and False Cape

Total distance (circuit): 23.7 miles

Hiking time: 3 days

Vertical rise: 120 feet

Maps: USGS 7½' North Bay; USGS 7½' Knotts Island; refuge map; state park map

Located in the southeast corner of Virginia, Back Bay National Wildlife Refuge and False Cape State Park are on a land unlike any other found in the commonwealth. Protecting the area from the ravages of the modern world, these two entities are situated on a mile-wide barrier spit sandwiched between the Atlantic Ocean and 6-mile-wide Back Bay. More akin to the barrier islands of Virginia's Eastern Shore and those found off the coast of North Carolina than to the mainland to which it is attached, this is an area of scrubby woodlands, salt and freshwater marshes, sand dunes, and an ocean beach devoid of the least bit of development. The coastline has remained essentially unchanged since the time the earliest settlers first set foot in the New World.

Until recently you could only reach the state park by walking or biking over 5.0 miles through the wildlife refuge or powering a boat across the waters of Back Bay. Now a tram for day visitors runs from Little Island City Park in Sandbridge through the refuge and into the state park. However, since full-sized backpacks are not permitted on the tram, you will still have to reach the park by foot if you wish to spend nights in the park as described below. Do not despair, though, as this is the only place in all of the Hampton Roads area where you are permitted to do any overnight backcountry camping on public lands. Camping will also allow you more time to explore the park– and you will experience much more than the day-trippers could ever imagine.

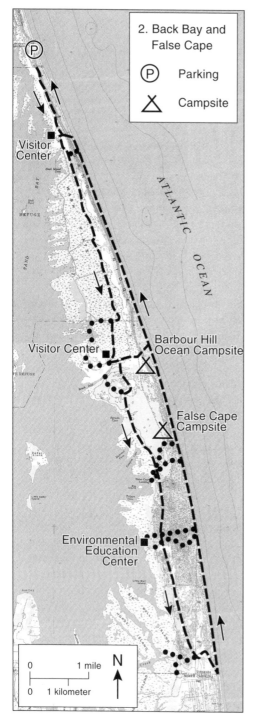

2. Back Bay and
False Cape

(P) Parking

△ Campsite

Visitor Center

Visitor Center

Barbour Hill
Ocean Campsite

False Cape
Campsite

Environmental
Education
Center

0   1 mile   N
0   1 kilometer

You do not need a permit if you are just going to do some day hiking, but overnighters must obtain one by calling 1-800-933-7275 at least two weeks in advance. (You may obtain the permit later than this, but must have a fax machine in order to receive the permit and other information that would otherwise be mailed to you.)

In a farsighted move, the citizens of Virginia approved the Parks and Recreational Facilities Bond in 1992, authorizing the state to expend funds for the purpose of bringing more acreage into the public domain and upgrading facilities at existing sites. One of those upgrades was the installation of potable water facilities at the False Cape State Park's visitors center and at two of the designated campsites. This will save you from carrying the previously suggested minimum of 1 gallon of water (which weighs 8 pounds!) for each day of your outing. Do remember, though, to carry enough with you to get you through the first 5.0 miles of the hike.

There is very little shade throughout much of this outing, so a tube of sunscreen of the highest SPF you can find is also a must, as are light clothing to protect you from the sun and a heavier layer for when the wind turns chilly. Of course, a hat and sunglasses should be a part of any walk on the beach. Mosquitoes, sand fleas, ticks, and a variety of flies, including nasty, biting deerflies, make insect repellent an essential item to pack—sometimes even in the middle of winter.

The tent pegs you use in the mountains just won't do here. The strong winds coming off the ocean will lift the short ones out of the soft sand in no time. Your pegs should be at least fifteen inches long, but don't expect to find any branches or downed wood around the campsites to use. Beach tent pegs can be purchased at a number of stores in Virginia Beach.

The beginning of the hike may be reached by taking I-64 to Exit 286 in Virginia Beach and driving southeast on VA 407 (Indian River Road) for 13.0 miles. Turn left onto VA 672 (New Bridge Road), continue an additional 1.2 miles, turn right onto VA 629, and drive 3.0 more miles to make one more right, this one onto Sandpiper Road. Another 3.7 miles of driving brings you to Little Island City Park, where you will pay the overnight parking fee and leave your car.

First Day

Total distance (one way): 6.1 miles
Hiking time: 2 hours, 30 minutes
Vertical rise: 10 feet

The foot journey begins by walking southward along the main paved roadway and coming to the refuge entrance station at 0.4 mile, where you will need to pay another fee. You are only permitted to be in the refuge during daylight hours, and pets are prohibited from April 1 to September 30. Also be aware that some routes through the refuge (including the one described below) are closed from time to time depending on wildlife use. However, there will always be a way to reach the state park by foot, so just follow posted directions.

The 7,732-acre Back Bay National Wildlife Refuge was established in 1938 to provide habitat for migrating and wintering waterfowl, especially greater snow geese. It is estimated that more than 10,000 of these geese visit the refuge during the annual peak in December and January. However, with its varied habitats, the refuge attracts a large number of bird species— more than 300 have been observed within its boundaries. Be on the lookout for loons, grebes, bitterns, swans, ducks, raptors, doves, woodpeckers, warblers, finches, wrens, and more.

As you walk along the road, notice that, protected from wind and salt spray, the vegetation behind the primary dune is larger and healthier looking than that found on the beach.

Stay to the right when you come to the T intersection at 1.6 mile, bypass the dirt road to the left for the moment, and, to understand your surroundings better, look over the displays in the refuge's visitors center.

When you are ready to resume walking, return to the main dirt road and follow it southward through the refuge, staying to the left at 1.8 miles and at 2.1 miles. The cross dikes to your right at 3.1 miles and 3.3 miles are closed to public travel. These water impoundments have been artificially created and are alternately drained and flooded to provide the optimum habitat for various species of visiting waterfowl.

Introduced from Europe into the northeastern U.S., the distinctive mute swan was not seen in the refuge until the 1960s. It was hard to misidentify, with its all-white plumage and orange bill with a black knob at the base. It holds its neck in a characteristic S-curve, as opposed to native swans, which hold their necks straight. Contact authorities if you happen to see one, as they seem to have once again disappeared from the refuge.

Stay straight when you come to the four-way intersection at 3.8 miles, bear left into False Cape State Park at 4.7 miles, and make use of the observation tower at 4.75 miles to look northward over the land you have walked across today; turn south to see what you will traverse tomorrow.

The state park contact station, where you may obtain water, is at 5.4 miles. (If it is early in the day and you are feeling energetic, consider taking an optional journey along the 2.4-mile circuit Barbour Hill Interpretive Nature Trail. Numbered posts keyed to a pamphlet you may obtain at the contact station will help acquaint you with the natural world you are walking through.)

Go left from the contact station on the route marked as leading toward the Barbour Hill beach campsite and arrive at your home for the night at 6.1 miles. After setting up camp (whose only amenities are a water spigot, picnic table, and chemical toilet), resting, and having dinner, consider walking the 3.0-mile round-trip journey to the Barbour Hill Boat Dock to watch the sun set over Back Bay.

Second Day

Total distance (circuit): 12.0 miles
Hiking time: 5 hours, 15 minutes
Vertical rise: 100 feet

Carpe diem! Hopefully, you walked over to Back Bay to watch the sun drop below the western horizon last night, so wake up early enough today to watch it rise over the ocean, having wended its way around the earth while you slept. Besides, you have much to do today and many miles of exploration to embrace.

After getting your camp in order, preparing a day pack with food and water, and hanging your food on the provided "raccoon racks," walk back toward the contact station. Turn left onto the dirt road at 0.6 mile that is signed as heading toward the Wash Woods Environmental Education Center. The shade you are walking through is courtesy of one of the most dominant trees in the park, the loblolly pine.

Adapting well to poorly drained, heavy soils, the loblolly grows straight and tall, with scales that become larger and smoother as the tree ages. One field guide claims its common name means mud puddle, a reference to one of its preferred environments. The loblolly has also been called the rosemary pine, an acknowledgment of the fragrant resin found within its needles.

South Inlet, the moist, swampy area you walk by at 0.8 mile, was formed during a hurricane in 1749; most of the downed trees you notice around the trail were toppled by the high winds of Hurricane Bonnie in 1998. Soon after you pass through the inlet, the live oak trees, whose acorns are a favorite food of the park's feral pigs, become some of the more dominant trees in the forest. You may notice that the earth under and around the trees looks like it has been churned over by a rototiller, but it's the work of the feral pigs. They are most active at dusk and dawn, and as they root around for food, they destroy the eggs and shelters of ground-nesting birds; they have become a serious threat to the area's native plants, as well.

Bypass the South Inlet Trail (which also leads to the remains of an old whiskey still) to the right at 1.2 miles. A mowed path of just a few feet to the right at 1.6 miles has a duck blind at its end overlooking the Spratts Cove area of Back Bay. Continuing southward on the main route, stay straight when you come to a four-way intersection at 2.7 miles. (The False Cape Landing beach campsite is 0.4 mile to the left and the False Cape Landing bay campsite is about 0.3 mile to the right, but neither of them has water available.)

Bypass the Ocean Bay Trail to the left at 2.8 miles. (Along its route is a concrete trough, known as The Dip, where cattle were once plunged into a solution to cleanse them of the ticks that are so abundant in this area.)

Stay straight again when you come to another four-way intersection at 3.9 miles. (The Wash Woods Beach Trail goes left about 0.8 mile to the ocean. The route to the right heads to the Wash Woods Environmental Education Center.) Once more you need to continue straight at the intersection, at 4.0

One of the refuge's impoundments

miles (right goes to the education center, left is the 0.7-mile Wash Woods Interpretive Trail). Less than 300 feet farther on, the route is less used and you will soon be walking on softer sand.

Continue straight, bypassing the Cemetery Trails at the four-way intersection at 4.5 miles.

The assemblage of rusting tin cans and old jars to the right at 5.9 miles is an indication that this narrow strip of land was once inhabited. Interestingly, since this is one of only a few such sites bearing witness to that habitation, this garbage pile has taken on sort of an aberrant historical and archaeological significance.

Keep to the left when the Dudley Island Trail (leading 0.4 mile to Inlet Creek) and the Monument Trail (0.4 mile to the Virginia/North Carolina border) come in from the right at 6.0 miles. Pass through the gate along the Virginia/North Carolina border at 6.8 miles and begin the return hike to your campsite by turning northward along the beach and the ocean's edge. No vehicles (except those of park personnel and a few commercial fishermen and North Carolina residents) are permitted on the sands and, since you are miles from any public road access point, you may well be the only person on the beach. It seems ironic that the land farthest to the east—an area that the earliest settlers would have most likely encountered first—is the place where you can be the most isolated in all of eastern America.

You may notice an old, weather-beaten black shape sticking out of the water during low tide at 7.5 miles into the hike. This is the bow of the 290-foot *Clythia*, which wrecked here during a storm in 1894 while transporting a load of marble for John D. Rockefeller.

The Wash Woods Interpretive Trail is to your left at 9.0 miles, while the Wash Woods Trail meets the beach at 9.1 miles. The primary dune along this stretch of beach is not natural but was constructed by the Army Corps of Engineers in the 1930s in an effort to protect the land behind it.

The largest portion of your foot travel for the day is over, so you might want to relax and take a swim in the ocean. Just remember, there are no lifeguards here to rescue you if you get into trouble.

Pass by False Cape Landing beach campsite at 10.2 miles and return to your tent in the Barbour Hill beach campsite at 12.0 miles.

Third Day
Total distance (one way): 5.6 miles
Hiking time: 2 hours, 45 minutes
Vertical rise: 10 feet
By walking back to the state park contact station and following the main route through the wildlife refuge, the final day of this outing could be a repeat (in reverse) of the first day. However, for variety, and especially if it is low tide, when the hard-packed sand will make for easy walking, head to the beach and follow it northward.

If you wish to take a dip in the ocean, be sure to do it soon after you begin, as you will enter the wildlife refuge at 0.6 mile, where swimming and sunbathing are prohibited.

Although there are few landmarks along the beach to mark your progress, there is still an amazing number of things to observe to occupy the hiking time. Maybe it is time to take a short break from dedicated hiking and just saunter a bit, engaging in the favorite activity of beachcombers everywhere—hunting for shells. With its fanlike appearance and two small wings at the bottom, the shells of the scallop are some of the easiest to identify. (Think of the logo for Shell gasoline.) These creatures are bivalves but unlike the oyster, whose entire body can be consumed, humans only eat the strong central muscle of the scallop. This is the muscle that snaps the two valves quickly shut, forcing a jet of water out of the scallop, enabling it to "swim."

If you are here at night from early spring to mid-autumn, you might witness a female sea turtle come ashore to lay eggs. Using both front and rear flippers, she digs a hole in the sand and lays from 50 to more than 150 white, Ping-Pong ball-sized eggs. Covering them with sand, the mother turtle returns to the sea, leaving the babies to fend for themselves when they hatch in 50 to 70 days. Please do not disturb the turtles, nests, or eggs; sadly, of the six sea turtle species found along U.S. coasts, all are designated either threatened or endangered.

You could turn inland via the Dune Trail at 3.6 miles, but to extend the oceanside walk as long as possible, continue along the beach. In winter you could possibly see humpback or fin whales go drifting by just beyond the whitewater of the surf.

The beach north of the Seaside Trail at 3.7 miles is closed to the public, so turn inland on the boardwalked pathway and arrive at the refuge's main paved road at 4.0 miles.

Turn right to retrace your steps from the first day and return to your car at 5.6 miles.

3

Northwest River

Total distance (circuit): 4.5 miles

Hiking time: 2 hours

Vertical rise: 20 feet

Maps: USGS 7½' Moyock

Even though Northwest River Park has a playground; ropes and initiative courses; picnic shelters; a miniature golf course; canoes, Jon boats, and paddleboats for rent; and a campground with hot showers, laundry, and a camp store (all of which are bunched together close to the park entrance), it is more like a nature preserve than a regional park. Except for the few miles of hiking trails and a network of old canals, most of its 763 acres have been left in an unspoiled state.

Finding a home within this natural area are 18 species of snakes, close to 300 types of plants, and several species of mammals, including mink, squirrel, nutria, otter, and white-tailed deer. At least 160 species of birds have been observed in the park at one time or another.

In addition, the park is a low-cost, quiet place to camp and explore the natural world while being only about a 30-minute drive from the resort amenities of Virginia Beach.

Northwest River Park may be reached from I-64 Exit 290 in Chesapeake. Drive VA 168 (Battlefield Boulevard) south for 12.2 miles (be sure to avoid Business VA 168 when the roadway splits in two so that you can escape traffic and numerous stoplights). Turn left onto Indian Creek Road, drive for 3.5 more miles, and turn right into the park. Bear left almost immediately into the Day Use Area, continue for another 0.2 mile and leave your automobile in Parking Lot 4.

Begin the hike by following the Molly Mitchell Trail into the woods and walking

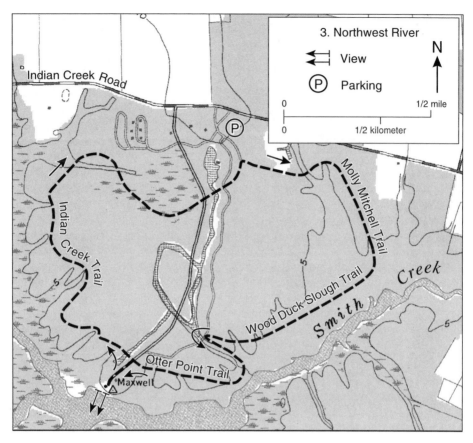

through switchgrass, with its tall-growing stems and long, thin blades. The pathway to the left at 0.15 mile leads to the playground area. Stay to the right here and once again, when you come to another intersection at 0.2 mile.

Swing by the first of many swampy areas at 0.5 mile and cross footbridges at 0.6 mile, 0.8 mile, and 1.1 miles. After another footbridge crossing, the name of the trail you are following magically changes to the Wood Duck Slough Trail.

Often overlooked by hikers are the half-inch white or purple flowers of the low-growing pennywort, which blooms next to the trail in this area in early to mid-spring. Gaining much of its nourishment from de-caying humus, this perennial's rounded leaves reminded people of the coins they carried in their pockets, giving rise to its common name.

You will cross two more footbridges, at 1.2 miles and 1.3 miles, where broad-based cypress trees and cypress knees grow out of the swampy lowland area. The maniacal laugh of pileated woodpeckers adds to the feeling of eeriness and isolation here. Turn left onto the gravel service road at 1.5 miles, pass by a swampy area bordered by dwarf trillium where turtles bask on floating logs, and make a left onto the Otter Point Trail.

Bear left at the intersection at 1.6 miles to stand upon an observation platform jut-ting into still and shallow Smith Creek, a

Cypress trees and knees in the Northwest River

quintessential southeastern Virginia body of water. Cypress trees and knees grow out of the dark-colored water, turtles make small ripples as they swim from log to log, and dragonflies dart about in search of tiny insects such as mosquitoes and midges.

People often confuse dragonflies–also called devil's darning needles–and damselflies. Probably the easiest time to tell them apart is when they are resting. The dragonfly extends its wings outward as if still in flight, while the damselfly folds its wings over its back.

Return to the main pathway, bear left, and continue along your way.

Turn left onto the gravel service road at 2.2 miles and follow it through a picnic area. Pass by rest rooms and a soda machine to come to the benches overlooking a wide expanse of the Northwest River, the perfect spot for a rest break. Bald cypress trees line the shore–it's a good place to observe that they shed their needles in winter, since it can be difficult to pick out individual trees in deep woods.

Take as much time as your schedule allows to enjoy this tranquil scene to which your feet have delivered you. Turkey and black vultures may soar overhead, egrets and herons might wade in close to the shore, and a nutria or muskrat might swim by–you'll know it by the V-shaped ripple pattern it will leave in its wake.

Larger than a muskrat, the nutria is sometimes mistaken for a beaver. Introduced from South America in the mid-1900s for its fur, it has no natural predators here, and its numbers continue to rise, causing increasing damage to wetlands. Burrowing into the soil, the nutria feed upon the roots of plants, causing them to die before being able to reproduce.

Retrace your steps and turn left onto the Indian Creek Trail at 2.4 miles. Although you can see the elevated boardwalks of a nature trail to your left at 2.6 miles, you want to remain on the Indian Creek Trail. Step over footbridges at 2.7 miles, 2.9 miles, and 3.3 miles. In the fall, you are likely to see squirrels busily harvesting the hundreds of acorns dropped here by towering oak trees.

Just like the pennywort found earlier in this hike, the wild ginger that grows along the trail in this area is easy to overlook. Its color closely approximates that of the soil around it and, as it rises no more than a couple of inches from the ground, it may also be hidden by its own foliage or fallen leaves.

There are a number of reasons why the flower has evolved into its particular color, shape, and size. Blooming in the early spring, the blossoms are some of the first to be located by small flies and gnats as they emerge from the ground in search of sustenance. Being carrion eaters, these insects are attracted by the flower's purplish-brown, rotting-flesh color. Once inside the jug-shaped flower, they can feast on the abundant pollen–protected from the chilly winds of springtime.

You cross equestrian trails at 3.9 miles and 4.1 miles, and you will need to turn right onto a service road at 4.2 miles–only to bear left into the woods less than 100 feet later. Walk over the bridge across the lake's outlet stream, ascend and descend wooden steps, and cross a gravel road at 4.4 miles. Barely 300 feet later, turn right onto the paved park road and return to your car at 4.5 miles.

4

Great Dismal Swamp

Total distance (round trip): 9.0 miles

Hiking time: 4 hours

Vertical rise: 10 feet

*Maps: USGS 7½' Suffolk; USGS 7½'
Lake Drummond; USGS 7½' Lake
Drummond, NW*

Unjustly called "dismal," the Great Dismal Swamp is a wondrous place of rich natural charm, with cypress knees rising out of tannin-darkened waters and a forest of pine, cedar, black gum (tupelo), sweet gum, and oak growing upon and around the soft peat bogs. In the center of the refuge is one of only two natural lakes in all of Virginia, 3,100-acre Lake Drummond. (See Hike 31, Mountain Lake, for the other one.)

George Washington first visited this place in 1763 and was so taken by it—proclaiming it a "glorious paradise"—that he helped form the Dismal Swamp Land Company, which purchased 40,000 acres. More entrepreneurial than naturalist in its philosophy, the company proceeded to drain and log portions of the swamp. Logging operations were so successful they continued until 1976; the exploitation was so extensive that the entire swamp has been logged at least once, greatly changing its ecology. In addition, continued agricultural, commercial, and residential development have destroyed much of the swamp, so much so that what remains is less than half of its original size.

Creation of the wildlife refuge began in 1973, when a lumber company donated 49,100 acres to The Nature Conservancy, which in turn transferred the land to the U.S. Department of the Interior. The Dismal Swamp Act of 1974 officially established the refuge, which now encompasses almost 109,000 acres of forested wetlands.

With more than 100 miles of old logging roads now open to hikers and bikers, you

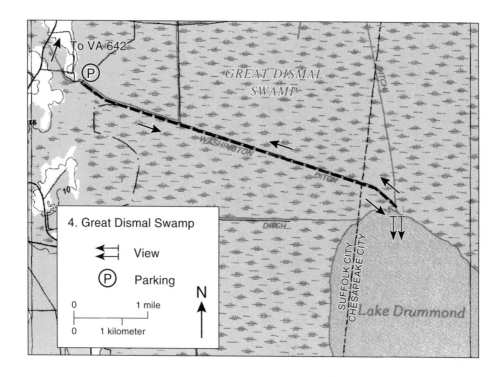

4. Great Dismal Swamp

⇄ View

Ⓟ Parking

0   1 mile

0   1 kilometer

N

could spend days exploring the area. The hike described below follows the arrow-straight route of the Washington Ditch to the heart of the swamp, Lake Drummond. This is not only the best-maintained and most popular pathway, it is also the most convenient and easiest route to experience just about everything the swamp has to offer.

The refuge may be reached from the intersection of I-664 Exit 13 and US 58/13/460 in Chesapeake. Drive US 58/13/460 west for 6.9 miles (making sure to take Business US 58/460 when the highway splits). Turn left onto VA 337 (East Washington Street), continue for an additional 2.4 miles, turn left onto VA 642 (White Marsh Road), and drive 5.5 more miles, bypassing the Jericho Lane entrance. Turn left onto the Washington Ditch entrance road and leave your car in the parking area 1.0

mile later. (The refuge headquarters, where additional information and a sketch map brochure may be obtained, can be reached by continuing southward on White Marsh Road for approximately 1.0 mile from the Washington Ditch entrance road. Bear left onto VA 604—Desert Road—and arrive at the headquarters in less than 2.0 miles.)

Begin the hike by passing through the gate and walking by both entrances to the Dismal Town Boardwalk Trail (see Hike 5). Just after passing the second entrance at 0.2 mile, look to the right across the ditch for your first view of a swampy area punctuated by cypress knees. There is still some disagreement about the purpose of these knees, which are a part of the cypress tree's root system. The most commonly accepted theory is that the trees send them up in order to draw oxygen out of the air and back to the roots. Notice that some knees appear

Harebell

to be growing not in the water but on dry land close to the trail. The swamp has evidently extended to these points at times, because the tree will not send up the knees unless its roots are under water.

As you walk along you will notice that jewelweed lines the ditch in prodigious amounts for more than half of this hike. Pokeweed joins the vegetative undergrowth about 0.5 mile into the journey. If you grew up in the country, or even close to an abandoned lot in the city, you are probably familiar with this tall plant with its 12-inch-long leaves and thick purple stem. It is a good bet that you were attracted to its dark violet berries, which begin to appear in midsummer. You might also have found out that the juice from these berries makes a great ink with which to stain your hands and clothes—sometimes indelibly. Luckily, you must not have eaten any, as they are poisonous.

The Lynn Ditch and its roadway come in from the left at 1.1 miles. To the right, in the

Washington Ditch, is a water control structure. Because the system of canals, dikes, and locks has significantly changed and dried the environment of the swamp, refuge management has installed these apparatuses and put pipes underneath the dike roads in an effort to restore the natural flow of the water.

One of the results of the unnatural drainage of the swamp has been the gradual encroachment of the red maple trees onto the tupelo, bald cypress, and Atlantic white cedar forests. At one time the most predominant forest types in the swamp, they now compose less than 20 percent of the total refuge cover.

Although they grow in isolated patches along the beginning of the trail, harebells join the floral display in large numbers about 2.6 miles after leaving your car. At one time, these beautiful blue flowers were referred to as witch's thimbles because of the Scottish belief that witches could transmogrify themselves into hares.

There are no hares living within the confines of the Great Dismal Swamp, but you are very likely to see a marsh or an eastern cottontail rabbit while here. The swamp, in fact, harbors a wide variety of mammals, including shrews, bats, chipmunks, squirrels, beavers, deer, foxes, raccoons, minks, river otters, and bobcats. With an estimated 200 to 300 individuals, the refuge is also home to the easternmost population of black bears in Virginia. Every once in a while one of them will make headlines by wandering off the refuge and into nearby farm fields and backyards.

Negotiate the curve at 4.0 miles, the only bend to the right on the entire trip. Turn to the right when you come to the T intersection at 4.4 miles and arrive at Lake Drummond and an observation deck at 4.5 miles. There is disagreement as to how the lake was formed. Some say it was the result of a meteorite slamming into the earth, though most experts feel that it was most likely formed by a fire that burned a depression into the peat during a severe drought. Although it is only between 4 and 6 feet deep, the lake can be an angler's dream, for within its waters are pickerel, catfish, perch, sunfish, bluegill, bass, crappie, and more.

This is by far one of the most isolated places you will ever find in eastern Virginia, so spend as much time as possible here, observing the natural world going about its business unfettered. If it were not for the naval aircraft that seem to be on constant training flights, you could easily imagine that you are no longer part of the 21st century.

As they have done for hundreds of years, snow geese and tundra swans visit here in the winter, double-crested cormorants and ospreys take up residence in spring and summer, and bald eagles have become a common sight during the fall and winter.

A number of wood ducks, both male and female, do not migrate and may be seen on Lake Drummond throughout the year. The male wood duck, one of the most colorful birds found here, has a red and white bill, red eyes, and luminescent green, purple, and blue feathers along its head. Because visitors must be out of the refuge no later than 30 minutes after sunset, you are eventually going to have to leave this peaceful place. Retrace your steps, noticing things you may have missed on the way in, such as the gnawings of beavers on trees next to the ditch, or the diminutive Asiatic dayflower. A member of the spiderwort family, the plant was imported from Asia and has escaped into the wild; now its range stretches from Alabama to Massachusetts in the east and as far as Kansas and Wisconsin to the west. Its small flower (less than an inch wide) consists of two rich blue rounded petals that last but a day.

The hike comes to an end when you return to your car at 9.0 miles. Since you now know that this is one of the most undervisited areas in Virginia, with its solitude, natural beauty, and outdoor adventure, you may find yourself returning here time and again.

5

Dismal Town Boardwalk

Total distance (circuit): 1.0 mile

Hiking time: 30 minutes

Vertical rise: 0 feet

Maps: USGS 7½' Suffolk

For those unable or unwilling to make the 9.0-mile round-trip journey to Lake Drummond (see Hike 4) to enjoy the Great Dismal Swamp National Wildlife Refuge, the 1.0-mile Dismal Town Boardwalk Trail is a viable and rewarding alternative. Although you will not become acquainted with the lake's environs, you will still be exposed to much of the beauty and human history of the swamp.

The National Wildlife Refuge System began in 1903, when one of America's most foresighted presidents, Theodore Roosevelt, pronounced Florida's Pelican Island the country's first such refuge. Administered by the U.S. Fish and Wildlife Service, the system has grown to include more than 500 sites throughout America that are managed specifically for the protection of wildlife and its habitat.

Mastodons roamed the Great Dismal Swamp a millennium ago, with human occupation beginning some time around A.D. 700. Few Native Americans remained in the area by 1665, when North Carolina governor William Drummond stumbled upon the lake that now bears his name. William Byrd III was commissioned to lead a party into the swamp in 1728 to survey the boundary between Virginia and North Carolina.

It was George Washington and his Dismal Swamp Land Company that had the biggest impact on the swamp. A decade before the Revolutionary War, Washington was involved in building a massive system of roadways and canals that drained much

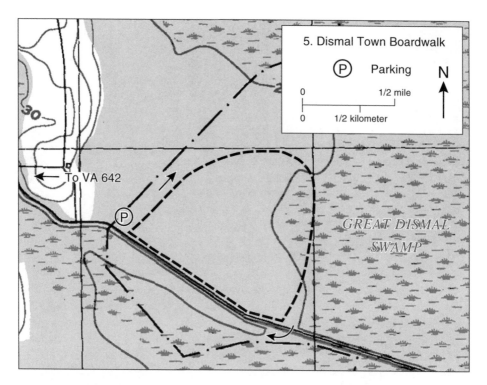

P Parking   N

0   1/2 mile

0   1/2 kilometer

To VA 642

P

GREAT DISMAL
SWAMP

of the land and made it accessible for nearly two centuries of large-scale logging.

Although the entire swamp has been logged over at least once, and it is now less than half of its original size, with greatly decreased biodiversity, it retains much of its primitive feel. Many of the animal and plant species that originally inhabited it are still there, as well. At least 35 mammals and close to 60 reptiles and amphibians roam the refuge, 70 tree and shrub species have been identified, and several score of wildflowers add color to the forest from early spring to late fall. One of the rarest and most localized of American ferns, the log fern, is more common in the refuge than anywhere else.

The refuge may be reached from the intersection of I-664 Exit 13 and US 58/13/460 in Chesapeake. Drive US 58/13/460 west for 6.9 miles (making sure to take Business US 58/460 when the highway splits). Turn left onto VA 337 (East Washington Street), continue for an additional 2.4 miles, turn left onto VA 642 (White Marsh Road) and drive 5.5 more miles, bypassing the Jericho Lake entrance. Turn left onto the Washington Ditch entrance road and leave your car in the parking area 1.0 mile later. (The refuge headquarters, where additional information and a sketch map brochure may be obtained, can be reached by continuing southward on White Marsh Road for approximately 1.0 mile from the Washington Ditch entrance road. Bear left onto VA 604—Desert Road—and arrive at the headquarters in less 2.0 miles.)

Begin the hike by walking through the gate and onto the Washington Ditch Road, which George Washington surveyed in 1768.

Dismal Town Boardwalk

The spot you are standing on was the site of Dismal Town, from which Washington oversaw the construction, primarily by slaves, of the cart road and the drainage ditch.

Turn left onto the boardwalk. Although logging removed a large percentage of the bald cypress and Atlantic white-cedar trees, permitting red maples to become the predominant cover throughout most of the refuge, you will be walking mostly through maple-gum and cypress-gum forests while on this hike.

Bear left at 0.3 mile, coming to benches in a quiet part of the refuge at 0.4 mile. The only sounds you are likely to hear will be the scampering of squirrels, the snorting of a deer, or the songs of an abundance of birds.

More than 25 species of warblers have been observed in the refuge, and two of them are more common here than in any other coastal location. Named after a 19th-century naturalist, the Swainson's warbler, with a drab olive color on the top of its body and a dull white breast underneath, can be hard to find amidst the lush foliage of the refuge. With its bright yellow face, Wayne's warbler, a subspecies of the black-throated green warbler, is a bit more colorful and easier to spot.

Return to the main portion of the boardwalk at 0.5 mile and bear left, only to turn left again onto another side route at 0.6 mile. This portion of the hike will deliver you to a small pool with broad-based cypress trees and knees rising out of the dark water. Since you are more than halfway through the outing, why not take a break? Notice a five-lined skink scamper across the boardwalk's handrail; listen to the *jug-o-rum* call of a bullfrog or the banjo-like *c'tung* of a green frog; watch a spotted turtle or eastern cottonmouth slip silently into the water.

Although they are rarely seen, the refuge is home to three species of poisonous snakes. The semiaquatic eastern cotton-

mouth, or water moccasin, can grow to be 6 feet long. They are olive brown with darker crossbands on their sides and backs. This pattern can fade as they age, and many adults become solid black. More commonly seen is the copperhead, with its light tan body decorated with darker hourglass markings. Now rarely found within the confines of the refuge (and, indeed, throughout most of what should be its home range) is the canebrake rattler. There has been much controversy among biologists about how to classify this snake. Some say it is merely a timber rattlesnake that is found in the lowlands, while others insist it is a species unto itself.

Return to the main boardwalk and bear left, passing by more cypress knees and listening to the Woody Woodpecker–like cries of pileated woodpeckers. They make their homes in tree trunks, usually excavating a hole several inches inward and up to 12 inches downward. Unlike many birds, they leave their nests unlined, save for a few wood chips. After she lays four or five white eggs, the female shares the brooding responsibilities with her mate.

Butterflies flit from the blossoms of jewelweed to those of the Asiatic dayflower where you turn right at 0.75 mile onto the Washington Ditch Road. Nearly 50 kinds of butterflies have been identified in the refuge; the several species of swallowtails are among the easiest to recognize. As their name suggests, most have short tails at the bottoms of their wings.

Pass through the gate and return to your car at 1.0 mile, having come to truly appreciate Henry David Thoreau's sagacious message in his book *Walking:* "When I would recreate myself, I seek the darkest wood, the thickest and most interminable and, to the citizen, the most dismal swamp. I enter a swamp as a sacred place, a sanctum sanctorum. There is the strength, the marrow, of Nature."

6

Hog Island

Total distance (circuit): 4.0 miles

Hiking time: 1 hour, 45 minutes

Vertical rise: 7 feet

Maps: USGS 7½' Hog Island; wildlife management area map

With close to 30 of them spread throughout the state, wildlife management areas (WMA) are probably the Old Dominion's most overlooked parcels of public back-country lands. Except during hunting season (usually late October to early January), when it might be best to avoid them, many of the areas can go for weeks on end without anyone visiting their inner reaches.

While state parks were established primarily to provide outdoor recreation, and state forests founded for silviculture, wildlife management areas were created with an emphasis on protecting and harvesting game animals. Habitat for waterfowl, white-tailed deer, ruffed grouse, fish, rabbit, squirrel, and others is often artificially created and maintained.

Within the last few decades, many people have come to also view these areas as places for conservation of nongame species and recreation sites for the public. In many ways, WMAs can't be beat if you are looking for a primitive experience in an uncrowded place. Amenities such as picnic areas, rest rooms, and the like are usually nonexistent, and trails are sometimes nothing more than informal, unmarked pathways created by the footsteps of occasional hunters.

Acquired by the state in the 1950s, the 3,908-acre Hog Island Wildlife Management Area contains three separate parcels. The Carlisle Tract and the Stewart Tract are small plots; the bulk of the acreage is located in the Hog Island Tract at the end of a peninsula jutting into the James River. The

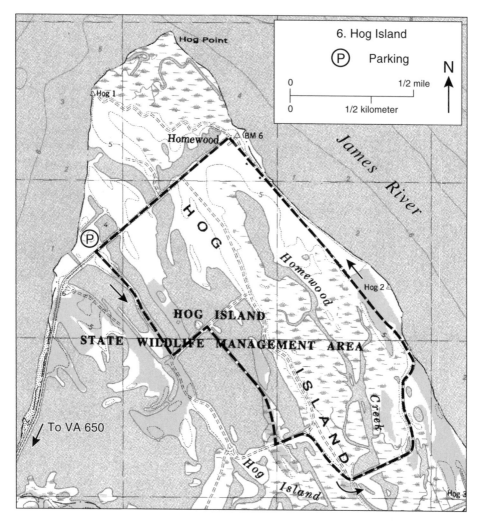

Hog Point

Hog 1

Homewood

BM 6

James River

H O G

Homewood

Hog 2

P

HOG ISLAND

STATE WILDLIFE MANAGEMENT AREA

I S L A N D

Creek

To VA 650

Hog Island

Hog 3

Hog Island Tract earned its name from the practice of 17th-century English settlers permitting their swine to forage freely upon the land. It is a flat, open area of pine forest mixed with tidal marshes and constructed water impoundments.

While a large percentage of the state's wildlife management areas have a tendency to concentrate on increasing the numbers of land animals, the emphasis here is on producing native plant foods for wintering waterfowl. They must know what they are doing; there have been years when there were more than 15,000 ducks and more than 10,000 Canada geese in the refuge all at the same time.

Following a network of service roads around the impoundments, this nearly level hike passes through the Hog Island Tract's varied ecological zones. With very little shade available, hikes during the summer can be exceedingly hot. In addition, be prepared for throngs of biting insects. Perhaps the best times to visit are in the early spring or fall, when temperatures are more moderate and bugs fewer in number. Remember that Hog Island is a wildlife management area with hunting permitted, and may be closed to the general public during hunting seasons and other occasions. It may be best to call ahead to see what regulation is currently in place.

The Hog Island Tract may be reached from the intersection of VA 10 and VA 617 in the small settlement of Bacon's Castle in Surry County. Drive VA 10 east for 0.8 mile and turn left onto VA 650. Follow that route for 5.7 more miles, where you will pass the information center for the Surry Nuclear Powerplant. Continue for an additional 0.6 mile to pass through the WMA entrance gate. You might consider stopping in another 0.3 mile to climb the observation tower to gaze upon the landscape you will be walking through. Leave your car at the parking area on the right in an additional 0.7 mile.

Begin your journey by passing through the gate and walking a grassy road, which is soon bordered on both sides by water impoundments. Perfectly at home in this moist environment, dragonflies dart across the road from one impoundment to another.

Most adult dragonflies capture their insect prey on the wing. In their immature stage as nymphs, they lie in wait in the water, some species sitting on aquatic vegetation, others buried at the bottom of the pond with only their eyes sticking out of the muck. When an insect or even a small fish or tadpole happens by, the nymph snatches the prey with its long labium. This odd, lip-like structure is folded under its head when not in use.

Come to an intersection at 0.5 mile. Because the land behind the gate in front of you is closed on a seasonal basis to protect eagle nesting sites, turn left onto a narrow strip of land between two impoundments. Bear right onto an even narrower strip of land at 0.7 mile, left at 1.1 miles, and right at 1.3 miles.

The distinctive reddish orange blossoms of the trumpet vine (also known as cow itch because it can cause contact dermatitis) that grows along the edges of the road usually begin to bloom in July. Aerial roots growing out from the stem enable the plant to hold on as it creeps and climbs over other vegetation; it sometimes becomes so aggressive and well established that it can be a nuisance plant.

You will dip slightly at 1.5 miles to cross Homewood Creek at a water control structure. This loss and rise of less than 10 feet is about the only change in elevation you will experience on the entire outing.

If you are here during the winter, look at the impounded waters of Homewood Creek to your left and you are likely to see at least a few, if not quite a lot, of Canada geese. Born during the summer in the Arctic regions of North America, they spend the winter in the lower 48 states. The impoundment is one of a number in the wildlife management area that are controlled wetlands. They are drained in spring, and various grains, such as millet, are sown or permitted to grow throughout the summer. The land is reflooded when the plants mature, and their seeds provide a source of food for the geese and other waterfowl.

Bend to the left at 2.2 miles and walk along the south bank of the James River, the Old Dominion's longest waterway. Rising as a narrow stream in the mountains along the Virginia/West Virginia border, the river has grown to be nearly 3.0 miles wide as it flows around the Hog Island peninsula.

Sweet gum trees provide a slight bit of shade just before you break out into the open again at 2.6 miles. A small, sandy

A small beach along the James River

beach at 2.9 miles might tempt you to rest for a few moments, remove your shoes, and wade into the cool water. (Be alert—the bottom drops off quickly.)

Pass by residences, maintenance buildings, and the WMA's headquarters before bending to the left onto the area's main roadway at 3.3 miles.

Make use of another observation platform at 3.6 miles to overlook the low-lying land of Hog Point to the north and the shimmering water of the James River to the west. Designated fishing sites along this portion of the hike allow anglers to fish for striped bass, channel and blue catfish, croaker, white perch, and carp. The outing comes to an end when you return to your car at 4.0 miles.

Other Virginia wildlife management areas worthy of your hiking time include:

The Havens WMA, which encompasses most of Fort Lewis Mountain west of Roanoke. A pathway ascends from VA 622 (Bradshaw Road) to the crest of the mountain, where a dirt road provides access to grandstand views of the Roanoke Valley and more than a dozen miles of ridgetop walking.

About 7.0 miles of the Appalachian Trail pass through the G.R. Thompson WMA, connecting with a system of more than 20.0 miles of pathways within the 4,160 acres.

Be sure to take a walk here in the spring when—literally—millions of trillium are in bloom. Easiest access is from VA 688 south of Paris.

Three of the trails in the 6,400-acre Hidden Valley WMA in far southwest Virginia actually have names. The Brumley Creek, Brumley Rim, and Long Arm Trails connect to make a circuit hike of close to 10.0 miles. Highlights include creekside walking and several vistas of Clinch Mountain. You can reach the area's main entrance by following US 19/Alternate 58 west from Abingdon for 11.0 miles to make a right onto VA 690.

Those who live in central Virginia, where vast acreages of public land are sadly quite scarce for backcountry tramping, should check out C.F. Phelps WMA. A network of about 15 miles of gated roads and unmarked trails twists through 4,500 acres, leading to some positively isolated camping spots. The area is accessible by driving US 17 northwest of Fredericksburg to VA 651 at Goldvein. Continue through Summerduck to the WMA.

Less than an hour's drive from downtown Richmond are the approximately 8.0 miles of trails and roadbeds in the 2,200-acre Amelia WMA (see Hike 9). Except for land adjacent to Saunders Pond and Amelia Lake, you are permitted to make camp anywhere.

Central Virginia

7

Petersburg National Battlefield

Total distance (circuit): 6.7 miles

Hiking time: 3 hours

Vertical rise: 360 feet

Maps: USGS 7½' Prince George; battlefield trail map

In the hope of finally bringing an end to the Civil War, Union troops under the command of General Ulysses S. Grant crossed the Rapidan River in May 1864 to engage Confederate general Robert E. Lee's Army of Northern Virginia. Recognizing the severity of the situation, Lee told one of his officers, "We must destroy this Army of Grant's before he gets to the James River. If he gets there it will become a siege and then it will be a mere question of time."

Although battles at Fredericksburg, the Wilderness, and Spotsylvania (see *50 Hikes in Northern Virginia*) brought no decisive victory for either side, Grant continued his movement toward the Confederacy's capitol in Richmond.

At Cold Harbor (see *50 Hikes in Northern Virginia*), a mere 9 miles from the capitol, Grant met such fierce resistance—and sustained so many casualties—in early June 1865 that he abandoned his idea of capturing the city by direct assault. Reasoning that if he could procure the "capture of [Lee's] army, Richmond would necessarily follow," he moved his troops to the south side of the James River in an attempt to seize Petersburg, a major rail center and re-supply line for the Confederate forces.

Cutting two of the railroad lines and gaining control of several roadways, but unable to take the city by direct combat, the Union forces began a siege of the city. Minor skirmishes occurred throughout the summer and fall months, with Grant's troops capturing other rail lines and diminishing the supplies for the Army of Northern Virginia.

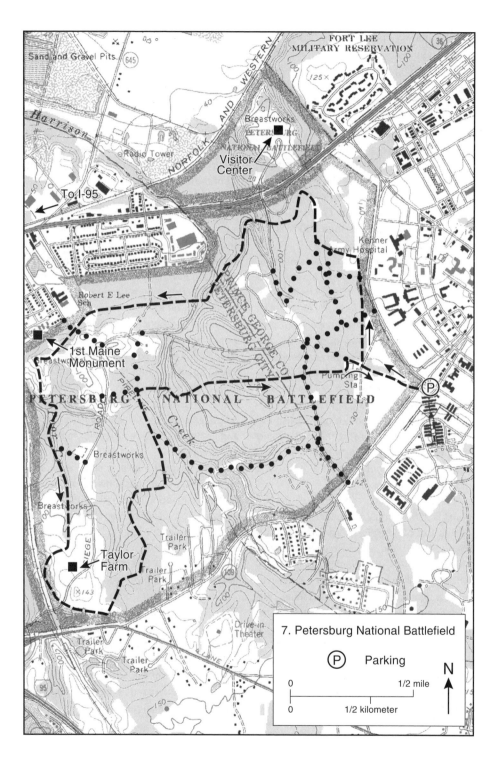

FORT LEE
MILITARY RESERVATION

Sand and Gravel Pits

Harrison

Radio Tower

Breastworks

PETERSBURG

NATIONAL BATTLEFIELD

Visitor
Center

To I-95

Kenner
Army Hospital

Robert E Lee
Sch

1st Maine
Monument

PETERSBURG   NATIONAL   BATTLEFIELD

Pumping
Sta

P

Breastworks

Creek

Breastworks

Taylor
Farm

Trailer
Park

Trailer
Park

Trailer
Park

Trailer
Park

Drive-in
Theater

7. Petersburg National Battlefield

P   Parking

N

0   1/2 mile

0   1/2 kilometer

Recognizing the weakening state of his forces, Lee took the offensive in March 1865, attacking Grant in an attempt to gain supplies with the capture of the Union's newly constructed U.S. Military Railroad. Although the move was somewhat successful, the tide of the battle turned in favor of Grant several days later. The 10-month struggle for the city, the longest siege in American warfare, came to an end with Lee's retreat and evacuation of Petersburg on April 2. His surrender to Grant at Appomattox Court House, less than 100 miles to the west, was just a week away.

Established in 1926 as a national military park, the 2,700-acre park was declared a national battlefield in 1962. Unlike many of the Civil War's other federally designated national battlefields, which have been preserved predominantly as open fields and meadows, the land at Petersburg has been permitted to grow into maturing forests. Therefore, most of this hike will be through deep woods with varying amounts of undergrowth. This allows you not only to visit the various sites pertaining to the battles and the siege, but also to enjoy plants and animals that would not be found living in a more open landscape.

Coming from Richmond, Petersburg National Battlefield may be reached by taking I-95 to Exit 52 in Petersburg. Drive east on Wythe Street for approximately 0.6 mile. Merge on VA 36 (Washington Street), which you will follow for another 1.4 miles to make a right and come to the battlefield visitors center, where you may obtain the required entrance pass.

In order to add more background information to your hike, take a few moments to look over the exhibits and multimedia programs in the visitors center. In addition to obtaining a brochure that describes a driving tour through the battlefield, you may also pick up a trail map here.

After driving back out along the visitors center road, continue east on Washington Street for 0.4 mile and make the first right onto Lee Avenue, entering Fort Lee. (You will have to obtain a parking permit at the entrance station.) Make another right only 0.2 mile later onto Adams Avenue and another right onto Mahone Avenue in an additional 0.9 mile. The parking area where you will leave your automobile is on the right. In addition to the usual ethical practices you should follow while on any hike, the park service requests that you not remove any relics you may happen to find, and preserve the breastworks by refraining from walking or climbing on them.

Initiate the outing by making use of the wide pathway to walk into a young forest of pine with a profusion of eastern red cedar trees. Squirrels often make use of the soft bark of the red cedar to line their nests. A native tree found in almost 40 states, its range extends as far as western Kansas and its berries provide forage for many birds and animals.

Pass by, at 0.1 mile, a short section of railroad tracks, all that remains of the U.S. Military Railroad that carried 50,000 tons of supplies from City Point on the James River to Union soldiers during the Petersburg siege.

Take the right fork onto the Meade Station Trail from the Y intersection at 0.25 mile.

Continue straight onto the Jordon Point Road Trail when you come to a four-way intersection at 0.4 mile. Many of the woods roads you follow during this hike, like the one you are on now, were major thoroughfares dating from decades before the Civil War and were used extensively by both sides during the siege.

Near Colquitt's Salient

Another pathway goes off to the left at 0.6 mile; stay right on the yellow-blazed route. Grassy routes come in from the left at 0.8 mile and 0.9 mile; stay right at both intersections. The road traffic on VA 36 is visible through the vegetation to the right at 1.1 miles. Use footbridges to cross ditches at 1.2 miles and 1.25 miles that were created when earthworks were built during the siege.

Cross paved Siege Road at 1.3 miles and descend to pass by earthworks covered by large trees. Black Union troops captured Confederate Battery 8 in this area, renaming it Fort Friend and using it as a supporting artillery position during the siege. The forest here is a bit older than what you have been walking through, with some large poplar and oak trees covered by thick, hairy poison ivy vines.

The Harrison Creek Trail is to the left at 1.9 miles, but you want to stay to the right and cross the creek, now following the Friend Trail. Confederate forces fell back to the creek and dug in for two days during the commencement of the battle in June 1864. The main advance of Lee's last offensive was stopped along the stream in March 1865.

Cross a paved service road at 2.1 miles and come to a T intersection at 2.3 miles where you need to turn left onto the Prince George Court House Trail. (*Please note:* The next mile or so of this hike is closed on a seasonal basis to protect nesting birds. If you find this to be the case when you're here, simply do not take the next right in a couple of hundred feet, but continue left to intersect Siege Road, turn right on it, and walk to the Fort Haskel site, where a short trail will bring you back to this hike close to the 3.1 milepoint.) The next intersection, a Y, is in less than 200 feet. Here you want to keep to the right fork, on the Poor Creek Trail.

Turn right onto the paved pathway at 2.5 miles and rise to the 1st Maine Heavy Artillery Monument. Follow the paved route to Colquitt's Salient, near the site of Lee's last offensive on March 25, 1865. About nine months before that date, Confederate forces had repulsed a charge from the 1st Maine Heavy Artillery, and that unit sustained the greatest casualties in a single action during the Civil War.

Continue the hike by following the yellow-blazed dirt road (the Poor Creek Trail), and you will soon pass Gracie's Salient. Enter the woods and follow Poor Creek upstream. Ironwood (also called American hophornbeam), enjoys the moist bottomland and thrives here. Its numbers are limited only because it is a low-growing tree that must make do with the decreased amount of sunlight that is able to penetrate the forest canopy.

Cross side streams on footbridges about 3 miles into the journey, swing away from the creek for a short distance at 3.1 miles, and walk by the remnants of the Fort Haskell earthworks. During Lee's final offensive, in March 1865, many federal troops were driven back into the fort, and they became so tightly packed that only those in the very front were able to fire weapons.

Rise on switchbacks at 3.3 miles and come to an intersection where you need to stay on the yellow-blazed Poor Creek Trail and avoid red-blazed Haskell Creek Trail. With railroad tracks visible to the right at 4.0 miles, come into an open area near the site of the Taylor farm, whose buildings were all destroyed at the start of the siege.

Cross paved Siege Road, reenter the woods on the yellow-blazed Encampment Trail, and cross a dirt service road at 4.3

miles. The ground is littered with pine cones, gumballs, hickory nuts, and acorns as you pass by a number of low earthworks around 4.7 miles.

Avoid the unblazed route to the right at 5.0 miles and stay left on the yellow-blazed Encampment Trail, lined by pine trees. The Encampment Trail continues straight ahead as a red-blazed route when you come to a four-way intersection at 5.5 miles, but you need to turn right onto the yellow-blazed Birney Trail. Cross a creek on a footbridge where there are massive earthworks at 5.6 miles.

There is a major intersection at 5.7 miles where yellow-blazed pathways run both right and left. Go left for just a few feet before turning right onto a red-blazed route for the first time during this hike. This is a lesser-used pathway and, therefore, those who do make use of it often see a number of white-tailed deer and squirrels.

All of us know that squirrels cache nuts for the winter, with many species burying their winter food supply in scattered locations throughout the forest. Although they cannot remember the specific sites, their acute sense of smell enables them to locate enough of the nuts. Studies have proven that they can even find what they are looking for through more than a foot of snow.

There is another four-way intersection at 6.2 miles. A red-blazed route comes in from the left, while yellow-blazed courses go right and straight ahead. Continue straight.

A red-blazed path comes in from the left at 6.4 miles; keep to the yellow-blazed trail on the right. Stay right again at 6.5 miles and return to your car at 6.7 miles.

8

Pocahontas State Park

Total distance (circuit): 2.5 miles

Hiking time: 1 hour, 10 minutes

Vertical rise: 130 feet

Maps: USGS 7½' Chesterfield; park map

Being so close to the large populations of Richmond, Petersburg, and other nearby settlements, Pocahontas State Park has come to be viewed by its neighbors as more akin to a municipal park than the typical state park. The commonwealth has catered to this perception by offering conference facilities, a swimming pool, a concession stand, Virginia's first Civilian Conservation Corps Museum (CCCM), a heritage center, an ecology camp, and an activity center. A large modern amphitheater has been constructed on a hillside and is extensively used. Recent offerings have included a variety of musical performances, including symphony, jazz, blues, and popular music. (Most shows require a ticket, which may be purchased at the park office for a small fee.)

All of this is in addition to the usual state park amenities, such as picnic areas and shelters, a playground, boat rentals and a launch area, and a campground complete with hot showers, hookups, a dump station, and rental cabins. Within a piedmont topography of gently rolling terrain, the Beaver Lake Trail winds its way through the forest and beside a scenic body of water.

More than 120 species of birds have been spotted on or near the trails, and more than 40 kinds of mammals make their home here as well. Underscoring the significance of preserving open spaces near growing population centers, the park is within the range of three scarcely seen creatures: bald eagles, eastern tiger salamanders, and loggerhead shrikes.

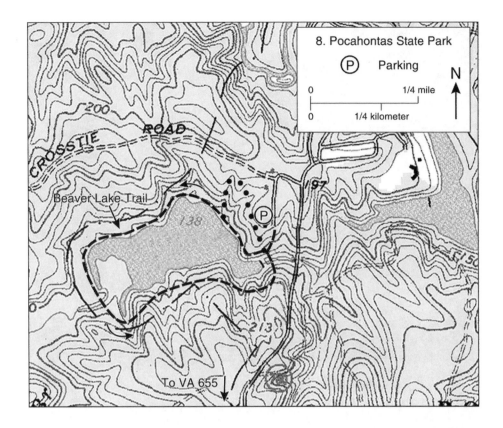

8. Pocahontas State Park

Ⓟ Parking

N

0   1/4 mile

0   1/4 kilometer

Pocahontas State Park may be reached from I-95 Exit 62, about midway between Richmond and Petersburg. Follow VA 288 west for approximately 7.0 miles, turn left onto VA 10 (Iron Bridge Road) and make a right onto VA 655 (Beach Road) in an additional 1.3 miles. Bear right into the park on VA 780 in another 4.2 miles. Continue along the main park road (pick up the Beaver Lake Trail brochure at the office), bypass the ecology camp and campground, and turn left 1.8 miles later. Leave your car in the lot next to the CCC Museum.

Begin the hike by walking behind the museum and onto the pathway marked as leading to the Spillway, Beaver Lake, and Ground Pine Trails. Turn right onto the Beaver Lake Trail at 0.15 mile and use the observation platform to look out upon the thousands of water lilies crowding the surface. Although the lake may appear clear and vibrant, it is on the decline. Silt from years of unsound land management is filling in the lake and causing the aquatic vegetation to die and decay.

Sensitive ferns and pawpaw trees grow near the pathway as you walk along it to cross the first of a number of footbridges at 0.3 mile. While the spores of many ferns develop on the bottom part of their leaves, those of the sensitive fern grow upon a separate, fertile frond.

Make use of another observation platform at 0.5 mile where you might observe

Beaver Lake

ducks paddling around, an egret trawling the water for a meal, or an osprey wending toward the trees with a fish grasped in its talons. The male osprey brings food back to the female to feed to their young. Each fledgling requires two pounds of fish per day in order to develop into a healthy adult.

A boardwalk delivers you across a wet area at 0.6 mile where ironwood and beech trees inhabit the moist soil. Sadly, the beeches are marred by the inevitable graffiti and love messages that thoughtless people just seem unable to refrain from carving into the bark. Swing away from the lake at 0.8 mile, soon walking next to a smaller pond that is also silting in.

A 350-foot boardwalk (slippery when wet!) at 0.9 mile allows you to observe the arrowhead-shaped leaves of freshwater marsh plants without getting your feet wet. Among the trees that grow here are sycamore, pawpaw, and ironwood. Spring beauty and jack-in-the-pulpit burst forth from the soil in early spring. The small brown balls you find on the ground in the fall are the fruits of the sycamore tree. Made up of numerous tiny nuts covered in tufts of hair, the ball comes apart as the temperatures cool in the winter months.

Swing to the left at 1.1 miles and follow Third Branch upstream in what is the quietest part of the hike. The Old Mill Bike and Third Branch Trails are to the right at 1.2 miles. You, however, want to turn left, cross the creek and pass by the site of a mill that operated here decades ago. Rise gradually as you walk beside more graffiti-defiled beech trees. Soon after walking above a small pond, where squirrels are often seen, you will make use of a footbridge at 1.8 miles to cross a gully created by erosion.

Return to the shore of Beaver Lake where the body of water's namesakes have built a number of lodges. Constructed primarily of sticks, mud, and leaves, the inside of a lodge, which is above the water's surface, is lined with soft grasses and shredded bark. A small hole in the top lets fresh air in. If you are here in early morning or early evening, and if you are lucky, you might spot one of these rodents swimming toward you or scurrying rather clumsily across the land.

Step across another footbridge at 2.1 miles and rise over a couple of low ridges through a forest of poplar, oak, and holly with an understory of Virginia creeper and blueberry bushes. An observation deck overlooks the dam spillway at 2.2 miles. Cross the concrete bridge below the dam spillway and come to an intersection. The bicycle trail goes right, but you want to bear to the left toward and beyond the spillway. Upon reaching the blacktopped pathway, turn right and follow it uphill to the CCC Museum and your car at 2.5 miles.

Pocahontas State Park was established in 1946 but was administratively combined with the surrounding state forest in 1989, making it the largest park within the state system. Mountain bikers will be interested to know that the 7,600 acres are no longer managed primarily for extractive purposes but for recreational opportunities. More than 50 miles of interconnecting old logging roads are now designated as bicycle trails (also open to hikers and equestrians). Some of the routes are wide and level, while others are narrower, less used, and somewhat challenging. The trailheads and some intersections are signed; an adequate sketch map is available from the park office.

9

Amelia Wildlife Management Area

Total distance (circuit): 7.75 miles

Hiking time: 3 hours, 20 minutes

Vertical rise: 480 feet

Maps: USGS 7½' Chula; wildlife management area map

In a part of the state that is somewhat lacking in large tracts of public land to hike and camp on, the Amelia Wildlife Management Area (WMA) helps to fill the void. Its 2,217 acres of nearly level piedmont land is primarily former farmland that remains open meadowland. Mature forests have developed in lowlands close to the Appomattox River and around Lake Appomattox. It is managed to enhance the habitat for game animals, so be on the lookout for rabbit, quail, deer, squirrel, turkey, dove, duck, and woodcock.

As with most of the state's WMAs, Amelia's roadway and trail systems are not marked and may only rarely be maintained. Intersections are not signed in any way, and some of the routes are little more than lightly mowed courses along the edges of cultivated fields. Although it would be hard to become hopelessly lost, it is suggested that you save this outing until you are comfortable with being outdoors and with having nothing to guide you but the hike description that follows. However, for those up to the challenge, the wildlife management area can provide some of the most primitive hiking and camping experiences to be found in Virginia's piedmont. Except for land adjacent to parking areas, safety zones, Saunders Pond, and Amelia Lake, you are permitted to set up a tent anywhere. The WMA may be reached from the intersection of VA 150 and US 60 southwest of downtown Richmond. Follow US 60 west for 24.3 miles and turn left onto VA 1002 (a short distance west of Powhatan). Make another left onto VA 13 in an

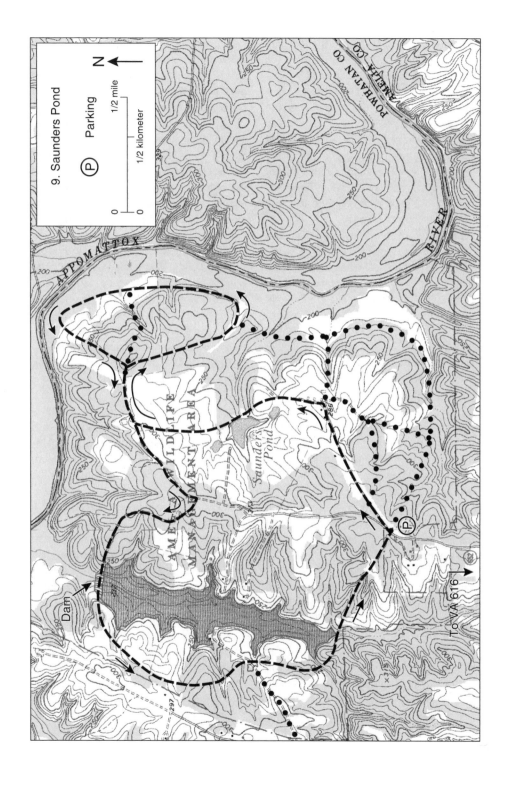

9. Saunders Pond

Ⓟ Parking

N

0   1/2 mile
0   1/2 kilometer

APPOMATTOX

POWHATAN CO
AMELIA CO

RIVER

AMELIA WILDLIFE MANAGEMENT AREA

Saunders Pond

Dam

Ⓟ

To VA 616

additional 0.5 mile, staying to the left onto VA 609 less than 2.0 miles later. There will be a T intersection in another 5.0 miles where you will need to turn left onto combined VA 609/VA 616. Be alert—only 0.4 mile after this intersection you will need to stay to the left on VA 616 when VA 609 breaks off to the right. A game and inland fisheries sign will instruct you to turn left onto VA 652 in another 2.7 miles. The WMA entrance and parking area are on the right 1.1 miles along this roadway.

Begin the adventure by taking the gated road from the parking lot and staying to the left when the road splits less than 0.2 mile later. There is a quail vegetation habitat demonstration project to the left of the road that is planted with silky dogwood, indigobush, Indiangrass, and American plum. The latter becomes festooned with clusters of white flowers early in the spring before its leaves develop. With a thick red skin, its juicy and somewhat sour fruit ripens in summer. In addition to being consumed by a variety of wildlife, the plums are used in jams, jellies, and preserves.

Swing by the buildings of an abandoned farmstead at 0.6 mile, after which the roadway becomes less used by vehicular traffic. If you visit during the warmer months, you may have dozens of blue swallowtail butterflies accompanying you as you walk away from you car.

Pass by a pond that was built by WMA personnel to create a wetlands habitat at 0.8 mile. Eastern red cedar trees grow along its banks, and dragonflies fly above its surface; it is used by birds and other wildlife, especially in times of drought. You will have already walked 1.0 mile when you come to larger Saunders Pond, so it might be time to take a short rest in this quiet, serene place where there are no sounds of road traffic.

As you continue along the journey, the roadway is bordered by an abundance of Queen Anne's lace, pokeweed, thistle, and goldenrod, all of which are able to survive in disturbed soils and bright sunshine.

You may also notice that the open fields and meadows are often bisected by long, narrow strips of woodlands. The use of these windrows (or hedgerows) is one of the oldest farming and land management techniques, dating back to at least the Middle Ages. In addition to providing a shield for their crops from wind and storms, farmers found the vegetation helped slow erosion, prevent floods, and conserve water. The windrows also serve as food sources and travel corridors for wildlife, and they increase the variety of wildlife home sites, appealing to a larger assortment of birds and animals than those found just in open meadows.

Come to a T intersection at 1.6 miles where you turn right, passing by a cinder block building. Be alert 1,000 feet later at a four-way intersection! Turn right onto a route that is not so much a road as it is a mowed passageway through taller vegetation. If it becomes unclear how to proceed, just stay close to the woods and keep the field to your right.

As you come to the end of the field at 2.1 miles, the mowed area splits into a Y. You need to swing onto the left fork and descend past lobelia and horse nettle. Although it has clusters of appealing, star-shaped flowers with white petals and yellow anthers, horse nettle can become a nuisance plant to farmers and ranchers. Also known as bull nettle and sand brier, it is a perennial whose stems are covered with sharp thorns. It can quickly saturate a meadow because livestock do not eat it and its deep-growing roots make it hard to destroy.

Be alert at 2.5 miles, as you once more come to the end of a field where the mowed

Amelia Lake

area splits into a Y. Again, bear left, passing by staghorn sumac; its leaves are some of the first to change color in the early fall. Another mowed area comes in from the left at 2.9 miles. Stay to the right and soon pass through a windrow and into another field. Merge with and keep to the right onto a road that comes in from the left at 3.3 miles.

Be alert at 3.4 miles! Turn left onto a mowed roadway area and rise. (If you continued straight at this point for 500 feet, you would come to a narrow woodland bordering the Appomattox River. Although it could not be considered a prime camping area, were you to look hard, you might find a couple of small tent sites overlooking the water.)

Turn right when you arrive at a four-way intersection at 3.75 miles. You are now within sound of the WMA's firing ranges, so the boom of a shotgun blast or the crack of a rifle may jar you out of your reveries. Having returned to the intersection with the cinder block building next to it at 3.9 miles, stay straight along the gravel road and bypass any routes to the left or right.

Pass through a gate at 4.4 miles, swing right onto the main WMA roadway, and gradually descend. When this gravel route comes to an end at 4.9 miles, pass through another gate and follow a grassy course onto Lake Amelia's earthen dam. Perched above the water, this is a nice place to rest on bright, sunny days. Small boats glide across the lake's 100 acres as fishermen cast for sunfish, crappie, largemouth bass, bluegill, catfish, and walleye.

Cross the dam and rise, staying on the main route, to arrive at a mowed area that splits into a Y at 5.2 miles. Bear left, pass through a windrow at 5.5 miles, and stay on

a mowed area to the right. If the route has not been maintained recently, you may find yourself walking, at times, through waist-high grasses and some entangling vegetation from here to near the end of the hike. Stay to the right again less than 250 feet later. This sector of the WMA is one of the most isolated and would be a great place to camp. (Be sure to set up your tent at least 200 feet away from the lake.)

Stay to the right once more at 5.9 miles, swing around a cove of the lake, and continue along the obvious route, walking through alternating woodlands and open fields. Asiatic dayflower grows close to a small creek you will step over on a roadway culvert at 6.2 miles.

A wide route goes off to the right when you come to a T intersection at 6.75 miles; you should turn left. Enter the woods at 6.9 miles and swing around the northern end of the lake, a place where ducks have a tendency to gather upon the undisturbed water. While wood ducks are often seen along the Appomattox River, the ones you will find here are likely to be mallards, ruddy ducks, and mergansers.

Cross the lake's main feeder creek on a culvert at 7.2 miles and rise to a four-way intersection where you want to continue straight. Turn left onto a mowed area at 7.5 miles and reenter the woods 500 feet later.

Cross the WMA entrance road and return to your car at 7.75 miles, secure in the knowledge that you have successfully negotiated a hike whose unimproved and unmarked routes could have led to quite a bit of confusion. Having gained experience and confidence here, you are now ready to tackle even more challenging outings.

10

Twin Lakes State Park

Total distance (circuit): 4.9 miles

Hiking time: 2 hours, 20 minutes

Vertical rise: 350 feet

Maps: USGS 7½' Green Bay; park map

Just as the citizens of Richmond and its surrounding suburbs think of Pocahontas State Park (see Hike 8) as a quasi-municipal or regional park, so do the residents of central Virginia think of Twin Lakes State Park. Because the amenities often associated with such facilities are quite absent in this portion of the commonwealth, Twin Lakes is a magnet for those looking for outdoor recreation. Contained within its 484 acres are picnic grounds and shelters, a swimming and canoeing area, a concession stand, a conference center, a developed campground with hot showers, and a network of hiking trails. Interpretive programs during the warmer months include morning hikes, evening campfire presentations, and canoe tours.

Events within the park's history parallel many of those that occurred in the rest of the commonwealth and, indeed, throughout much of the southern United States.

Just as it had obtained the property for Shenandoah National Park (see *50 Hikes in Northern Virginia*) and Greenbelt Park (see *50 Hikes in Maryland*), the federal government purchased land for this state park from despondent farm families during the Great Depression. Subsequently, two parks, one focused around each lake, were established in 1939.

In the late 1940s, Maceo C. Martin, an African American resident of Danville, sued the state after being denied access to Staunton River State Park (see Hike 13). As the commonwealth's response in 1950,

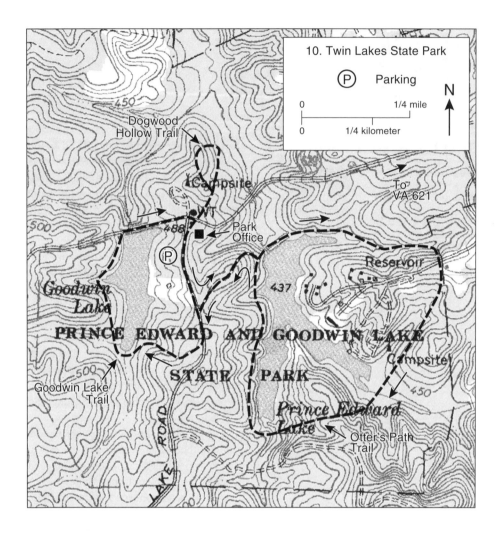

Governor William M. Tuck–justifying his action upon the basis of "similar and equal"–designated one of the parks as the Prince Edward State Park for Negroes. This segregation finally came to an end with the passage of the federal 1964 Civil Rights Act. The two entities merged into Twin Lakes State Park in 1986.

The park may be reached from the intersection of US 360 and US 460 in Burkeville. Drive west on US 360 for 2.8 miles and turn right onto VA 621. Follow this route for an additional 1.1 miles and turn left onto VA 629, which you travel on for another 0.8 mile. Soon after entering the park, turn left onto the roadway marked as leading to the day-use area. Leave you car in the picnic area parking lot.

Begin your investigation of the lakes and their surrounding piedmont woodlands by walking out of the parking lot and following the road marked as leading to the boat launch. Walk above the concession stand and swimming area on Goodwin Lake and

Central Virginia

turn left onto to the Connection "Between the Lakes" Trail at 0.15 mile. Actually a service road for park personnel, it passes through a forest of oak, red cedar, Virginia pine, and red maple. Having the greatest distribution of all tree species in eastern North America, red maple can be found as far south as Florida, as far north as Canada, and as far west as eastern Texas.

Gradually descend to Prince Edward Lake at 0.4 mile. You will be walking around this 36-acre body of water for the next hour, so pause for a few moments to appreciate what it has to offer. Let your eyes sweep across the scenery, taking in the wavering shapes of the shoreline trees as they are reflected on the wind-rippled surface of the water. The images may become even more misshapen if one of the resident beavers jumps from the bank and slaps its tail on the surface to alert others that you have walked into their home territory.

Turn left onto the Otter Path Trail and walk across the earthen dam. Once across, swing right and follow a footpath around a small cove.

Be alert at 0.6 mile! Just as you round the top of the cove you need to leave the trail along the lakeshore and switchback to the left. Ferns enjoy the moist ground along this pathway, which winds upstream along a feeder creek.

Swing away from the stream at 0.8 mile and rise, crossing the paved road to the Cedar Crest Conference Center and descending on the footpath through a carpet of crow's foot. The facility, which includes group campsites, a full-service kitchen, and a large pavilion overlooking the lake, may be reserved for business, church, and educational meetings as well as banquets, family reunions, and youth camp sessions.

From June through August, the bluish purple petals of lobelia blooms can be seen next to the trail where it crosses a footbridge, at 1.1 miles. There are several species of lobelia, many of which are so similar that a number of wildflower guidebooks don't try to identify them but simply mention that there are "variations."

Bear left onto a woods road through a stand of shortleaf pine trees at 1.2 miles. Eventually this wide route dwindles to a footpath around a backwater area of the lake. Turn left onto another woods road, lined with dogwood and sweet gum, at 1.6 miles. Dogwood becomes a deep crimson in the fall, while sweet gum's leaves turn lemon yellow. Just a few steps before you would have to wade across a stream at 1.9 miles, turn right and follow the pathway to a rock-hopping crossing of the creek.

After returning to the lake at 2.1 miles, walk along its western shoreline, possibly startling dozens of turtles and causing them to leave their log perches. The interesting movements of their feet as they paddle through the water may make you remember a tidbit of information you learned in high school biology: unlike other vertebrates, the hips and shoulders of turtles are inside their ribcages, not outside.

The crimson petals of cardinal flowers and the orange-yellow blossoms of jewelweed line the bank at 2.2 miles throughout the summer. Cross the boat launch road at 2.4 miles and continue along the Otter Path Trail, only to make a left onto the Connection "Between the Lakes" Trail at 2.6 miles and rise to retrace your steps.

Several hundred yards ahead, turn left onto the gravel road (your car is only 700 feet to the right at this point, if you have run out of time) and bear right only 200 feet later to descend the boat launch road to Goodwin Lake. Comprising only 16 surface acres, it is less than half the size of Prince Edward Lake. At the far end of the launch

Goodwin Lake

turnaround, follow the Goodwin Lake Trail into the woods.

As they tend to favor small, wooded streams instead of large bodies of water, the footbridge over the main feeder stream at 3.2 miles is one of the places in the park you are likely to spy wood ducks. Usually born in tree cavities, young wood ducks can have a rude introduction to the outside world as, not being able to fly yet, they must fling themselves 30 to 60 feet onto the ground or water below. If they survive the plunge, they need to be wary of numerous predators; snapping turtles are especially fond of them.

There is another footbridge only 300 feet later where you pass through a forest of shagbark, pignut, and mockernut hickory; sourwood, white oak, and ironwood trees. Eastern newts and red efts, the small red or orange juvenile form of the red-spotted newt, are often seen here as they scramble across the damp lumber of the footbridge. When they mature, the adult red-spotted newts are completely aquatic, but as efts they roam the forest floor.

Turn right onto paved VA 629 at 3.7 miles, cross over Goodwin Dam, and continue past the campground entrance (your car is several hundred feet to the right at this point), just before making a left into the woods and onto the Dogwood Hollow Trail.

Once on the Dogwood Trail, you will come to the loop trail intersection at 4.1 miles where you need to keep to the right and walk into a bottomland forest of sycamore and ironwood trees. Rise from the stream and, at 4.3 miles, pass by some large sweet gum, oak, and poplar trees.

The trail to the right at 4.4 miles leads to the campground; you will know you are close to it as smoke from the campfires drifts through the woods. Stay to the left, descend, and return to the loop trail intersection at 4.5 miles.

Swing right and rise, noticing the rattlesnake plantain plants you might have missed the first time you passed this way. Having returned to the campground entrance at 4.75 miles, swing around the park office building and follow the day-use area road back to your car at 4.9 miles.

An additional traipsing opportunity in this area is the 9.0-mile (one way) Prince Edward-Gallion Bridle, Boot and Bike Trail in the neighboring state forest. A map of its route is available in the state park office.

11

Kerr Reservoir

Total distance (one way): 7.2 miles

Hiking time: 3 hours, 15 minutes

Vertical rise: 300 feet

Maps: USGS 7½' Tungsten, VA/NC

Between 1899 and 1945, the Roanoke River (also known as the Staunton River) overflowed its banks at least 200 times, causing extensive damage to property and the loss of many lives. Eventually, in response to area residents' pleas—and the worst of the floods, which occurred in 1946—Congress authorized a plan for flood control.

A dam site was chosen along the Roanoke River several hundred feet above small Buggs Island, named for an early settler. During its construction in the late 1940s and early 1950s, the dam was known as the Buggs Island Project. Although its official name is now John H. Kerr Reservoir, in honor of a North Carolina congressman, most Virginians still refer to it as Buggs Island Lake.

Straddling the Virginia/North Carolina border and stretching for 39 miles along the Roanoke River, the lake has more than 800 miles of shoreline. The largest federally owned property in Virginia's piedmont, the surrounding 55,000 acres of rolling land dissected by deep drainages are a mix of large and fragmented forests, open fields, and beaver swamps. Before the early settlers arrived, the Occoneechee Indians lived in the area, and reminders of both cultures have been found in a number of the small, hidden coves.

The property is now managed by the U.S. Army Corps of Engineers for electric power production, land and water recreation, forest production, environmental protection, and flood control. In addition to two state parks (see Hikes 12 and 13), more

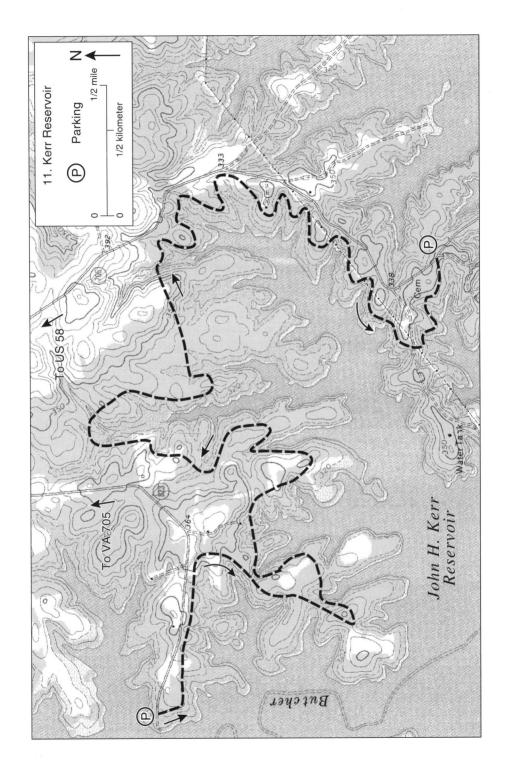

Ⓟ Parking

N

0   1/2 kilometer
0   1/2 mile

To US 58

To VA 705

Ⓟ

392

195

1333

350

336

Cem

Water Tank

350

364

Ⓟ

Butcher

*John H. Kerr
Reservoir*

than a dozen camping and recreation areas are dispersed along the shoreline, while wildlife management areas (WMAs) provide large tracts of land to wander. Most just have service roads or hunters' trails running through them, but within the Greenwood WMA is the marked and maintained Robert Munford Trail. Munford was a prominent 18th-century citizen of Mecklenburg County who lived on the land the trail passes through. Although the Kerr Reservoir area receives more than 4 million visitors annually, almost none of them (except during hunting season) make use of this pathway, making it a pristine and quiet walk in the woods.

Since this is a one-way hike, a car shuttle will be necessary. You can drive to the lower trailhead by taking I-85 to Exit 12 in South Hill, following US 58 west for 18.5 miles, and turning left onto VA 756 (Jefferson Street). Make a right onto VA 705 (Taylor Ferry Road) just 0.2 mile later, continuing for an additional 5.1 miles to the Robert Munford Trailhead parking on the right. Leave one car here and retrace your route for 2.7 miles to make a left turn onto VA 823, on which the other trailhead parking area will be found on the left in 2.0 miles.

Initiate the excursion by crossing through the gate and following the white-blazed pathway (a dirt and gravel road at this point) into the woods. The sound of your approaching footsteps may cause scores of frogs to jump into the safety of the roadway's mud puddles. Although they live much of their lives in the water, frogs don't drink it the way people do. Instead, they have a permeable skin through which liquid and gasses can pass. Additional water comes from the food they eat and, in times of drought, they are able to redirect it back into their bodies before it becomes a waste product.

As you travel this route, which is lined with a wide variety of trees—dogwood, oak, sweet gum, holly, poplar, beech, pine, and cedar—you will soon pass by a private cabin on the left. After the cabin you will see a small clearing at 0.7 mile that is rapidly becoming overgrown.

Beside a small dip in the road is a maple tree with several trunks, most likely the result of sprouts that sprang from a single stump after the tree had been cut. A second clearing is at 1.1 miles. Virginia pine and cedar trees line the clearing, whose openness lets you look up to the sky. You are obviously on a narrow point of land at 1.2 miles as water is visible through the vegetation on both sides of you.

At 1.4 miles is the cemetery that contains the grave of Robert Munford, but the only legible headstone still standing is that of Col. Sam L. Locket, who passed away in 1850.

Be alert after exploring the graves—you want to swing to the left along the cemetery's fence line. The trail may be a bit obscure at first, but follow the white blazes for a few hundred feet and it will become more obvious. After walking along the wide gravel road for so long, it is pleasant to be walking upon a narrow pathway with fallen leaves and pine needles to soften your steps. Swing around a point where small patches of rattlesnake plantain grow.

The most striking thing about rattlesnake plantain is not its flower but its leaf. Remaining green throughout the year, the mottled leaves are said to resemble the markings on the skin of a rattlesnake, hence the plant's common name. (In addition, if you use your imagination, the flowered spike reminds some people of a rattlesnake's tail.) Following the Doctrine of Signatures, this plant, which is common in both moist and dry woodlands, was often

Munford Cemetery

used to treat snakebites. Since there appears to be no special agent in the rattlesnake plantain to act as a remedy, it must be assumed that any victims who recovered only did so because their bodies were somehow able to fight off the poison.

The pathway curves around the top of a small inlet at 1.7 miles, giving you one of the best views of the lake so far. Cross a woods road at 1.9 miles and skirt the edge of a clearing, swinging around another inlet at 2.1 miles and passing by a developed spring at 2.3 miles. This is all that remains of an old springhouse, but it is another reminder of the era during which this land was inhabited.

Cross a woods road at 2.4 miles, merge onto an old road 200 feet later, and veer off it to the right in less than 50 feet more. Cross another woods road, which connects the two clearings on either side of you, at 2.75 miles. Merge right onto an old lane at 3.0 miles and follow it for a short distance, perhaps encountering more frogs. Crow's foot, a club moss that resembles miniature evergreen trees, is along the route at 3.25 miles.

Cross another woods road at 3.4 miles. Begin a long swing around a pond and inlet at 3.6 miles and cross a creek at 3.7 miles. You are a bit more than halfway through the hike, so taking a break will not only allow you a few moments rest, but also permit you to study the land you are walking through a little more thoroughly.

It is always amazing how much life is packed within a few feet of earth. Be careful to avoid the poison ivy growing nearby, but feel free to lift up and examine the tube-like blossoms of the false foxglove. The small, round hickory nuts that have fallen from the hickory trees towering above may make it a bit uncomfortable to sit on the ground; birdsong and perhaps the hoot of

an owl let you know you are not alone in the forest.

Where it crosses a small stream at 4.7 miles, the trail may disappear into heavy summer growth of nettle and poison ivy; watch for the blazes and pass by a pond at 4.8 miles.

There is a private cabin to the left at 4.9 miles, and an inlet of the lake and a private dock are to the right. Be sure to watch for blazes taking you back into the woods after crossing the dirt road because the treadway may be very faint for the first few hundred feet. Cross another dirt road at 5.25 miles and walk behind another private residence.

Merge right onto an old woods road at 5.4 miles, turning left onto a pathway less than 100 feet later where there is a view of the lake and private boat docks. Unless one series has been eliminated by the time you take this hike, you will come across two sets of white blazes going in different directions through the forest. Be sure to take the largest and newest ones so that you will come to eye-pleasing views of the lake.

Covering 50,000 acres, Kerr Reservoir is Virginia's largest inland body of water. This large expanse attracts boating enthusiasts of all kinds. Near the developed campgrounds and boat ramps, scores of power-boaters, water skiers, sailboaters, and jet skiers skim across the water, seemingly trying to outdo each other in speed. Yet, from the Robert Munford Trail you will probably only see a few canoeists or kayakers searching out hidden coves and inlets.

Abundant sunlight reaches the ground and nourishes the undergrowth of a utility line right-of-way you walk across at 5.9 miles. Expect to get scratched arms and legs from the entangling briers and brambles, but do enjoy the delicate Asiatic dayflower, which prospers in open areas. Pass under another utility line at 6.1 miles.

Cross a narrow ravine on a footbridge (which, if it has not been repaired, may not be here when you arrive) at 6.4 miles and another one at 6.5 miles.

The openness of one last utility line right-of-way at 6.7 miles provides the sunlight that allows greenbrier and Virginia creeper to grow well. Because it can also be a climbing vine, the latter is often confused with poison ivy. Creeper, however, has five leaves (which turn a deep crimson in late summer/early fall), as opposed to poison ivy's three leaves.

Be alert at 7.1 miles! Although there may be a pathway to the right, you need to swing to the left when you come to an old concrete-block foundation so you can return to your car and end the hike at 7.2 miles.

12

Occoneechee State Park

Total distance (circuit): 2.4 miles

Hiking time: 1 hour

Vertical rise: 190 feet

Maps: USGS 7½' Clarksville North; park map

For more than four centuries, the Occoneechee Indians lived on lands that are now under the waters of Kerr Reservoir. Making camps on small islands in the Roanoke River, they prospered by trading with other Native Americans who used the waterway as a natural travel route, but their existence as a cohesive tribe began to unravel in the early part of the 17th century.

Arriving in May 1607 upon the *Susan Constant, Godspeed,* and *Discovery,* a band of 104 men and boys from Great Britain set about establishing a colony on the James River. Ill-equipped for the task at hand, they were held together in large part by the determination of Captain John Smith. Yet the London Company, which had sponsored the venture, continued to send more settlers. During the winter of 1609–1610–known as the starving time–the colony of 500 was reduced to no more than 60.

Life remained a struggle for many years. In addition, continuing Indian raids and a growing disillusionment with the British governor's failure to deal with them brought about a rebellion in 1676. Seeking revenge, a band of colonial settlers led by Nathaniel Bacon murdered scores of Native Americans, which nearly wiped out the entire tribe; the few who survived fled into what is now North Carolina.

Occoneechee State Park is on the site of where much of this took place. Situated along the northern shore of Kerr Reservoir, the park's 2,690 acres are leased by the commonwealth from the U.S. Army Corps of Engineers. (The Corps constructed the

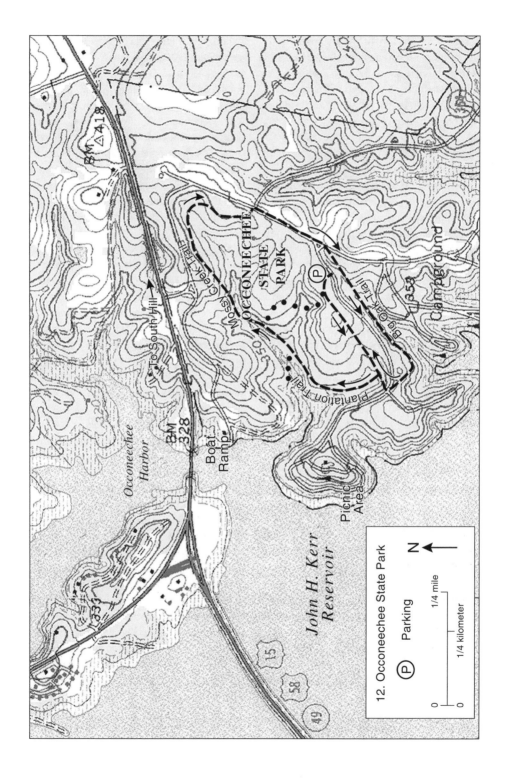

12. Occoneechee State Park

P   Parking

N

0 _____ 1/4 mile
0 _____ 1/4 kilometer

Occoneechee Harbor

John H. Kerr Reservoir

OCCONEECHEE STATE PARK

Moss Creek Trail

Plantation Trail

Big Oak Trail

To South Hill

Boat Ramp

Picnic Area

Campground

BM △418

BM 328

49
58
15

reservoir and has management responsibility for its shoreline acreage (see Hike 11.) Within the park are hiking trails, picnic areas and shelters, a playground, a campground with flush toilets, hot showers, and a dump station. Two boat ramps give motorboaters, jet skiers, water skiers, and sailboaters access to the lake. Interpretive programs, including Native American crafts, nature and cultural programs, campfire presentations, and night hikes, are offered every weekend from Memorial Day to Labor Day.

Although the traverse of the park's network of trails is rather short when compared to many other outings in this guidebook, it is an easy and pleasant stroll that the whole family should be able to enjoy. Most visitors to the park are here to engage in some kind of activity on the reservoir, so it is a very real possibility you may be the only one on the trails. Being on these pathways is a great way to start your day or to escape the hustle and bustle of the campground in the evening. Remember, as in all of Virginia's state parks, pets must be kept on a leash.

Occoneechee State Park may be reached by taking I-85 to Exit 12 in South Hill and following US 58 west for about 17.0 miles to the US 58/VA 92 intersection near Boydton. Approximately 8.0 miles beyond the junction, turn left off of US 58 into the park on VA 364. (If coming from the west, this would be a right turn about 1.5 miles east of downtown Clarksville.) Pass through the contact station in just a few hundred feet and turn left toward the campgrounds. Bear right onto the road to Campground B 0.7 mile later and leave your car at the Terrace Gardens parking area on the right in an additional 0.1 mile.

Start the hike by following the rock-lined pathway into the woods, arriving within a few feet at the remains of the five terraced gardens of the Occoneechee Plantation.

Although that term was applied to any large farm in the 1800s, Occoneechee would certainly qualify as a *Gone With the Wind*-type plantation. Encompassing 3,105 acres, it ran as a self-sufficient operation, complete with icehouse, mill, smokehouse, slaves' quarters, and a pottery and carpentry workshop. The main house, a 20-room mansion built by William Townes in 1839, overlooked the gardens. The plantation's demise begin in 1898, when the mansion burned to the ground in a fire started by Christmas tree candles.

Come to a Y intersection less than 300 feet after leaving your car and bear to the left, passing by the site of an old 30-foot water well and the deep pit that is all that remains of the icehouse. Walking along the edge of the woods, it is easy to discern each garden terrace as you drop down onto the different levels. The boxwood trees on the terraces were planted as part of the landscaping scheme to provide a pleasant view from the mansion.

Take the short trail to the right at 0.1 mile and walk the few feet to the Crudup gravesite, surrounded—and grown over—by periwinkle. Try to memorize this trailing plant with its purplish-blue flowers. It was often cultivated as an ornamental border plant around gardens or yards, and you will often find patches of it growing in the most unlikely places throughout woodlands in Virginia—an almost-sure sign that a homestead once existed on that spot.

Return to the main route, turn right, and look to the left for the sign marking the Plantation Trail, which you should follow into the woods. Cross a dirt road at 0.2 mile, reentering a wood with sweet gum trees growing above you and crow's foot spreading over the forest floor.

The Campground B Trail comes in from the left at 0.3 mile; keep right and begin to

The only evidence of bygone days

walk parallel to a gully; it was created because past unsound farming practices accelerated the erosive power of rainwater. Through the vegetation to the left, you may be able to make out the sunlight playing upon the water of the lake.

The Warrior's Path goes left to a boat launch at 0.4 mile; stay to the right. The long, narrow mound to the left of the trail at 0.5 mile was built to dam the creek and create a small pond that was just a few feet deep. When it froze over in winter, the ice was cut out and brought to the icehouse, where it was covered with straw and sawdust, creating a cool place in which to store food even during the summer.

Rise gradually along the stream, where lobelia, with its purple flowers, grows among several different species of ferns.

Switchback to the right at 0.6 mile, then to the left, and come to an old brick chimney, the only evidence that a house once stood here. Turn left and descend along the Mossy Creek Trail, crossing the stream on a footbridge at 0.7 mile. Swing left and descend along the creek, noticing the varied pinks, oranges, and purples of the fungi pushing their way through the disturbed soil of the footpath.

Swing to the right at 0.8 mile, heading up a different watercourse. Large beech trees—with the inevitable initials and love messages carved into their smooth bark—line the pathway. An abundance of large pine cones dropped onto the ground from the high branches of the Virginia pines are scattered between the evergreen leaves of rattlesnake plantain and the thin blades of yellow star grass. Just as its common name suggests, the flowers of the latter are tiny, yellow, star-shaped blossoms growing from grasslike leaves. Depending on a particular year's weather conditions, you could possibly find the plant blooming all the way from March through September.

Soon you will rise from the creek and turn to the right along the grassy shoulder of the main park road at 1.2 miles. Bypass the private roads and the Campground B road, make a right turn into the woods on the Big Oak Trail at 1.5 miles, and descend into a small stream valley. Pass under a utility line at 1.8 miles and ascend.

Turn left onto the Campground B road at 2.0 miles and bear right almost immediately at the Y intersection. Be alert less than 500 feet later as you need to turn right into the woods on the path marked as leading to the Plantation Trail and Warrior's Path. Once again, periwinkle becomes a part of this hike.

Using a footbridge to cross a small creek at 2.1 miles, turn right onto the Plantation Trail and retrace your steps through the mansion site with its terraced gardens. The hike ends when you return to your car at 2.4 miles.

For additional walks within the Kerr Reservoir area, Staunton River State Park (see Hike 13) is less than a 45-minute drive to the west, while a ramble (see Hike 11) that winds around isolated coves of the reservoir is only a 20-minute car trip to the east.

13

Staunton River State Park

Total distance (circuit): 7.5 miles

Hiking time: 3 hours, 40 minutes

Vertical rise: 700 feet

Maps: USGS 7½' Buffalo Springs; park map

Established in 1936–one of the six original state parks in Virginia–and located at the confluence of the Staunton and Dan Rivers, Staunton River State Park sits at the head of Kerr Reservoir (see Hike 11). Within the park are a swimming pool, rental cabins, campground with hot showers, picnic areas and shelters, tennis and volleyball courts, children's playgrounds, and a network of pathways open to hikers, bikers, and equestrians. The Civilian Conservation Corps (CCC) constructed most of these facilities in the 1930s.

The river (and thus the park) was named in honor of Captain Henry Staunton, whose troops protected early settlers from Indian attacks in the days before the Revolutionary War. As the area prospered, large plantations were established along the river, which became an important transportation route.

I have always enjoyed my walks here. Not only does the park have the distinction of possessing one of the longest single pathways that can be hiked in central Virginia, it also has wonderful views of the rivers, and wildlife sightings can be quite frequent. Be on the lookout for ducks, geese, herons, turtles, and frogs in the water, while deer, turkey, raccoons, and snakes may draw your attention back to the land. The River Bank Trail leads not only through the forests, but also beside all three bodies of water that crowd in upon the land.

To reach the park, drive US 360 east from South Boston for a little more than 8.0 miles and make a right onto VA 344. You will enter the park 10.1 miles later. Continue

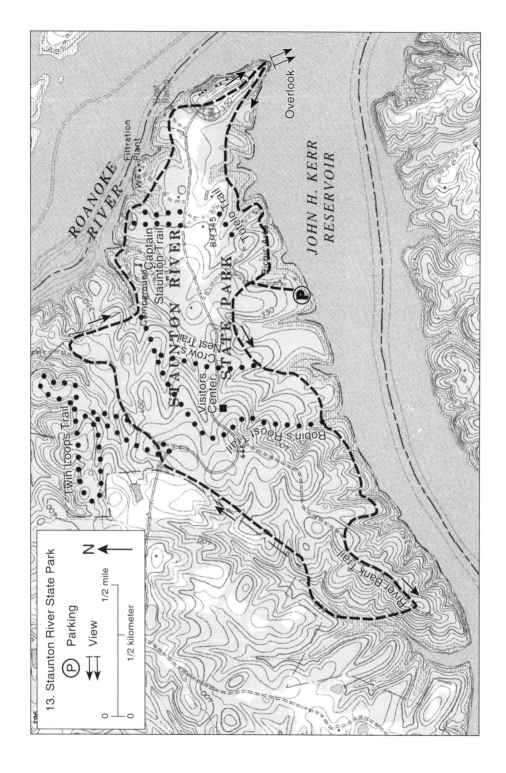

13. Staunton River State Park

ⓟ Parking

View

N

0   1/2 mile

0   1/2 kilometer

ROANOKE RIVER

Filtration Plant

Boat Ramp

Overlook

JOHN H. KERR RESERVOIR

STAUNTON RIVER STATE PARK

Staunton Trail

Campground

Captain Staunton Trail

Totero Trail

BM 345

ⓟ

Crow's Nest Trail

Visitors Center

Robin's Roost Trail

Twin Loops Trail

River Bank Trail

an additional 1.0 mile to make a right onto VA 782 toward the picnic area, and turn right again toward Picnic Area #2 in less than 0.1 mile. Parking is on the left, 0.3 mile later.

Walk back up the road, turn left onto the blue-blazed River Bank Trail, and enter the woods. Loblolly pine and cedar trees grow tall in this forest, while poison ivy creeps along the ground and onto tree trunks. Cross the paved boat dock road at 0.5 mile. If you are getting tired, running out of time, or just wish to shorten this hike by about 3 miles, you could turn right onto the orange-blazed Crow's Nest Trail at 0.6 mile, follow it across the main park road, turn right onto the Robin's Roost Trail, and rejoin this description at the 4.7 milepoint. To continue along the River Bank Trail, turn left, walk about 500 feet, and swing right.

Views of the Dan River are visible through the vegetation at 1.0 mile, where you swing away from it to join up with and walk the combined route of the River Bank/Robin's Roost Trails. However, the Robin's Roost Trail goes off to the right at 1.2 miles where you want to stay to the left to continue along the River Bank Trail, which brings you back to a view of the river through a forest of beech and sweet gum trees at 1.5 miles.

Once more, the pathway swings away from the river at 1.9 miles, this time coming to a Y intersection at 2.2 miles where it bears left to descend. Never quite returning to the river, the trail veers to the right at 2.6 miles (next to the state park's boundary with the Army Corps of Engineers property) and begins the long traverse across the ridge that separates the Dan River from the Staunton River. Rattlesnake plantain grows in small patches beside the trail as you descend and rise through several small stream valleys. Cross VA 344 diagonally to the right

next to the park entrance at 3.7 miles and reeneter the woods. Just a few hundred feet later, stay left to avoid the trail to the right that leads a short distance to a horse trailer parking area. However, at 3.8 miles you will want to swing to the right to avoid a spur of the pink-blazed Twin Loops Trail. (Around the turn of the 21st century, the park obtained almost 1,000 more acres and plans call for the Twin Loops Trail to connect with many miles of pathways winding their way through these new lands. Inquire at the park office to see if additional hiking opportunities are available by the time you visit the park.)

The road to the right at 3.9 miles also leads to the horse trailer parking area. The River Bank Trail turns left and descends in a younger forest than what you have been hiking through, and greenbrier vines snake onto the vegetation and sweet gum balls lay on the ground. Stay to the right at 4.3 miles when another spur of the Twin Loops Trail comes in from the left.

At 4.7 miles, step over a small stream on a nicely constructed footbridge where, at its far end, the Robin's Roost Trail comes in from the right. The River Bank Trail bears left. Although it is barely more than a foot wide, the stream (when flowing well in the spring or after a heavy rain) sparkles as it reflects the green of the growth above it. The water does become wider as it empties into the Staunton River at 4.9 miles. With a variety of ducks—including mallards, mergansers, and wood ducks—found on both the lake and the two rivers around the state park, it is a good bet that they have been a part of your hike. They glide about quite easily in the water, but on shore their gait is more of a waddle than a walk. This is because a duck's legs are positioned close to the rear of its body, where they provide the most efficient forward thrust while the bird is swimming.

A backwater area of the Staunton River

Swing right along the river at 5 miles and pass by a trail to the right that leads a short distance to the campground. Great blue herons are often seen close to shore, wading in the shallow water in search of a meal.

Pass by the red-blazed Captain Staunton's Trail coming in from the right at 5.1 miles. You might see a box turtle lumbering up from the river to a drier site on the hillside; they live throughout the park. These land turtles do not have one particular nest or burrow, but rest in "forms," depressions dug about an inch into the vegetation and soil. From spring to fall they sleep in the forms and stay in them until late in the morning, waiting for the sun to warm them before heading out to eat. In winter, box turtles hibernate below the leaf litter in forms that are a few inches deeper. Since this is not deep enough to keep frost from reaching them, scientists do not yet know how they avoid freezing to death.

As you swing around a few inlets, you may notice that, sadly, when the level of the lake drops, these small coves and inlets show just how much garbage must be in the lake. Cross a dirt road at 5.5 miles, pass under a utility line at 5.6 miles, and step across the boat ramp gravel road at 5.9 miles. (Pit toilets are to your left.)

Swing away from the Staunton River and, once again, rise over the land that separates the two rivers—at this point much narrower than it was earlier in the hike. Cross the main park road at 6.0 miles and descend beside pawpaw trees. In an example of how important it is to understand the interdependence of all life, researchers have found that the pawpaw is the only food source for the zebra swallowtail butterfly. As the lands where pawpaws grow are being consumed for development, the numbers of zebra swallowtails have decreased. What as yet unknown effect is this loss of butterflies having on other creatures or plants?

The River Bank Trail makes a hard turn to the right at 6.1 miles, but before following it, continue straight (on a pathway that may not be marked) to an overlook of the confluence of the Staunton and Dan Rivers, where they form Kerr Reservoir. Egrets may be wading around close to shore while a great blue heron takes wing into the blue sky. Great blues have been known to nest on the ground, but because there are numerous predators living on the land around the reservoir, the population in this area has a tendency to nest in colonies in the treetops. Watch for flocks of them returning home as the day wanes.

Retrace your steps back to the intersection, bear left, and proceed through the woods with the Dan River, once again, visible through the trees. The sound of kids playing in the park's swimming pool is often audible as it seeps into the forest's thick summer vegetation. Turn left at 6.9 miles, walk under utility lines for a few feet, and turn right back into the woods to swing around the amenities of Picnic Area #1 before coming to a small clay beach on the river's edge. Be alert as you continue along the River Bank Trail, for at 7.0 miles it makes an abrupt turn to the right and does not follow the pathway that descends to the left. You will make a left turn to walk under utility lines at 7.1 miles, where horse nettle thrives in the open sunshine. Less than 800 feet later, turn right into the woods, go a few hundred feet, turn left onto the paved Picnic Area #2 road, and return to your car at 7.5 miles.

14

Appomattox History Trail

Total distance (one way): 4.0 miles

Hiking time: 2 hours

Vertical rise: 390 feet

Maps: USGS 7½' Appomattox; USGS 7½' Vera; park History Trail map

Upon the fall of Petersburg to Union forces (see Hike 7), Confederate general Robert E. Lee evacuated both Petersburg and Richmond and, in an attempt to regroup, marched his men westward. When anticipated and much-needed supplies failed to reach the troops, Lee recognized that the end was near. Setting up camp next to the Appomattox River, he sent word to Ulysses S. Grant, general-in-chief of all United States forces, that he wished to discuss terms of surrender. Although minor skirmishes continued throughout the South for the next few months, the Civil War effectively came to an end on April 12, 1865, when Lee's Army of Northern Virginia laid down its arms in the small village of Appomattox Court House.

Although a historic site, the town was neglected and soon fell into disrepair. Finally, in June 1930, Congress passed a bill providing for a monument at the site—which was never built. However, legislation was signed in 1935 to restore the village, and on April 6, 1954, the area was designated the Appomattox Court House National Historical Park.

Weaving onto open meadows and into quiet forests, the Appomattox History Trail provides the means to explore much of the park's rolling piedmont terrain. What is so interesting about hiking in national historical parks such as this is that there are so many levels to appreciate. You can enjoy the restful scenery and delight in the various plants and animals, all the while obtaining a better understanding of our nation's history.

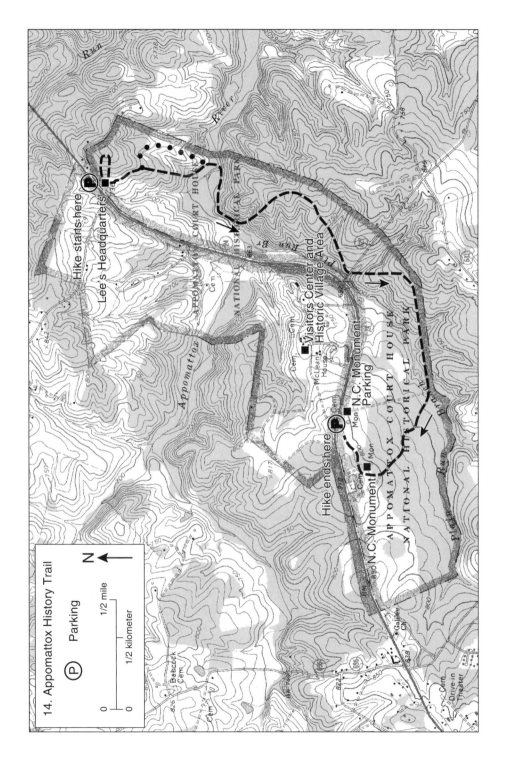

14. Appomattox History Trail

Ⓟ Parking

N

0   1/2 mile

0   1/2 kilometer

Hike starts here

Lee's Headquarters

Visitors Center and
Historic Village Area

N.C. Monument

Parking

McLean
House

Hike ends here

N.C. Monument

APPOMATTOX COURT HOUSE
NATIONAL HISTORICAL PARK

At one time, the Appomattox History Trail was a circuit hike of 6.1 miles that took in both the historic village area and the woodlands across the road. Concerns about the safety of pedestrians crossing busy VA 24 resulted in the trail being broken into two unconnected sections. This hike description follows the longer section in the woods, but, in order to gain a better appreciation for the history of the area you will be walking through, you are strongly urged to take in the displays at the visitors center and walk through the historic village area before beginning the hike. (There are hopes that one day the trail may once again be a circuit; check at the visitors center to see if that has happened by the time you arrive here.)

The park may be reached from the intersection of US 460 and VA 24 in Appomattox County. Drive VA 24 east for 1.2 miles and leave one car in the parking area marked for the North Carolina monument. Continue eastward for 0.4 mile and turn left into the national historical park entrance.

After gathering background information for your outing by obtaining brochures and watching interpretive multimedia presentations at the visitors center, walk into the village. Guided tours of the reconstructed McLean House, where Lee formally surrendered to Grant, are given on a regular basis (check at the visitors center for times and dates). The 1852 Meeks' Store served as a store, pharmacy, private residence, and Presbyterian church, and the jail was under construction in 1865. Keep to the right at the triangle, which the defeated Confederate Army marched by on the way to surrender their arms. The small building across from the corner of the triangle was the law office of Crawford Jones, an ardent local secessionist.

Turn left here and then right onto a grassy route, and you will soon pass by a vista of the surrounding provincial countryside. Grant and Lee met here on April 10, 1865, for the second time before the surrender parade on April 12. Retrace your steps back to the car, having walked less than 0.75 mile. Drive eastward again on VA 24 for 0.4 mile to park in the lot for Lee's Headquarters.

Upon evacuating Petersburg, Lee's army was soon blocked in at this site by Union troops. After holding his final war council on April 8, Lee sent the message about discussing surrender to Grant the next day. Begin the hike by taking the trail to the left into the woods and coming to the place, at 0.1 mile, where Lee's headquarters tent was situated. Swing to the right and continue along a pathway lined with dogwood, oak, and poplar.

Bear left at 0.2 mile (your car is a few hundred yards to the right) to continue along the combined History and Nature Trails. If you are wondering what kinds of trees you are walking by, small signs placed by the American Society of Foresters will help you to identify white oak, red maple, yellow poplar, black gum, southern red oak, and flowering dogwood. Remember, though, that a large percentage of the property you are walking through during this hike was planted in fields of tobacco and small grain during the Civil War. The piles of rocks in the woods are evidence of just how much work it took to make this land tillable.

Be alert at 0.4 mile. This description follows the route of the Nature Trail, which goes to the right. You could just as easily stay to the left and follow the History Trail, as the two rejoin in a short distance. Following the Nature Trail, descend past Virginia pine, mockernut hickory, mountain ash, mountain laurel, and eastern red cedar. Stay to the right again at 0.5 mile, where a route comes in from the left and beech trees are part of the forest.

The open meadows of the park

Make use of a footbridge at 0.6 mile to cross a small gully. The trail is no longer a woods road, but a narrower footpath winding its way beside black cherry, American sycamore, and black walnut. Walk through an open field for a few hundred feet at 0.7 mile, where in late summer the seeds of the tall grass add a subtle pinkish hue, and the Nature Trail comes to an end. At the far edge of the field, turn right into the woods on the History Trail and cross the Appomattox River at the site where the Sweeny mill operated after the Civil War. Local farmers brought the small grain they had raised in their fields to be ground into meal. Keep to the right to follow the river upstream, swing left at 1.3 miles, and rise a bit before leveling out to bear right at a T intersection at 1.5 miles. In order to avoid a utility line right-of-way, the trail swings to the right at 1.7 miles.

Cross the Prince Edward Court House Road at 2.2 miles and rise into the woods, soon coming to the site where Union major general George Armstrong Custer (later of Little Bighorn fame) received a flag of truce from Captain Robert M. Sims on the morning of April 9, 1865. The Confederates asked for a cessation of hostilities until Lee could confer with Grant.

Bypass the pathways coming in from the left at 2.6 miles and 2.8 miles, but be sure to seek out the blossoms of the lobelia that grow beside the small stream crossing in late summer. Cross Plain Run on a footbridge at 3.1 miles and bypass Sears Lane, which goes to the right at 3.2 miles. This is part of the route Grant used on the way to meet Lee.

Rise on a wide grassy swath through the woods, where you might spot numerous animal droppings. Taking a few moments to study these can provide clues to some of the animals living here. Cylindrical scat indicates skunks, raccoons, opossums, and foxes, while piles of pellets show that deer or rabbits were here.

Swing right to stay in the woods at 3.7 miles, coming to the North Carolina monument at 3.8 miles. It is interesting to note that the monument states that, throughout the war, this southern state lost 14,522 men during battle; 5,151 later died from their wounds; and 20,602 died from disease. Both sides suffered heavy casualties during the Civil War, and more men were lost to disease—most often severe cases of dysentery—than to wounds inflicted during battle.

Follow the obvious dirt roadway to a low ridge at 3.9 miles, the site of the last organized volley by Lee's Army of Northern Virginia, on the morning of April 9. Turn right onto the trail marked as leading to the Confederate Cemetery and follow it to end the hike when you return to your shuttled car at 4.0 miles.

If you feel like braving the traffic of VA 24, you can cross the road for a final bit of history before heading home. The Appomattox Court House Confederate Cemetery is the final resting place of 18 Confederate soldiers and one Union soldier. A plaque erected in 1926 by the Appomattox Chapter of the Daughters of the Confederacy is a vivid expression of how a large number of southerners viewed the end of the war more than a half-century later:

AFTER 4 YEARS OF HEROIC STRUGGLE
IN DEFENSE OF THE PRINCIPLES BELIEVED
FUNDAMENTAL TO THE EXISTENCE OF OUR
    GOVERNMENT
LEE SURRENDERED 9000 MEN THE REMNANT
    OF AN ARMY
STILL UNCONQUERED IN SPIRIT

(The plaque is somewhat inaccurate; Lee actually surrendered more than 28,000 men.)

Just beyond the cemetery, and lined by a split-rail fence, is the route of the Richmond–Lynchburg Stage Road. On April 12, 1865, the Confederates marched on this road and into the village to give up their arms and receive their paroles.

15

Blackwater Creek

Total distance (circuit): 5.7 miles

Hiking time: 2 hours, 40 minutes

Vertical rise: 280 feet

Maps: USGS 7½' Lynchburg

As far back as 1934, decades before other municipalities had even begun to think about greenways, the citizens of Lynchburg were envisioning such places. Although their plans did not materialize at that time, the concept was reintroduced in the early 1970s. Encouraged by the volunteer members of the Friends of Lynchburg Stream Valleys and other supporters, the city included the idea into its master plan, acquired the needed property, and developed a network of bikeways and hiking trails. Located within the center of the city, and officially dedicated on May 17, 1979, the Blackwater Creek Natural Area and its trails were recognized by the federal government to be of such significance that they were proclaimed a part of the National Recreational Trail System in 1981.

In addition to furnishing an easily accessible place in which the city's citizens and visitors can recreate in the outdoors, the natural area serves as a much-needed green space for the urban area. Its lush vegetation acts as a filter for water borne pollutants and soaks up gallons of water, helping to moderate floods during times of heavy rain. The linear greenway provides homes and a migration route to many animals not often found within a city's boundaries. Be on the lookout for deer, foxes, raccoons, snakes, beavers, hawks, owls, blue herons, and a wide assortment of songbirds. Even wild turkeys, which need expansive plots of undisturbed land, have been seen here. This is probably the best hike one can take within the limits of any of Virginia's cities;

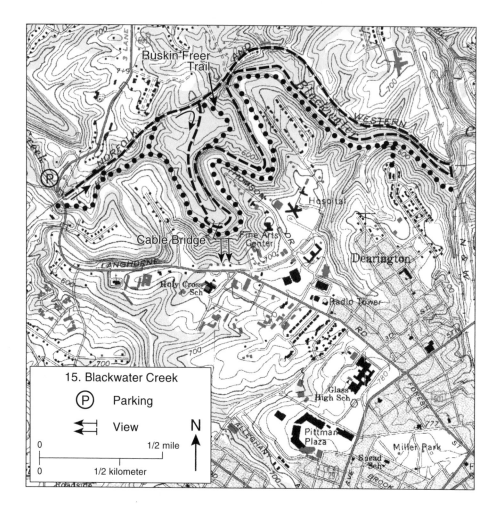

15. Blackwater Creek

(P) Parking

⇆ View   N

0 _____ 1/2 mile

0 _____ 1/2 kilometer

you could easily find yourself believing you are in some of the state's remotest back-country.

There are numerous access points to the natural area, but to reach the trailhead for the hike described here, drive (with many twists and turns for each of the routes described; follow road signs) US 29 Business north from the US 29/US 460 intersection south of Lynchburg for 5.0 miles. Turn onto US 501 Business, continue for 3.1 miles, make a right onto Old Langhorne Road, and almost immediately make a right into the

parking lot. Be aware that the natural area is open only from sunrise to sunset, and that pets must be kept on a leash.

Begin the hike by walking the paved Bikeway into the woods. The bike route follows an old railroad bed, so the first and last portions of the hike are on a nearly level grade. The terrain is certainly not flat, though, and you will walk through numerous areas where the builders of the railroad had to cut through the hillside or fill in small ravines in order to lay down the track on a suitable railroad grade.

The trail to the right at 0.2 mile descends to the creek; stay on the Bikeway here and do the same at 0.4 mile, when another pathway drops to the right. However, be alert at 0.7 mile because you do want to take the trail that enters the woods to your right. Within a few feet, bear right on the path marked as leading to the Freer Trail. Rise into a mixed hardwood forest, with dogwood and redbud as part of the understory.

Descend at 0.8 mile, but you will soon begin a gradual rise and make a right turn onto the red-blazed Freer Trail at the loop trail intersection. You have just entered the Ruskin Freer Nature Preserve. Named in honor of a local biology teacher, the preserve's 115 acres are in various stages of forest succession. Much of the Blackwater Creek area was once open agricultural land, and nature is in the slow process of returning it to a climax forest.

Begin to descend into the creek gorge at 1.0 mile, where crow's foot lines both sides of the path. A number of the trees, such as tulip poplar and Virginia pine, are tagged at 1.4 miles in order to help you identify them throughout the hike. Reach the creek at 1.5 miles and turn left to follow it downstream. Almost immediately there is a cable suspension bridge that you could use to cross the stream. You, however, want to remain on the left bank.

This portion of the hike along Blackwater Creek is by far the prettiest and most isolated. Down inside this deep canyon, the sound of the moving water overcomes any traffic noise. The abundance of wildflowers, such as mayapple, bloodroot, Indian pipe, dogtooth violet, and robin's plantain, add to this nice illusion of wilderness.

The rocks in the creek at 1.7 miles make small ripples and rapids while jack-in-the-pulpit and poison ivy grow along the bank. The other section of the Freer Trail comes in from the left at 2.0 miles. Stay right along the creek, watching for wood ducks and other waterfowl. A swinging bridge would make it possible for you to cross the stream at 2.1 miles, but stay left instead and rise high above the creek, beginning the descent back to it at 2.3 miles.

The trail to the left at 2.5 miles rises to the Bikeway, but you should stay right and continue to descend. Upon returning to the creek, you might notice the tracks of deer, opossum, or other creatures impressed into the soft mud.

Pass by a small, overgrowing clearing at 2.7 miles. Joe-pye weed, goldenrod, asters, and black-eyed Susans all flourish in the bright sunshine. In a perfect example of how humans affect the makeup of the natural world, black-eyed Susans are not native to the eastern United States but rather were originally found only in the plains and prairie lands of North America. It is believed the flower made its way eastward in the 1830s, when its seeds became mixed with shipments of the red clover seeds that eastern farmers were eager to plant in their fields. Today the plant is found in nearly every state in the U.S. and in many Canadian provinces.

Step over sewer line rights-of-way and footbridges across side streams at 2.9 miles and 3.1 miles. Avoid the trail rising to the Bikeway at 3.15 miles and step over a concrete culvert stamped with the date 1943 on it at 3.5 miles. Be alert at 3.7 miles. With an old railroad trestle rising more than a hundred feet above you, take your leave of the creek and make a sudden switchback to ascend to the left.

Turn left onto the paved Bikeway ᴬ miles. Once again you are on thᴬ the old railroad bed, so thᴬ major ups and downs tᴬ will be rising at a vᴬ begin this return portion of the hike back to your car. Asiatic dayflower lines much of the pathway and grapevines drape themselves over the vegetation of the understory.

The trail to the left at 4.4 miles descends to the creek; stay on the paved pathway as it goes through a major cut through the rock strata of the hillside. Mullein, a member of the snapdragon family, reaches heights of almost 5 feet as it grows from the disturbed soils here.

The trail to the right at 4.6 miles leads to Brunswick Road; the East Randolph Place parking lot is next to the Bikeway at 4.7 miles. Walk underneath a utility line at 5.0 miles, soon bypassing the pathway to the left that you followed onto the Freer Trail about two hours ago. From here it is a simple matter of retracing your steps along the Bikeway to return to your car at 5.7 miles.

Looking for additional walking opportunities within the city? There are many, many more miles of pathways for you to discover in the Blackwater Creek area and along the James River. The Blackwater Creek Bikeway connects to the River Walk, which then extends across Percival's Island and on into Amherst County. Additional hiking places include Ivy Creek Greenway, the Bill Foot Natural Area, and numerous other trails. Contact the Lynchburg Department of Parks and Recreation (see the section entitled Addresses in the Introduction of this book) for maps and the most up-to-date information. Other municipalities would be wise to emulate this city's forward-looking example.

16

Fairy Stone State Park

Total distance (circuit): 6.4 miles

Hiking time: 3 hours, 10 minutes

Vertical rise: 880 feet

*Maps: USGS 7½' Charity; USGS 7½'
Philpott Reservoir; park map*

Situated next to a western arm of Philpott Lake, Fairy Stone State Park is named for the cross-shaped staurolite stones found only in this area of Virginia. A local legend holds that they are the crystallized tears of fairies who wept upon hearing the sad news of the crucifixion of Christ. Less fancifully, geologists say they are the result of intense heat and pressure produced during the formation of the Appalachian Mountains. Since you are permitted to search for and keep any of the cross-shaped stones you may happen to find on specified park property, it might be a bit more romantic to believe the fairy story.

Within the park's 4,570 acres are 168-acre Fairy Stone Lake, a bathing beach, a campground, picnic areas, cabins, rowboats, canoes, and paddleboats for rent. The lake has been known to yield walleyes and bluegills to anglers; catfish in the 20-pound range are not uncommon.

For a state park in Virginia, Fairy Stone has an amazing amount of land devoted to hiking trails—more than 25 miles of pathways in all. Although considered by most people to be in central Virginia, the park is more in the mountains than in the piedmont, so there is a great variety of terrain suitable for all levels of fitness.

This hike begins in the developed part of the park and follows a system of wide and well-marked pathways. Highlights include numerous stream valleys and a stretch along the shore of the lake. Since it's on the eastern rampart of the Blue Ridge, there are several spectacular mountain vistas. This is

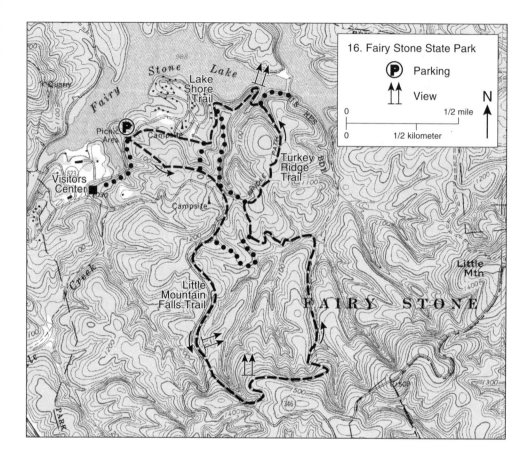

a great morning walk to work up a little sweat before an afternoon swim in the cooling waters of the lake.

From US 220 a few miles north of Martinsville, Fairy Stone State Park may be reached by driving westward on VA 57 for 13.0 miles and then turning right onto VA 346. You will enter the park 1.0 mile later. Turn left where the road splits in two at the visitors center and continue for an additional 0.5 mile to the trailhead parking.

Walk across the park road, enter the woods, and head toward the campground on the combined Little Mountain Falls, Turkey Ridge, and Lakeshore Trails marked by orange, blue, and yellow blazes. Ascend

at a gradual rate through hardwoods and pines.

The trail to the right at 0.15 mile ascends to the campground; stay left on the combined trails and walk below the campground. Avoid the trail to the left at 0.3 mile that leads to the cabins. Stay to the right again just a few feet later, when the Lakeshore Trail takes off to the left. An unmarked trail descends to the left at 0.4 mile; continue right and rise above the first of a number of narrow creek defiles you will encounter on this journey.

The next intersection, at 0.5 mile, is where you want to keep to the right to follow the orange blazes of the Little Mountain

Falls Trail. Less than 200 feet later, stay to the left to avoid the path to the campground and the Mountain View Trail. The pine trees, which have been quite prevalent, become less common as you descend.

Arrive at a small clearing at 0.9 mile. The trail to the left is a connector route, while the trail to the immediate right leads to the Mountain View Trail. You want to swing progressively to the right, continuing to follow the orange blazes.

Gradually descend, swinging around another narrow hollow. This is a jumbled landscape you are walking through, not at all like the Blue Ridge area just to the west, which has long, narrow ridges separated by well-defined valleys.

Rise for a short distance at 1.2 miles, resuming the descent once you reach the top of a low ridge. The oaks are probably the most dominant trees in this part of the forest. When you realize that there are at least 1,000 species of insects that feed upon the oaks, you may marvel that the trees exist at all. There are a few pests in particular whose work on the oaks is easy to recognize: Because of the heavy infestations within the last couple of decades, many of us are familiar with the gypsy moth, which may kill a tree within two to three years after attacking it. Leaves that have been folded and tied together by strands of silk are the work of the oak leaftyer, a moth that feeds inside the folds. The thin trails or tunnels on the upper surface of the leaves are the result of oak leaf miners.

Even the oaks' seeds, the acorns, are not safe from insect parasites. The female black acorn weevil bores a hole through the acorn and lays eggs in it. The larvae then feed and pupate inside the acorn. After these insects vacate the premises, the holes they leave behind are, in turn, used by the acorn moth to lay its eggs.

Rise again at 1.4 miles, quickly gaining elevation as the route becomes lined by mountain laurel and galax.

A created viewpoint at 1.7 miles provides a sweeping vista across the foothills to some of the higher peaks along the eastern edge of the Blue Ridge. Upon reaching the height of the land, bear left and descend amid the galax. (Directly ahead is the Mountain View Trail.) However, you will soon begin to rise again, coming to a second created viewpoint at 2.1 miles before resuming a rapid descent.

Switchback to the right at 2.5 miles and parallel Little Mountain Falls Creek. Cross the stream at 2.8 miles and descend next to the falls. Although it is a very minor drop when compared to falls found in the western part of the state, the sparkling water does add beauty to the hike. Cross the creek again at 2.9 miles and once more just 150 feet later.

The trail to the right at 3.2 miles leads to the backcountry campsite—sadly no longer open. (Since all regulations have a tendency to change over time, it might be worth it before you embark upon this hike to check with the authorities. This is a lovely and isolated spot and would be a great place to spend the night if so permitted.) Cross the creek for the last time and ascend to the right, avoiding the crossover trail along the creek. Deer tracks in the soft mud provide evidence that the stream is frequented by woodland creatures.

The Little Mountain Falls Trail bears to the left at 3.8 miles. You want to turn right, though, now descending and following the blue blazes of the Turkey Ridge Trail. Be alert just 300 feet later, as you need to swing to the right to continue along the Turkey Ridge Trail.

The vagaries of the land will take you on a few ups and downs as you walk through a

Looking into the Blue Ridge from the second view

forest punctuated by the tall trunks and long needles of the eastern white pine. By far the largest conifer found in this part of the state, you can recognize it by its needles; it is the only evergreen in Virginia to have five needles in each bundle.

Begin to descend at 4.4 miles, coming to an arm of Fairy Stone Lake at 4.7 miles. Turn left onto the yellow-blazed Lakeshore Trail (right leads less than 0.5 mile to the dam spillway).

Rise to an intersection at 4.9 miles where the Turkey Ridge Trail comes in from the left. Stay right on the Lakeshore Trail, coming to a view overlooking the lake. This would be a grand place to be at sunrise or sunset as you could watch the lengthened rays of the sun reflect upon the lake's mirrored surface. Descend to near water level, where you might find some old evidence of beavers.

When you see a couple of state park cabins directly in front of you, swing left to stay on the Lakeshore Trail and turn right just 300 feet later to avoid the Turkey Ridge Trail coming in from the left. Swing left and turn right again less than 200 feet later to once again stay on the Lakeshore Trail.

Walk behind a large picnic shelter at 5.4 miles, reenter the woods, swing left and rise to stay on the yellow-blazed Lakeshore Trail; do not continue straight on the unmarked pathway.

Come to a familiar-looking intersection at 6.0 miles and bear right onto the combined Little Mountain Falls, Turkey Ridge, and Lakeshore Trails marked by orange, blue, and yellow blazes. The trail to the right 100 feet later goes to the cabins; stay left, but in an additional 300 feet you should bear right when a path takes off to the left, heading toward the campground.

Return to your car and complete the hike at 6.4 miles.

There is another network of pathways in the park, but you should feel comfortable about being in a more isolated area before embarking upon the Iron Mountain, Whiskey Run, or Stuart's Knob Trails. Totaling almost 4 miles in length, the trails interconnect to take hikers by old iron mine sites, past azaleas and redbuds in bloom in the spring, and up to rocky Stuart's Knob.

If you want to hunt for fairy stones, drive out of the park on VA 634 and turn left onto VA 57. There will be an old service station on the left after about 3 miles. Park your car here and walk into the woods on the left side of the station. You are permitted to hunt for (on the surface, no digging allowed) and take home a small number of the stones for your personal use. Good luck!

The Blue Ridge Region

17

The Appalachian Trail and the Mount Rogers National Recreation Area

Total distance (one way): 17.1 miles

Hiking time: 9 hours, 20 minutes

Vertical rise: 2,400 feet

Maps: USGS 7½' Troutdale, USGS 7½' Whitetop Mountain; USFS Mt. Rogers High Country map

On all four of my complete traverses of the 2,000-mile Appalachian Trail, the Mount Rogers area has always been one of the most eagerly anticipated sections. Below summits covered with spruce and fir are thousands of acres of open meadows dotted by clusters of rocky outcrops. With such far-off vistas, the entire region reminds me more of walks along the Continental Divide in Montana and Wyoming than of hikes in Virginia. Herds of grazing cattle and wild ponies add to the feeling of being in the American West.

Boasting the state's highest mountain, Mount Rogers (5,729 feet), as its centerpiece, the Mount Rogers National Recreation Area (MRNRA) was established in 1966. More than 400 miles of pathways wend their way through the area's 200,000 acres. Although the hiking possibilities here are nearly limitless, the section of the AT described herein is a great introduction to the area, cutting across miles of open terrain and experiencing the best of what the crest zone has to offer. This is one of the most scenic hikes in the state; do not miss it.

The outing could be accomplished as a very long day hike, but to enjoy it to its fullest, consider backpacking it overnight. Nothing beats gazing at the stars as they appear in the expansive night sky and then waking in the morning to a herd of wild ponies grazing in the drifting fog. Except for a few posted sections and Grayson Highlands State Park (GHSP), camping is permitted anywhere. There are even three trailside shelters to choose from.

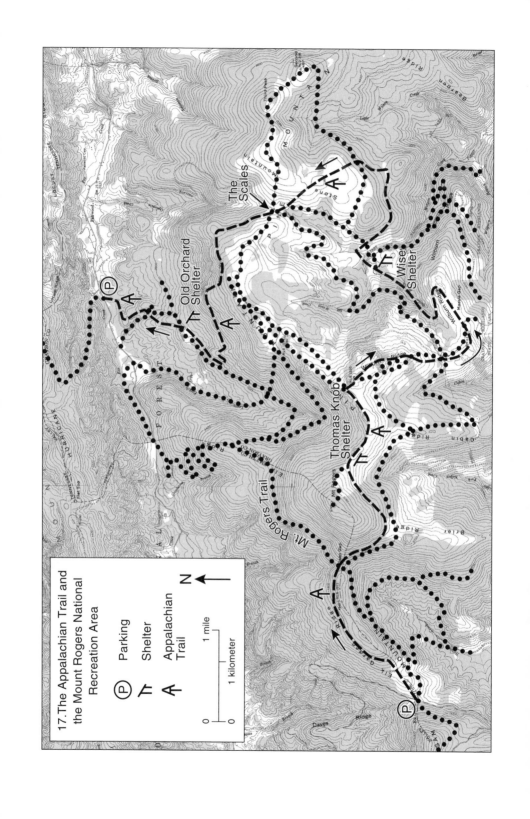

17. The Appalachian Trail and the Mount Rogers National Recreation Area

Parking

Shelter

Appalachian Trail

N

1 mile

1 kilometer

0

0

The Scales

Old Orchard Shelter

Wise Shelter

Thomas Knob Shelter

Mt Rogers Trail

Because this is a one-way hike, a car shuttle will be necessary. Take I-81 to Exit 45 in Marion and drive south on VA 16, passing by the Mount Rogers National Recreation Area visitors center in 6.1 miles, where it is worthwhile to check out the exhibits, video presentations, and information. Continue for another 11.2 miles to Troutdale and turn right onto VA 603. The AT parking lot, where you will leave one car, will be on the left about 4.0 miles later.

Turn left out of the parking lot, continue on VA 603 for nearly 6.0 miles and make a left onto VA 600. Gain elevation for 3.5 miles and park in the large area on the right.

Cross the highway, walk through the wooden fence, and gradually ascend into the open meadow on the white-blazed AT {FS 1}, enjoying the first of miles of vistas. Closest to you are Bluff and Whitetop Mountains (see Hike 19), while dominating the distant southeastern horizon are Grandfather and Sugar Mountains in North Carolina.

The views fade for a while once you step over a stile and into the Lewis Fork Wilderness at 0.6 mile, descending into forestland. The wide, flat area within Deep Gap at 1.8 miles used to contain a trailside shelter. It was removed in the 1980s due to overuse, and the area is now recovering, with understory vegetation and hardwoods reclaiming what used to be bare ground.

Shortly after you begin to rise, the blue-blazed Mount Rogers Trail {FS 166} descends to the left; stay to the right along the AT, crossing the south-facing slope of Mount Rogers. The open meadow to the right at 2.8 miles provides a repeat of the earlier vista.

When the trail makes a hard turn to the right at 3.8 miles, you have the option of turning left onto the Mount Rogers Spur Trail {FS 4590} and making a 1.0-mile

(round-trip) side journey to the zenith of the commonwealth. (See Hike 18 for a description of that route.)

Continuing along the AT, walk out of the Lewis Fork Wilderness and come to the Thomas Knob Shelter at 4.2 miles. Situated just about 100 yards in elevation below Mount Rogers, this is Virginia's highest AT shelter. Be sure to climb the rocks behind the structure, where the high, open meadows look onto some of North Carolina and Virginia's loftiest peaks.

Upon leaving the shelter and crossing a stile at 4.6 miles, you will see views of Wilburn Ridge—which you will be walking on shortly—and Haw Orchard Mountain in GHSP (see Hike 21). There is a major intersection of pathways in Rhododendron Gap at 5.0 miles. The blue-blazed Pine Mountain Trail {FS 4595}, a former route of the AT, veers off to the left. Clamber onto the top of the rocks before making the right turn along the white blazes of the AT. A heath bald, hundreds of acres in size (see Hike 19 for a discussion of balds), becomes an ocean of evergreen leaves adorned by the purple waves of thousands of Catawba rhododendron blossoms in early June.

Less than 100 feet from the intersection with the Pine Mountain Trail, the blue-blazed Crest Trail {FS 4605} comes in from the left; again, stay to the right along the AT. However, you will need to stay to the left when the Wilburn Ridge Trail {FS 4597} heads off to the right at 5.1 miles. Although you are not on the main crest, the rocky pathway you are walking upon provides its own rewarding views.

At 5.6 miles, the AT passes between two large boulders known as the Fatman Squeeze Tunnel (which in this day and age someone will surely think is a politically insensitive reference). A short distance to

Along the crest of Stone Mountain

your left are the wide, connected ridgelines of Pine and Stone Mountains, which you will be traversing within the next few miles.

Continue to follow white blazes, bypassing or stepping over any side routes, such as the Wilburn Ridge, Rhododendron Gap {FS 4612}, or Virginia Highlands Horse Trails {FS 337}. Temporarily leave the national recreation area by passing through a wooden fence at 6.6 miles and entering GHSP.

The wild ponies, for which the highlands area is so well known, tend to graze in the area where the AT crosses the blue-blazed Rhododendron Gap Trail at 7.2 miles. Resembling the famous ponies of Assateague Island off Virginia's Eastern Shore, they are the descendants of once-domesticated animals that were brought here generations ago. Although their grazing is keeping the highlands from growing over, thereby providing a useful service, there is some concern that the ponies are detrimental to the

alpine environment. They run free until the fall roundup, when some are auctioned. A portion of the money raised goes toward keeping the herd healthy and running wild.

The feeling of being in Montana remains as the trail rises to a series of rock cliffs upon the crest of Wilburn Ridge. Be sure to turn around and take a last look at all you have crossed thus far, for once you begin to descend at 7.7 miles, you will be taking your leave of this part of the world.

Enter a rhododendron thicket and cross Quebec Branch at 8.4 miles. Step over a stile, and leave state parklands. Turn right onto an old railroad grade and cross a series of small water runs. Most of the woodlands you walk through on this hike were heavily logged near the beginning of the 20th century, and the many old rail grades are reminders of how the timber was extracted.

Use another stile and return to state parklands at 8.8 miles. Two club mosses, running cedar and crow's foot, grow inter-mingled beside the trail. Soon you will enter a semi-open area where the blueberry bushes would rise above the head of a 6-foot-tall person. The berries are so abun-dant in August that you could pick handfuls in just a few minutes.

The blue-blazed trail to the right at 9.2 miles leads to a spring; 300 feet later you will arrive at the Tom and Clara Wise Shel-ter, constructed in 1996 by volunteer mem-bers of the Mount Rogers Appalachian Trail Club.

Continue along the AT and come a Y in-tersection at 9.3 miles, where you want to follow the white blazes to the left. Use yet an-other stile to step over a fence and then cross Big Wilson Creek on a footbridge, walking out of state parklands for the final time. Once you have made it over a soggy area, you will drop down to step over the Wil-son Creek Trail {FS 339} at 9.7 miles and a bridged crossing of the East Fork of Big Wil-son Creek. The trail passes through a gate at 9.7 miles and crosses the Scales Trail {FS 4523}, entering the Little Wilson Creek Wilderness on another old railroad grade.

Now on the semi-open southern slope of Stone Mountain, the trail turns left off the railbed at 10.0 miles and ascends gradually toward the ridgeline. Just as you enter a small wooded area at 10.1 miles, it begins to follow an old logging road, passing by a spring at 10.7 miles. Only a few steps be-yond this water source you must turn left off the old roadbed. Cross a fence and the Bearpen Trail {FS 4525}, which comes into an open meadow and leaves the Little Wilson Creek Wilderness.

Ascend gradually to the broad ridgeline of Stone Mountain at 11.9 miles, obtaining great views of Pine Mountain to the north and the twin pinnacles of Haw Orchard Mountain in GHSP to the south. You might come across a few riders unloading their horses from trailers when you walk through The Scales, an area once used to weigh cattle, at 12.2 miles.

Just outside the wooden fence is a maze of dirt roads and interconnecting pathways. Bypassing all trails not marked with the white blazes of the AT, rise into a full-fledged forest of yellow birch and red spruce at 12.5 miles, pass through a fence, and climb toward Pine Mountain's ridgeline. Another fence crossing at 13.4 miles brings you into a semi-open area with more blue-berry bushes. Bid farewell to the high coun-try after crossing the fence again; you will bypass the blue-blazed Pine Mountain Trail coming in from the left and descend into the deep forest of Lewis Fork Wilderness.

Next to the trail at 15.3 miles is the Old Orchard Shelter. Looking out on the crest of Iron Mountain to the north (see Hike 22), it is one of the few shelters in all of Virginia to have a view.

Descending from the shelter, cross the Lewis Fork Trail {FS 4533} at 15.4 miles and the Old Orchard Spur Trail {FS 4533.1} at 16.2 miles. Make use of a foot-bridge to step over a small water run at 16.9 miles and leave the Lewis Fork Wilder-ness. If, like me, once you have returned to your shuttled car at 17.1 miles you discover that you just have not had enough of the Mount Rogers area, look to Hikes 18 and 19 for additional high country adventures.

18

Mount Rogers

Total distance (circuit): 19.2 miles

Hiking time: 9 hours, 50 minutes; 3-day backpack

Vertical rise: 3,080 feet

Maps: USGS 7½' Whitetop Mountain

This journey rises from lowlands covered in the deep shade of hardwood and evergreen coves to ramble over high, open meadows with 360-degree views and cool mountain air that blows across your face. Hiking just doesn't get much better than this.

At 5,729 feet, Mount Rogers is the highest point in the commonwealth. The northern limit of the Fraser fir tree, close to the southern limit of the red spruce, it is an environment unto itself. Rarely-seen salamanders hide in the moist areas of its slopes, while the equally elusive sharp-shinned hawk has been seen flying over its grasslands. In addition, bear, deer, fox, bobcat, raccoon, red squirrel, chipmunk, and woodchuck all make their homes within the Mount Rogers National Recreation Area (MRNRA), and wild ponies graze the alpine meadows.

There are more than 400 miles of pathways within the recreation area, and you could spend weeks exploring them. This three-day hike guides you over what many consider to be the best of its 200,000 acres.

Drive to the trailhead by taking I-81 to Exit 45 in Marion and heading south on VA 16, passing by the MRNRA visitors center in 6.1 miles. Continue for another 11.2 miles to Troutdale, where you turn right onto VA 603. Identified by a small sign, the trailhead parking is on the right 5.7 miles later.

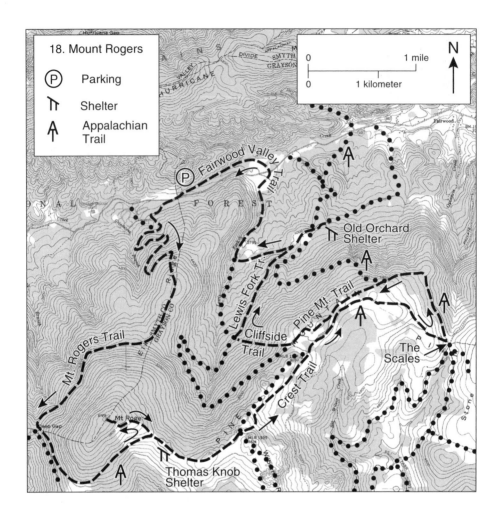

First Day

Total distance: 7.6 miles
Hiking time: 4 hours, 25 minutes
Vertical rise: 2,120 feet

The outing commences by crossing VA 603, walking into the woods on the blue-blazed Mount Rogers Trail {FS 166}, and taking the boardwalk over a wet area crowded with great rhododendron. Immediately begin the climb that will last for several miles.

The trail to the right at 0.4 mile leads to the Forest Service's Grindstone Campground; stay to the left and use a series of short footbridges to step over small water runs. At 0.9 mile, negotiate the first of a number of switchbacks as your climb runs along a pathway bordered by ferns, gnarled beech trees, Indian pipe, and star moss. Forming compact mats, mosses are capable of storing large amounts of moisture, making them an important part of the forest's survival during times of drought. The ascent levels out for a bit as you come to a natural shelf amid a younger forest. Here you will bypass the Lewis Fork Spur Trail {FS 4598}, which comes in from the left at 2.4 miles.

Conspicuous crimson bee balm flowers grow in a wet area–at 3.6 miles–during the summer, while Turk's-cap lily rises beside the trail at around 3.8 miles. This latter is quite a showy plant, with as many as 40 individual flowers blooming at the same time, nodding their heads downward and swinging back and forth in response to the lightest of breezes. Its species name, *Lilium superbum,* means superb lily and acknowledges its glamour and charm. The common name comes from the flower's backward-curving petals and sepals, thought to resemble a martagan, a turban-like cap worn by Turks centuries ago.

Unless the route has been recently cleared, expect to be scratched where nettles and thorn bushes droop over the path, around 4.1 miles. The water you hear but can't see is an underground system close to the surface.

The Mount Rogers Trail comes to an end at 4.25 miles; turn left and continue ascending, now along the white-blazed Appalachian Trail {FS 1}. The first of the vistas comes into view as you break out of the vegetation to look upon Whitetop Mountain (see Hike 19) to the southwest.

Be sure to swing to the left at 5.25 miles and not go through the fence into the meadow on your right. Walk into open fields again at 5.9 miles; now you will understand why you had to huff and puff for so long. Alpine meadows spread out before you and slope gradually away, furnishing dazzling views across Helton Creek Valley and onto some of North Carolina's highest mountains; there are almost no signs of modern civilization.

When the MRNRA was established in 1966, some people saw it as a way to develop the region and proposed that a major ski resort, complete with multiple runs, lifts, and condominiums, be constructed in the high country. Thankfully, for those of us who like our recreation areas more natural, those ideas faded away.

Bear left onto the Mount Rogers Spur Trail {FS 4590} at 6.2 miles and make the final push to the state's highest point. The rich perfume of fir and spruce is an olfactory delight when the path enters the forest at 6.5 miles. White wood sorrel blossoms, with their shamrock-shaped leaves, dot the thick mats of green moss that cover trailside boulders.

Negotiate several rock steps and, at 6.7 miles, arrive at the summit, marked by a USGS triangulation plaque on the highest rock in the state of Virginia. There may be no view from here, but the rustling sound of the wind, the flow of a variety of birdsongs, the continuous hum of dozens of insects, and the wonderful aroma of the forest will entice you to tarry.

In 1840, William Barton Rogers, head of the University of Virginia's natural philosophy department, was hired by the commonwealth as the state's first geologist and commissioned to explore the highlands region. Walking onto what he called Balsam Mountain, Rogers sent back glowing reports about the area's resources. Soon after his death in 1882, the Virginia legislature honored him by declaring that the summit would bear his name.

Return to the AT and turn left, coming to Thomas Knob Shelter, your home for the night, at 7.6 miles. Consider having your dinner on the boulders behind it, where you can enjoy a repeat performance of the vistas you surveyed earlier in the day.

Second Day

Total distance: 8.7 miles
Hiking time: 4 hours, 10 minutes
Vertical rise: 680 feet

Continue your journey along the AT, reaching the top of a knob at 0.5 mile where a

The Pine Mountain Trail

whole new world opens up. Say goodbye to the Mount Rogers ridgeline and gaze out upon the expanse of Wilburn Ridge and Grayson Highlands State Park (see Hike 20).

Pass through a fence and come into a semi-open area at 0.7 mile. The Pine Mountain Trail {FS 4595} comes in from the left at 1.0 mile. Keep to the right on the AT, but less than 100 feet later, bear left onto the Crest Trail {FS 4605}, breaking out into the open and descending along switchbacks.

Begin to rise at 1.4 miles and follow Pine Mountain's undulations to a knoll at 2.2 miles. The Lewis Fork Trail {FS 4533} comes in from the left, but stay to the right along the Crest Trail, entering a 600-foot-long rhododendron thicket at 2.3 miles. Just as you top a short rise at 3.1 miles, be sure to stay on the Crest Trail, even though the white blazes of the AT become visible to the left. Buttercups, Queen Ann's lace, and a mint–heal all–populate the meadow you descend into. Turn left onto the AT at 4.1 miles. (Chemical toilets and The Scales, once a cattle weighing station, are just below you at this point.)

Enter a forest of yellow birch and red spruce at 4.3 miles and pass through a fence. Just a few miles south of here (on Whitetop Mountain), the red spruce reaches its natural southern limit. Swing to the left at 5.0 miles, begin the climb back to the Pine Mountain crest, pass through another fence at 5.3 miles, and come into a semi-open area where there are tall blueberry bushes.

Just before passing through the fence again, take a short side trip to the rocks on your left to view the Mount Rogers ridgeline and much of the terrain you traversed yesterday. Return to the fence, pass through it, and continue along the AT.

Reenter the woods and turn left onto the blue-blazed Pine Mountain Trail; you are now standing at an elevation of exactly 5,000 feet above sea level. Walk by a well-established campsite, enter a semi-open area at 5.7 miles, and pass through another fence.

As you descend an open area at 6.2 miles, the views of Mount Rogers, Whitetop Mountain, and the mountains of North Carolina can't be beat. Your focus changes at 6.5 miles as you turn right onto the Lewis Fork Trail and gaze upon Iron Mountain (see Hike 22) to the west and the north. Reenter the woods at 6.7 miles and bear right onto the lightly-used Cliffside Trail {FS 4533.2}; pay close attention when it veers to the left away from the small water run. The rate of descent quickens and you may find yourself slipping and sliding on rocks and in the mud.

Turn right onto the wide and level Lewis Fork Trail at 7.3 miles, soon crossing a Lewis Fork tributary and gradually descending. The lower the elevation you achieve, the lusher the vegetation grows, the more songbirds you hear, and the higher the temperatures become. Sadly, horse traffic has churned the route into rocky, muddy muck from which you cannot easily escape.

The Lewis Fork Trail makes a switchback left turn at 8.3 miles; continue right onto the Old Orchard Spur Trail {FS 4596}. Ascend into a younger forest whose floor is covered almost exclusively with crow's foot.

Come to a four-way intersection at 8.6 miles, where you want to turn right onto the white-blazed AT and arrive at the Old Orchard Shelter at 8.7 miles. With luck, you have arrived here early enough to watch the sunset's glow envelop Iron Mountain's ridgeline, visible from the front of the shelter.

Thomas Knob Shelter

Third Day

Total distance: 2.9 miles
Hiking time: 1 hour, 15 minutes
Vertical rise: 280 feet

Your final day is an easy one of downhill walking, so sleep in if you wish. Return to the four-way intersection, bear left onto the Old Orchard Spur Trail, and retrace your steps to the Lewis Fork Trail switchback. Bear right and descend into an area that seems to teem with roving deer.

Avoiding the Cliffside Trail to the left at 0.9 mile, keep right and continue along the Lewis Fork Trail, dropping at a barely perceptible rate along the creek. Bee balm covers the banks of Lewis Fork, which you will cross on a footbridge. Keep to the left onto a lesser-used route just a few hundred feet later as the horse trail veers right. Be sure to turn around and gaze upon all of the

elevation you have lost since leaving the highlands yesterday.

Cross VA 603 at 1.8 miles. There may be no discernible pathway, but continue straight across the field, aiming for the trees in front of you. Copious amounts of clover, Queen Ann's lace, heal all, daisy, aster, and buttercup color the meadow.

Turn left onto the Fairwood Valley Trail {FS 4631} at 1.9 miles, pass through a fence, and enter the woods. Cross a small water run at 2.0 miles and make the final little uphill climb of the hike. Thousands of roots exposed by the cut of this woods road show what an extensive support network trees have hidden underground.

Begin a gradual descent at 2.6 miles, keep left when a trail rises to the right, and, at 2.9 miles, return to the car you walked away from two days ago.

The Blue Ridge Region

19

Buzzard Rock

Total distance (one way): 3.3 miles

Hiking time: 1 hour, 20 minutes

Vertical rise: 60 feet

Maps: USGS 7½' Whitetop Mountain

The previous two outings (Hikes 17 and 18) are rather extensive excursions into the Mount Rogers area. This hike is for those occasions when you do not have the time or inclination to walk for such long periods. Although much shorter, it still provides you with a sense of the high country and the expansive vistas for which it is so famous. If you do not have two cars for a shuttle, or do not want to walk the entire distance, you can still have a great 1.5-mile round-trip hike by simply going just to Buzzard Rocks and then returning to your car.

If you wish to do the entire hike, a car shuttle will be necessary. Take I-81 to Exit 45 in Marion and drive south on VA 16, passing by the Mount Rogers National Recreation Area visitors center in 6.1 miles. Continue for another 11.2 miles to Troutdale and turn right onto VA 603, which you follow for more than 10.0 miles to make a left turn onto US 58. Approximately 1.0 mile later, turn left onto VA 601, follow its gravel surface for 1.0 mile more, and leave one car in the Appalachian Trail (AT) parking area.

Return to US 58, turn right, and make the next right back onto VA 603, which you follow for a little more than 2.0 miles. Bear right onto VA 600 and gain elevation until 3.5 miles, where there is a large AT parking lot on the right. Pass by the lot, continue for 1.0 mile more, and make a hard right onto FDR 89. Climb toward the summit of Whitetop Mountain, crossing over the AT 2.6 miles later. Continue just a few hundred yards farther and park in the picnic area. (The 5,520-foot summit of Whitetop, the

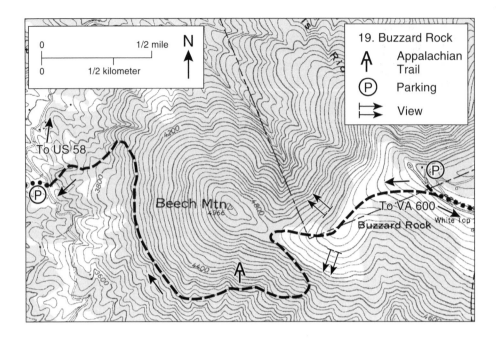

second highest point in Virginia, is several hundred yards beyond the picnic area.)

Walk back down the road and turn right onto the Appalachian Trail {FS 1}, gradually descending into the open field with a vista looking onto the surrounding ridgelines. Closest to you in the northwest is Iron Mountain, but more than 20 miles behind it are the Clinch Mountains, located across the unseen Great Valley of Virginia. To the south are some of the tallest peaks to be found in northern North Carolina, including Grandfather Mountain about 40 miles away. Directly behind you is the summit of White-top, the northern limit of Fraser fir, and the southern limit of red spruce. As you continue to descend, you might want to think about the origins of the open area you are walking through, a natural Appalachian bald.

Balds are still a mystery to those who have studied them. Heath balds, sometimes called slicks by local inhabitants, are made up of plants in the heath family, predomi-

nantly mountain laurel and rhododendron, but including huckleberry, blueberry, and azalea. Grass balds have no such shrubs but may include sedges and other low-growing vegetation and grasses; the two types of balds can commingle. When you first see them, you may be inclined to conclude that they are alpine summits above tree line. Yet there is no tree line this far south and, as you can see, this bald occurs below a tree-covered peak.

There are numerous theories on how balds came to be. One states that they were caused by fires that completely eliminated the trees. However, fires occur in many areas other than balds, and trees have reestablished themselves over time. Some researchers propose that Native Americans, especially the Cherokee, originally cleared the areas of trees and intermittently burned them for sacred sites, or so that mountain oat grass and berries would flourish. Others say that the balds are simply areas that

Whitetop Mountain's natural bald

were cleared for mountain pastures by early settlers. Yet it is an established fact that at least some balds were in existence when homesteaders first began to move into the mountains.

Other theories abound. A certain soil has been proposed, but there is no one type found to occur in all of the balds. Insect infestation, an overpopulation of browsing animals, or tree destruction from harsh conditions such as drought, ice storms, or heavy winds have all been put forth as reasons for the existence of the balds.

Finally, a number of noted ecologists say that the hot and dry climatic conditions of several thousand years ago killed the spruces and firs that were near their southern limit. This permitted maples, beeches, and a few other deciduous trees to invade and dominate. The earth then entered a phase of cooler temperatures, killing the broad-leaved trees. Because they need shade to establish themselves, the spruces and firs were unable to repopulate the open areas, permitting the grasses and/or heaths to gain the upper hand.

Take a break when you reach Buzzard Rock at 0.75 mile. This jumbled rock formation, whose origin is from lava that flowed more than 400 million years ago, is the perfect perch from which to immerse yourself in your surroundings. In addition to the aforementioned vistas, you could lie down and watch the procession of clouds floating across the sky.

Incidentally, despite the rock's name, there are no buzzards in the eastern United States. The large birds you may happen to spot riding the hot air that rises from the valleys are most likely vultures. Although black vultures (with light patches on their wingtips) are seen in the Appalachians, turkey vultures are much more common. In flight, their 6-foot wingspan forms a distinctive and easily identifiable black-and-white V shape.

Resume the hike by continuing downhill and making a sudden swing to the left at 1.0 mile to avoid a former route of the AT straight ahead. Small trees and bushes, such as cedar and gooseberry, have begun to invade the bald here near its edge. With leaves resembling those of the maple tree, gooseberry produces a fruit that ripens some time in July. Although it is possible to eat this half-inch round relative of the currant right off the shrub, it will taste better when sweetened and cooked into a jam or jelly.

Enter the deep forest about 1.6 miles after leaving the Whitetop Mountain picnic area and continue to descend, working your way from the southern to the western slope of Beech Mountain. Oaks become some of the dominant trees; their roots are parasitized by the false foxglove, whose yellow, funnel-shaped flowers bloom throughout most of the summer. A whimsical folk legend asserts that fairies gave the flowers to foxes to wear over their paws so that they would not be heard when raiding henhouses.

In order to avoid private property, the trail makes a sudden switchback to the left at 2.6 miles and continues its downward trend. Cross a water run at 3.0 miles, coming to your shuttled automobile parked along VA 601 at 3.3 miles.

If you feel the need to keep walking, you could continue south along the AT for 4.0 more miles to join up with the Virginia Creeper Trail, described at the 6.3 milepoint of Hike 20.

20

Virginia Creeper Trail

Total distance (one way): 17.4 miles

Hiking time: 7 hours

Vertical rise: 80 feet

Maps: USGS 7½' Damascus; USGS 7½' Grayson; USGS 7½' Konnarock; USGS 7½' Park; USGS 7½' Laurel Bloomery

Thanks to the rails-to-trails movement, Virginia is blessed with a number of excellent pathways it probably would not have had otherwise. The W&OD Trail stretches for 45.0 miles from the urban atmosphere of Alexandria to the countryside in Purcellville. Coursing for 7.0 miles from Lexington to Buena Vista along the Maury River is the Chessie Nature Trail (see Hike 38). For 57.0 miles, the New River Trail runs from Pulaski to Galax, with close to 40.0 miles along the river, while the Blackwater Creek Trail system (see Hike 15) provides a backcountry experience in the heart of Lynchburg.

While these and others found throughout the state are worthy projects and good trails in their own way, many people consider the Virginia Creeper Trail (VCT) {FS 4575} to be the most enjoyable and scenic. Beginning on the heights of the Mount Rogers National Recreation Area and almost always within sight of a stream, it runs for 34.0 miles to Abingdon, passing by farmland and natural meadows, through lush forests and rural landscapes, and into small communities dating from the railroad's heyday of the early 20th century.

This hike, which takes in about half of the VCT, is a great way to introduce someone to the joys of outdoor walking (and possibly backcountry camping), without subjecting them to the rigors of harsh or isolated terrain. The walking is continuously downhill, and road crossings are frequent if the need for help should arise. In addition, there are public rest rooms at several sites along the trail.

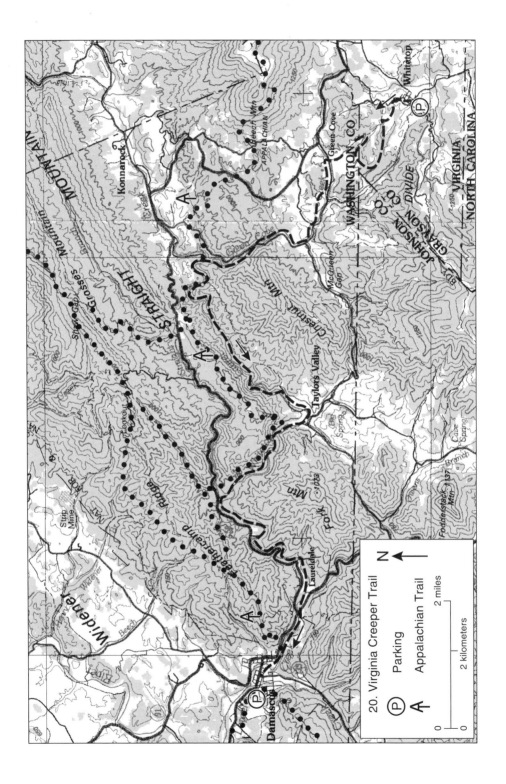

20. Virginia Creeper Trail

(P) Parking

Ⓐ Appalachian Trail

N ←

0   2 miles

0   2 kilometers

At least 60 kinds of trees, more than 170 different wildflowers, and close to 150 species of birds have been identified along the trail's route. There is also the possibility of seeing bats, beavers, black bears, flying squirrels, deer, chipmunks, bobcats, and more. The historic aspects of the journey are an added bonus.

Originally part of a Native American footpath, the trail was used by early explorers and settlers, among them Daniel Boone. The railroad was built in the early 1900s to extract lumber as well as transport iron ore, supplies, and passengers. With scores of bridges and trestles, it was constantly beset with floods, washouts, and rock slides. By the 1920s, unsound logging practices had nearly denuded the hills, adding to the area's economic woes. The rise of the automobile and changing population patterns caused passenger service to be discontinued in the early 1960s. Mounting maintenance costs, many due to recurring floods, finally forced the company to abandon the line, and the last train ran on March 31, 1977.

Since this is a one-way hike, you will need to do a car shuttle. Take I-81 to Exit 19 at Abingdon and drive US 58 east for almost 10.0 miles to Damascus. Just as the roadway makes a sharp left into the main part of town, you want to bear right onto Beaverdam Avenue and leave one car in the lot next to the city park. (The train caboose serves as an information center for the town and the Forest Service.)

Continue following US 58 east for another 16.0 miles (watch out for its many intersections and twists and turns) and make a right turn onto VA 726. Reach the parking lot at Whitetop Station 1.7 miles later. Be aware that the VCT is a multi-use trail, also open to equestrians and bicyclists. Pets must be on a leash.

Walk slightly uphill along the trail for just a few feet, cross VA 726, and then it is down you go for the rest of the journey! Birch trees, common in New England but found only in the higher elevations of the Southern Appalachians, are part of the forest along the trail here. As you walk along the smooth pathway, you should take note of how low gaps in the terrain were filled in by the railroad builders in order to provide a level bed on which to lay tracks.

You will cross the first trestle, almost 300 feet long and 65 feet above the stream, 0.9 mile into the journey. The narrow cut in the topography at 2.4 miles was primarily done by hand, without the aid of modern bulldozers or other heavy, earth-moving equipment.

Shortly after this, you will walk by a Christmas tree farm, one of many such operations located throughout the highlands region. Looking for a cash crop to replace dwindling income from cattle and tobacco farming, landowners began converting to tree farms in the late 1970s. They mostly grow Fraser fir, an evergreen that occurs naturally only in the higher elevations of the Mount Rogers area, North Carolina, and Tennessee. In addition to being well suited to the climate, it is one of the most prized of Christmas trees because of its beauty, aroma, and ability to hold its needles.

The Green Cove Station at 2.9 miles will be familiar to railroad buffs—it was made famous in O. Winston Link's 1956 photograph of the steam locomotive Old Maud. Today it serves as a Forest Service information center; if not open, the rest rooms, water, and picnic tables will still be accessible.

Just beyond the station, the VCT begins to parallel Green Cove Creek, its rushing water and lush green vegetation producing a natural scene worthy of its own photograph.

Continuing downstream, the water gathers strength and width and descends via small cascades and waterfalls. The deep red petals of bee balm add to the attractiveness of the walk from July into September.

Cross VA 726 at 4.0 miles and VA 859 at 5.3 miles. Small campsites, most of them hidden within the twisted branches of rhododendron thickets, can be found along the trail for the next several miles.

Just after the Appalachian Trail {FS 1} comes in from the right at 6.3 miles, vertigo may set in when you cross the most impressive span of the VCT. Known as High Trestle, the 563-foot bridge soars close to 100 feet above the confluence of Green Cove and Whitetop Laurel Creeks. Beyond the trestle is a major road access point, and the dirt road below you has handicapped-accessible fishing platforms along the creek.

The AT takes its leave of the VCT by turning right and ascending the hillside at 7.0 miles. More campsites, many adorned by bee balm, are along the trail about 8.0 miles into the journey.

Be aware, though, that you will be crossing private property as you pass through the small community of Taylors Valley at around 10.7 miles. (Public rest rooms are available beside the parking lot at the far end of town.) When the VCT was in the planning stages, local governments held meetings to discuss the pros and cons of the trail. Although some adjacent landowners voiced fears at that time, recent surveys have found that the majority now favor the trail.

Walk back into woodlands and onto Forest Service land, where an access trail to the AT comes in from the right at 11.0 miles. At 12.9 miles is the Forest Service's Straight Branch parking area, with picnic tables and chemical toilets. Several hundred yards

beyond this is a well-used campsite within the confines of a grove of white pines.

Walking along this next stretch of pathway, with its rhododendron thickets, cascades, and waterfalls, warblers' songs drifting through the mixed hardwood and evergreen forest, and detachment from the modern world, you should utter a word of thanks for those who work hard on behalf of the VCT. It was designated a National Recreation Trail in 1985. There is some confusion as to how the railroad that once came through here got its name. Some people say it was named after the Virginia creeper vine that grows so profusely along the route, while others claim it is because the trains had to creep along the tracks due to steep grades and sharp turns.

Soon after crossing the distinctive Iron Bridge, be sure to use caution when the trail goes over busy VA 91 at 15.9 miles. The pathway is now beside US 58, and the AT rejoins it at 16.3 miles, having dropped off Feathercamp Ridge. The AT leaves the VCT once again at 16.7 miles, just as you come to the eastern end of Damascus. Across the highway is Dot's Inn, a local watering hole that contains what many AT thru-hikers describe as the best jukebox from Georgia to Maine.

Cross Laurel and Beaverdam Creeks and walk beside houses in the main part of Damascus before returning to your car at 17.4 miles.

Hopefully you have made arrangements ahead of time to stay in one of the town's many bed and breakfasts so you can spend tomorrow completing the VCT. The hosts of the Apple Tree B&B (115 East Laurel Avenue, 276-475-5261) have an affinity for hikers; Dancing Bear Vacation Rentals (203 Laurel Avenue, 276-475-5900) is another good choice.

Coming into Taylors Valley

A nice option for doing the western segment of the trail, which passes primarily through rural farmland and private property, is to contact the Blue Blaze (Laurel Avenue, Damascus, 276-475-5095). They will rent you a mountain bike and shuttle you to Abingdon, and you will have a (mostly) downhill ride back to Damascus.

Billing itself as the friendliest town on the Appalachian Trail, Damascus hosts Trail Days every May. Conceived in 1987 as a way to celebrate the 50th anniversary of the AT's completion, the event now attracts thousands of hikers, locals, and visitors for a week-long series of events focusing on the AT.

21

Grayson Highlands

Total distance (circuit): 8.3 miles

Hiking time: 5 hours

Vertical rise: 1,820 feet

Maps: USGS 7½' Whitetop Mountain; USGS 7½' Troutdale; USGS 7½' Grassy Creek; USGS 7½' Park; park map

Adjacent to the Mount Rogers National Recreation Area (MRNRA), Grayson Highlands State Park (GHSP) contains the highest 4,822 acres of land owned by the state. With open meadows, vistas stretching for miles, cascading waterfalls, and forests reminiscent of New England, it is also one of Virginia's most scenic possessions. Established in 1965, it was the first of eight parks to be acquired through Virginia's State Park Expansion Program. It has since become one of the most visited.

Equestrians are drawn here because of the stables and access to miles of trails open to horseback riders—including the 57-mile Virginia Highlands Horse Trail in the MRNRA. Mountain bikers come to use the same routes open to the horses, while many families simply set up in the campground (with hot showers and dumping station) to enjoy the cool mountain air. The hike described below takes you over the GHSP's highest point for 360-degree views, into grasslands for chance meetings with wild ponies (see Hike 17), and beside a series of tumbling cascades.

The trailhead is reached by taking I-81 to Exit 45 in Marion, driving VA 16 south for almost 20.0 miles to Volney, and turning onto US 58 west. Gaining elevation as you continue, make a right turn into the park on VA 362 in an additional 7.6 miles. Bypass side roads to the picnic area, campground, and horse stables, driving all of the way to the visitors center parking lot, 4.5 miles from the park entrance.

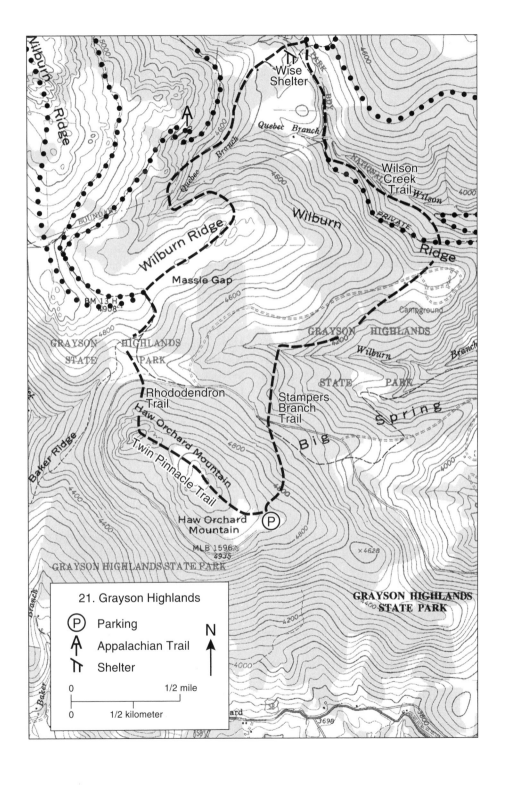

Wilburn Ridge

Wise
Shelter

Quebec Branch

Wilson
Creek
Trail

Wilburn

Wilburn Ridge

Massie Gap

GRAYSON HIGHLANDS

Wilburn

Branch

BM 13 H
4908

GRAYSON
STATE   HIGHLANDS   PARK
PARK

Campground

STATE   PARK

Rhododendron
Trail

Haw Orchard Mountain

Baker Ridge

Twin Pinnacle Trail

Stampers
Branch
Trail

Big   Spring

Haw Orchard
Mountain

MLB 1596
4935

P

×4628

GRAYSON HIGHLANDS STATE PARK

GRAYSON HIGHLANDS
STATE PARK

21. Grayson Highlands

P Parking

A Appalachian Trail

T Shelter

N

0   1/2 mile

0   1/2 kilometer

Walk uphill, swing to the left of the building, and begin following the red-blazed Twin Pinnacles Trail through a forest of yellow birch. (Numbered posts correspond to a brochure about the area's human and natural history that is available in the visitors center.) Much of the land within the park was cleared of trees in the early 1900s to graze livestock, but the forest has been returning and is now on its way to becoming a mature woodland of red spruce, yellow birch, and sugar maple.

Stay to the left when you come to the loop trail intersection at 0.15 mile. Fireweed, a flower most often associated with recently-burned areas, bursts forth in July and August. Rise on rock steps at 0.25 mile, making sure to look to your left once you level out to see the tree whose roots are engulfing a large boulder.

The vast number of hawthorn trees growing here at one time gave rise to the name of the mountain you are walking on, Haw Orchard Mountain. Pass by a small shelter surrounded by some hawthorns at 0.35 mile. You will encounter a number of these structures on the hike which, not designed for overnight stays, can provide a convenient rest spot or shelter from a sudden rain.

The summit of Little Pinnacle, the high point in the park (5,089 feet), provides the first of many views to come, with the ridgelines of North Carolina and Tennessee visible to the south and west. You will shortly be traversing the terrain you see when you turn your gaze northward.

Descend into a small gap at 0.7 mile and rise to another trailside shelter, where the upper end of the loop trail comes in from the right. Stay to the left and immediately come to another intersection; bear left again and rise steeply to the summit of Big Pinnacle (5,068 feet). The vista from here is much the same, except that you now have a

view onto Massie Gap and the open lands of the MRNRA. Even though you have only been walking a short time, take a break and observe the aerial acrobatics of the park's birds. Turkey vultures and (to a lesser extent) black vultures soar along, taking advantage of thermals rising from the lower elevations, while crows and red-tailed hawks fly from one tree to another.

Retrace your steps to the intersection, turn left, and descend somewhat steeply along the yellow-blazed Big Pinnacle Trail, lined with star moss.

Come into Massie Gap and cross the road diagonally to the right. (Pit toilets are about 800 feet to the right along the road.) Although artifacts found in the gap indicate that Native Americans used it many centuries ago, this area is named for the Lee Massey family, homesteaders here in the late 1800s and early 1900s. The name was misspelled on an early United States Geological Survey map and has never been changed.

Begin following the blue-blazed Rhododendron Trail, passing through the gate and rising on a moderately steep grade through a meadow dotted with Queen Anne's lace and buttercups. The jagged rock formations on Wilburn Ridge, named for Wilburn Waters, become more prominent as you gain elevation. Waters was a locally famed bear and wolf trapper whose final years were spent in a cabin high atop Whitetop Mountain (see Hike 19).

Swing left onto a service road at 1.6 miles, avoiding an orange-blazed route coming in from the right a few hundred feet later. The white-blazed Appalachian Trail {FS 1} runs both left and right at 1.8 miles; turn right onto it and reach the rocky ridgeline 800 feet later. You might be lucky enough to wander into an entire herd of wild ponies grazing among the tall blueberry

Wild ponies of the Highlands Area inspect the author's measuring wheel.

bushes. Reach a high point at 2.3 miles and then descend into forestland.

False hellebore flourishes in the seepage area you pick your way through at 3.6 miles. One of its other common names, Indian poke, refers to the story that some chiefs of Native American tribes were permitted to ascend to the position only after they had survived eating the noxious plant. A recent Appalachian Trail thru-hiker who mistook the plant for a ramp (a strong, onionlike wild green) earned the trail name "Chief" Frodo after enduring a night of sweating, vomiting, and severe stomach cramps!

The blue-blazed trail to the right at 3.8 miles leads to a spring; 300 feet later you will arrive at the Tom and Clara Wise Shelter, constructed in 1996 by volunteer members of the Mount Rogers Appalachian Trail Club.

Continue along the AT and come to a Y intersection at 3.9 miles. Follow the white blazes to the left, use a stile to step over a fence, and cross Big Wilson Creek on a footbridge. Come to the unmarked Seed Orchard Road (open to equestrians) at 4.2 miles and turn right to take your leave of the AT—do not take the footbridge across the creek.

The Scales Trail comes in from the left at 4.3 miles; stay to the right, ford Big Wilson Creek, and continue downstream along the dirt road. Pass through a gate at 4.6 miles and walk beside a Fraser fir seed production plot. (See Hike 20 for a discussion about fir plantations in the highlands area.)

Cross a side creek at 4.7 miles and ascend for the first time in more than 2 miles. In order to enjoy a different aspect of the park—and to escape the horse droppings—turn left onto the red-blazed Wilson Creek Trail at 5.0 miles. Coming to what appears to be a four-way intersection at 5.1 miles, make a left turn upstream along an unblazed route for 250 feet to enjoy a beautiful waterfall unseen by most park visitors. Return to the intersection and proceed downstream along

Rhododendron tunnel

the red-blazed route on a path that will become rough and rocky, and go up and down every few feet. As compensation, it delivers you to one grand waterfall after another. Some drop in a series of cascades, some through narrow chutes, and others in wide channels. The Bridal Veil Falls at 5.5 miles is particularly striking, with the water taking on a mirror-like appearance as it clings to the smooth rock surfaces over which it flows.

Rise away from the creek at 5.7 miles, making sure to follow the red blazes and not continue downstream on the unmarked angler's route. Step over a woods road at 6.0 miles and continue to rise. Cross the campground road diagonally to the right at 6.3 miles (rest rooms are a few hundred feet to the left), pass by the country store (with a soda vending machine), and begin to follow the yellow-blazed Stampers Branch Trail.

Descending into a hardwood forest typical of those found throughout Virginia's mountains, cross Wilburn Branch at 6.9 miles. The narrow stream drops down small boulders surrounded by rhododendron tunnels; you will rise through them on the way to passing by the final trailside shelter at 7.0 miles.

At 7.2 miles, swing around a spring, the headwaters of Stampers Branch, as the ascent steepens. Cross the paved park road at 7.5 miles and continue to rise beside cinnamon, lady, New York, and Christmas ferns. The ascent steepens once again around 7.7 miles, where you might notice that you are climbing back into the yellow birch forest where you began this hike. Arrive at the visitors center at 8.2 miles, descend the steps, and return to your car at 8.3 miles.

22

Iron Mountain

Total distance (circuit): 14.1 miles

Hiking time: 8 hours, 20 minutes

Vertical rise: 2,720 feet

Maps: USGS 7½' Konnarock

Located within the boundaries of the Mount Rogers National Recreation Area (MRNRA), the Iron Mountain area is often overlooked by hikers, who tend to gravitate toward the Appalachian Trail's passage through the highlands region. On nice weekends when the trails of the high country can begin to resemble overcrowded highways, the pathways on and near Iron Mountain are usually peaceful and almost devoid of human activity. Yet, this hike, which makes use of four different trails, offers much of what most outdoor travelers desire. There are miles of rolling mountain streams, vistas looking out upon wave after wave of towering ridgelines, thickets of mountain laurel and rhododendron growing within maturing hardwood forests, and backcountry camping permitted anywhere along the route.

Because the hike begins and ends in the Forest Service's Beartree Recreation Area, this outing can be a good choice for families or groups with diverse outdoor interests that want to go somewhere together but not necessarily do the same activities together. Those looking for the most rugged adventure can take the hike, choosing to spend a night in one of two trailside shelters or at a tent site of their choice along the way. Others can stay in the developed campground, with its modern toilets and warm showers. During the day, they could swim in the lake, cast a line in hopes of hooking one of the stocked trout, or lazily paddle a canoe (bring your own) across the water.

The Beartree Recreation Area can be reached by taking I-81 to Exit 19 at Abingdon

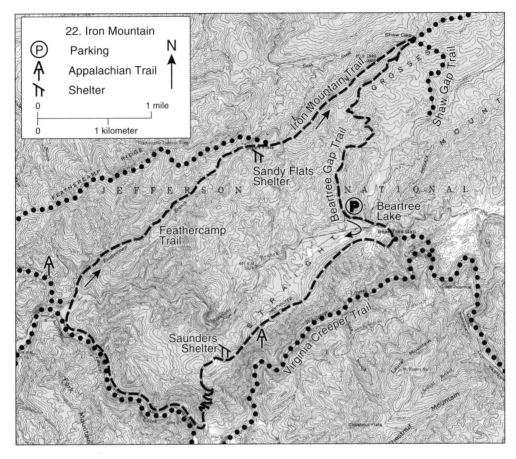

22. Iron Mathere

(P) Parking

A Appalachian Trail

T Shelter

0   1 mile

0   1 kilometer

and driving US 58 east for 10.0 miles to Damascus. At the intersection with VA 91 on the far side of town, make a right turn, continue following US 58 east for another 6.6 miles, and turn left onto FDR 837. Just a short distance up this roadway, make a right turn and leave your car in the angler's parking lot. (The campground is another mile or so up the Forest Service road.)

Begin the hike by taking the paved Beartree Gap Trail {FS 4551} into the woods near the upper end of the parking area. The Beartree Lake Trail {FS 4563} takes off to the left at 0.3 mile, leading to the swimming and picnic areas near the head of the lake. You want to stay to the

right and cross the dam, enjoying the expansive view overlooking the lake. Immediately after the dam, stay to the right on the Beartree Gap Trail (now blazed with purple), avoiding another portion of the lake trail that comes in from the left.

Descending at a gradual rate, cross US 58 at 0.5 mile and come to Beartree Gap Trail's southern terminus with the Appalachian Trail at 0.7 mile {FS 1}. Make a right turn onto the white-blazed AT, which is making use of an old railroad grade at this point, to negotiate the southern slope of Straight Mountain.

One of the best vistas of the hike comes into view when the trail makes a hard left at

---

Iron Mountain

1.1 miles. To the east are the common-wealth's two loftiest peaks. Whitetop Mountain (see Hike 19) appears to be the highest because it is closest to you, but it is Mount Rogers (see Hike 18), a bit farther in the distance, that has claim to the greatest elevation. Continuing along the ridgeline, there are several views of Beartree Lake and the crest of Iron Mountain to the northwest.

The terrain gradually slopes into a gap at 1.9 miles, where you will cross a small creek and avoid the blue-blazed logging road coming in from the right. After regaining the elevation you lost, you can thank trail maintainers for opening up the view, at 2.4 miles, of Whitetop Laurel Gorge, Chestnut Mountain, and some of the jagged peaks along the North Carolina/Tennessee border.

Merge onto a woods road at 2.8 miles, but pay attention: You need to follow the AT when it leaves the road and turns left no more than 50 feet later.

It is time for a break, so take the blue-blazed side trail to the right at 3.0 miles, coming to Saunders Shelter a few hundred yards later. With funds provided in memory of Walter T. Saunders, the structure was built by Appalachian Trail Conservancy volunteers in 1987. In case you are in need of water, the blue-blazed route leading beyond the shelter goes to a spring.

Return to the main route and continue the journey along the AT, rising to the 3,500-foot crest of Straight Mountain at 3.6 miles. Receding to the southeast, getting progressively higher, you will see a succession of ridgelines—Laurel, Chestnut, Beech, and Whitetop Mountains. Within a few hundred feet of this overlook, the AT begins a long descent on a series of switchbacks constructed by the Civilian Conservation Corps in the 1930s.

Make a hard turn to the right at 5.0 miles, avoiding the side trail to the left. The sound of Whitetop Laurel Creek is audible as it is less than a hundred feet below you (the Virginia Creeper Trail is also close—see Hike 20).

Swing away from the creek at 6.8 miles, soon crossing a footbridge above the confluence of Straight and Feathercamp Branches. Just a few feet beyond, step across US 58 and ascend into woodlands. Less than 500 feet later, cross a footbridge over Feathercamp Branch. The AT turns off to the left, but you want to stay to the right, now following the blue-blazed Feathercamp Trail {FS 169} along the stream.

As the waterway rises at a moderate grade, you will cross it eight times within the next 0.5 mile. A low-growing club moss, running cedar, covers the forest floor close to the pathway, while the creek drops in eye-pleasing cascades and riffles on its journey to mingle with the waters of Whitetop Laurel Creek.

The valley begins to widen a bit at 8.2 miles; around 8.5 miles you might be able to find a few flat but rocky tent sites. Galax becomes the dominant trailside plant in this area just after you cross a small side stream.

It is next to impossible to take a full day's hike anywhere in the mountains of Virginia and not come across some galax. The plant forms dense carpets beside paths and upon the forest floor, covering extensive areas of the mountains with its evergreen leaves. Early in the spring the leaves are almost a yellowish green, but they turn to a rich and shiny deep green in the middle of the summer. During the cooler fall and winter months, the leaves can provide a bit of welcome color as their edges become a greenish bronze or a dull crimson hue.

The route becomes a woods road as you pass through a wildlife clearing that could serve as a campsite at 9.0 miles. Intersect

Beartree Lake

another road at 9.1 miles, bear right, and, in a few feet, turn right off of the roadbed and onto the yellow-blazed Iron Mountain Trail {FS 301}, the route of the Appalachian Trail until the early 1970s. The Sandy Flats Shelter at 9.4 miles makes for a convenient rest spot. There is a spring about 50 feet to the right of the shelter.

Continue following the yellow blazes of the Iron Mountain Trail beyond the shelter. First you will notice that wintergreen is the dominant ground cover, but it soon yields to ferns. Descend to cross FDR 90 at 9.8 miles and rise on an older road. Less than 200 feet later, come to a Y intersection where you need to stay to the right. (Both routes may be yellow-blazed; be sure to take the one to the right.) Rise along the crest of the ridgeline, populated by patches of mayapple, striped maple, and cancer root.

Despite its name, the mayapple's fruit, which looks more like a yellowish-green, egg-shaped berry than an apple, does not begin to develop until mid- to late summer. Those who have eaten the fruit of the mayapple describe it as tasting like a sweet lemon, or being tasteless, or downright nauseating. Euell Gibbons, the late wild edible plants expert, felt that a bit of mayapple juice squeezed into lemonade improved the drink's flavor. Some hikers use the juice to help mask the taste of iodine-purified water. Just be careful if you decide to try it; the fruit is a strong (and quick-acting) laxative! Other parts of the plant contain a poison that Native Americans are said to have used to commit suicide.

Begin a quick descent at 10.9 miles, coming into Shaw Gap at 11.3 miles. Leave the Iron Mountain Trail by turning right and descending a few feet to another intersection. The Shaw Gap Trail {FS 4545} heads off to the left, but you want to stay to the right and descend along the upper portion of the same pathway you started this hike on, the Beartree Gap Trail. Stay to the right once more, when the Yancy Trail {FS 4627} comes in from the left at 13.0 miles.

The small pond that the Forest Service constructed on the left side of the pathway at 13.2 miles serves as a water source for wildlife, especially during times of drought. Although artificially created, the pond has now become a part of its environment, and the sound of your approaching footsteps may cause some of the resident frogs to make a hopping retreat into the water.

A footbridge at 13.8 miles permits you to make it over a stream without getting wet feet. Cross FDR 837 diagonally to the left and walk through a moist bottomland forest, an environment you have not encountered on this hike until now.

The outing comes to an end once you emerge from the woods and onto the pavement of the angler's parking lot at 14.1 miles. If it has been a hot and sticky day, it just might be worth your time to continue walking to the bathing area at the far end of the lake for a long, cooling swim.

23

Comers Creek Falls

Total distance (circuit): 8.9 miles

Hiking time: 5 hours, 15 minutes

Vertical rise: 1,840 feet

Maps: USGS 7½' Troutdale; USGS 7½' Whitetop Mountain

Never underestimate the power of voicing your opinion. In response to statements of opposition during a series of public meetings and hundreds of letters of protest by Virginia residents and other Appalachian Trail supporters, the Virginia Department of Transportation canceled plans in 1996 to build a four-lane highway across the trail and through the Mount Rogers National Recreation Area. The road would have split the recreation area in two and turned Comers Creek and Comers Creek Falls into a concrete culvert.

This hike along portions of the Appalachian and Iron Mountain Trails will show you how much would have been lost. Not only would the creek have become a conduit for highway runoff, but an area rich with plants and wildlife would have become greatly disturbed, resulting in the fragmentation and loss of a diverse array of habitats.

Backcountry camping is permitted anywhere along the route of the hike, but you also have the option of staying in the Forest Service's Hurricane Campground, with its modern rest rooms and warm showers. It also makes a good base from which you may explore a number of other nearby treks, such as Hikes 17, 18, 19, and 24.

This journey's trailhead is accessed by taking I-81 to Exit 45 at Marion, driving south on VA 16 for approximately 14.0 miles, and turning right onto VA 650 at the sign for the campground. Turn left onto Hurricane Campground Road 0.6 mile later, make another left onto FDR 84 at the entrance to the campground in an additional

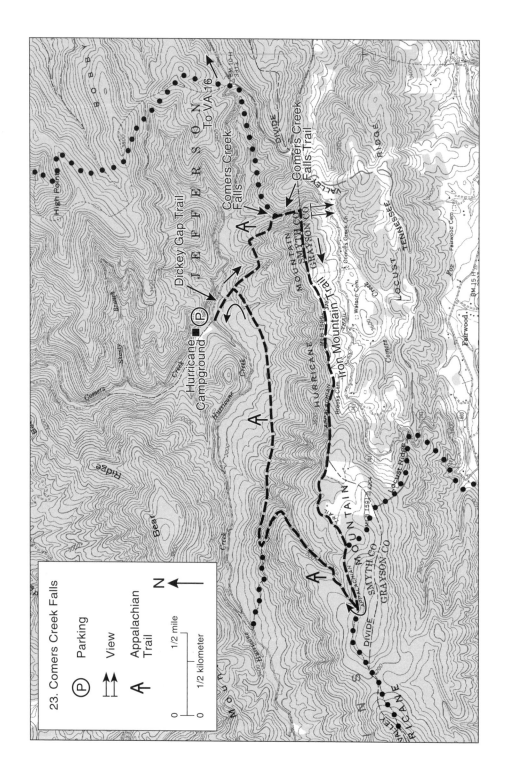

23. Comers Creek Falls

Parking

View

Appalachian Trail

N

0   1/2 mile

0   1/2 kilometer

0.4 mile, and leave your car in the small pull-out on the left side of the road.

Walk back to the intersection, turn right on the blue-blazed Dickey Gap Trail {FS 4518}, and rise gradually into a woods that stays green throughout the year because it has profuse quantities of rhododendron, hemlock, and crow's foot. The route makes a bit of a swing to the right as the ascent steepens at 0.3 mile.

The Appalachian Trail {FS 1} runs both left and right when the Dickey Gap Trail comes to an end at 0.4 miles; turn left to follow white blazes and continue to rise. The *drink-your-tea* song and *to-wheee* call of the rufous-sided towhee provides a fitting soundtrack for the snack of ripe raspberries you can indulge in beside the trail in mid-July at around 0.8 mile.

When you turn left at an intersection at the 1.0 milepoint to stay on the AT and come to Comers Creek Falls, it's time for a break. As you immerse yourself in the cooling waters of the pool at the base of the 10-foot cascade, you will surely realize what a special place this is and how lucky you are that other people worked hard to preserve it. There is much to regard besides the falls—the leathery leaves of the rhododendron, the flat needles of the hemlocks, the feathery fronds of the ferns, and the thick mats of mosses covering the boulders with a soft, cushiony pad. Within the water, you might spot a small school of minnows or have your toes nibbled upon by a crayfish.

When you are finally ready to resume the hike, return to the intersection, bear left, and ascend along the blue-blazed Comers Creek Falls Trail {FS 4526}. The stream continues to descend in small cascades, but your eyes may be drawn to two interesting plants along the side of the trail, both lacking chlorophyll. Squawroot has a yel-lowish-brown countenance, while Indian pipe is a translucent white.

With a small falls on your left at 1.4 miles, turn right onto the yellow-blazed Iron Mountain Trail {FS 301} and continue to rise alongside the tiny white wintergreen flowers that bloom in July, almost hidden by their own leaves.

Pass through a fence at 1.5 miles and swing right into an overgrown field that provides a view of Hurricane Creek Valley and the southern flank of Hurricane Mountain. Make use of another stile at 1.6 miles and continue to rise, rather steeply in spots. Mayapple grows beside an old rock wall as you attain the height of the land at 1.9 miles.

Pass through a fence into a narrow, semi-open field at 2.0 miles where cattle may be grazing. Deptford pink, asters, and daisies grow at your feet, while the highlands of the Mount Rogers area rise to the horizon on your left. Just after obtaining a final good view of the land to the south you will reenter the woods at 2.3 miles, where sassafras and greenbrier are part of the understory. Ascend for a short distance before descending quickly to pass through another fence. Be alert at 2.6 miles! You need to stay to the right on the yellow-blazed Iron Mountain Trail, avoiding the route to the left that leads to VA 741 in 0.5 mile. Butterfly weed grows to eye level, but if you look to the ground, you will notice that horses are now permitted on this section of trail.

The trail levels out and passes under a utility line at 3.2 miles; be sure to keep to the right at 3.3 miles and do not mistakenly go into the field on your left. Continue with the small ups and downs, staying to the right when the Virginia Highlands Horse Trail {FS 337} comes in from the left at 4.0 miles. In times of wet weather, the pathway here can become a quagmire of churned-up mud.

Comers Creek Falls

Descending to a four-way intersection in a broad area known as Chestnut Flats at 4.4 miles, you will turn right and continue to lose elevation, once again following the white blazes of the AT. I am amazed that I have seen at least one black bear every time I have taken a walk in this area; they are usually quite elusive.

The fall is probably the time of year when you have the best chance of seeing a black bear. Fall is when they are on the move, searching for acorns, beechnuts, honeycombs, berries, and insects. This final gorging before hibernation can put a layer of fat on them as much as 5 inches thick, all of it needed to get them through their impending winter slumbers. As cooler temperatures become the norm and food supplies fade, bears will begin to seek out individual dens, with the females retiring first, then the yearlings, and finally the older males.

Switchback to the left at 4.6 miles, walking by squawroot and Indian pipe growing beneath two large-leafed trees, Fraser magnolia and striped maple. A couple of switchbacks later, at 5.2 miles, you will be heading down a stream that is lined by such a heavy growth of rhododendron that you cannot see the water, though you can hear it. This gurgling of the stream, in addition to the songs of dozens of birds, hemlocks rising to great heights, and moss draping itself over rotting logs, can make you feel you are in a primitive forest, far removed from the modern world.

The sound of the creek begins to fade once you swing to the left at 5.5 miles. At 6.0 miles, make a switchback off the old road you have been following and onto a footpath, crossing a small boulder field at 6.4 miles. At 6.7 miles, step over the creek you walked away from a few minutes ago and rise for the first time in more than 2.0 miles, with rattlesnake plantain and running cedar bordering the pathway. The unmistakably pungent odor of galax assaults your nose when you walk through a rhododendron thicket at 7.8 miles.

At 8.4 miles, return to the very first intersection you encountered on this hike and turn left to descend along the Dickey Gap Trail, looking for deer prints in the soft mud that may have not been here when you passed this way before.

Break out of the woods at the Hurricane Campground entrance, turn left onto FDR 84, and return to your car at 8.9 miles. Perhaps now, after experiencing this part of the natural world that has been saved from the ravages of modern development, you may be willing to lend your voice to help protect other areas.

24

Rowlands Creek Falls

Total distance (circuit): 11.8 miles

Hiking time: 6 hours, 15 minutes

Vertical rise: 2,100 feet

Maps: USGS 7½' Whitetop Mountain

Using guidebooks dedicated to the subject of tumbling cascades, waterfall devotees flock to the Blue Ridge and Allegheny Mountains, searching out such well-known spots as Crabtree Falls and Whiteoak Canyon (see *50 Hikes in Northern Virginia*), Fallingwater Cascades (see Hike 39), and The Cascades (see Hike 30). However, very few people—and almost none of the books—know about, or make mention of, Rowlands Creek. Located along the northern edge of the Mount Rogers National Recreation Area, this mountain stream is rarely visited by anyone other than a few locals from nearby towns.

A tributary of the South Fork of the Holston River, the creek descends more than 2,000 feet from its headwaters near Round Top. Along the way, it drops down not just one but a succession of waterfalls—a couple of them more than 100 feet in length and one rushing into a narrow chute that it has carved out of the bedrock. Factor in another bubbling creek, the possibility of seeing a black bear or two, and the option to set up a tent anywhere along the route, and you have the makings of a perfect overnight outing.

The trailhead is reached by taking I-81 to Exit 45 in Marion, driving VA 16 south for 9.6 miles, and turning right onto VA 601. This route makes a turn to the right in another 2.7 miles; the designation for the road you want to follow straight ahead is now VA 670. Bear left onto VA 656 5.5 miles later and make another left onto VA 668 in 1.8 additional miles. Follow this roadway, which

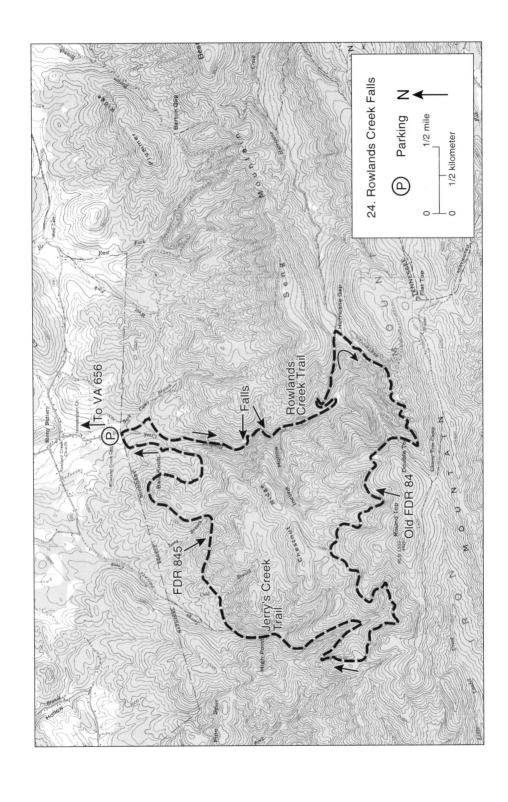

24. Rowlands Creek Falls

Ⓟ Parking   N ←

1/2 mile
1/2 kilometer

becomes FDR 643, for a little more than 3.0 miles. Almost immediately after it changes to an unpaved road there will be another road coming in from the right. Bypass it and continue for only 200 feet more to the parking pullout on the left.

Begin the hike by walking along FDR 643 in the direction in which you were driving, but in less than 400 feet, make a right turn onto the Rowlands Creek Trail {FS 164}. There may be no sign, and the beginning of the pathway may be somewhat obscure, so watch for its orange blazes. Once on the trail, though, the route will be obvious.

Immediately begin to ascend along Rowlands Creek, walking onto a woods road shaded by tall hemlock trees and great rhododendron. When this shrub begins to bloom in mid-June, its flowers appear as tightly closed, rich pink pods, but then they open into large white blossoms. Take a close look and you will notice that the uppermost petal of each bloom is decorated by a pattern of small green dots.

The trail levels out at 0.3 mile, passing by an established campsite that, judging by the number of beer cans, is a favorite partying spot. The first ford of the creek occurs 200 feet later. An old road turns off to the left at 0.5 mile; stay right and continue to rise alongside striped maple and squawroot. As the rate of ascent increases around 0.9 mile, the creek descends at a steeper grade, dropping down small waterfalls and cascades.

At around 1 mile, it is time to slow down and really begin to appreciate your surroundings. The stream is now dropping down a series of cascades, each one with its own unique arrangement and design. According to the Forest Service, the overall drop is more than 150 feet. Be sure to watch for the segment of the cascades where all of this water is funneled into a narrow rock chute.

Ford the creek for the second time at 1.1 miles and make a switchbacking ascent— first right, then left onto a footpath. When you step over a side stream at 1.3 miles, you are high above Rowlands Creek, perhaps thanking the builders of this trail, who did such an excellent job of carving it out of the steep and rocky hillside.

There is another succession of falls at 1.5 miles, with the most impressive one plunging at least 100 feet. Although you are still gaining elevation, the path is on more of a level plane and partridgeberry grows alongside it. The third ford of Rowlands Creek is at 1.8 miles, the fourth at 1.9 miles, and the fifth at 2.0 miles. Next to a small wildlife clearing at 2.1 miles is the final crossing of the creek, this one on a road culvert. A woods road comes in from the left at 2.9 miles; stay right.

The Rowlands Creek Trail reaches its terminus as you walk into the dead end area of a forest service road 250 feet later. Turn right, walk just a few feet, and make another right onto Old FDR 84. Be sure that you take the orange-blazed route that runs level and not the trail ascending to the left of it.

Large amounts of great rhododendron once again become part of the hike when the woods road rises along a gentle grade at 3.2 miles. Although it stays on this upward trend for some distance, it does not attain the high points of the two knobs it is skirting, Double Top and Round Top.

Crossing a series of water runs (which may be dry in summer) along this old road, kudzu drapes itself over every bit of vegetation, creating wild, eerie green sculptures— and killing nearly everything it comes into contact with.

The second crossing of Rowlands Creek

Pass a wildlife clearing to the left at 3.9 miles. You are now as isolated as you are going to get on this hike, and the copious amounts of bear scat and paw prints in the soft soil of the old roadbed can only add to the feeling of being far removed from others of your species. A black bear's front paw prints show five toes; they are about 4 inches long and 5 inches wide. The back prints are 7 to 9 inches long, 5 inches wide, and almost resemble a human footprint, except that the longest toe extends from the middle of the paw. In soft soil or mud, it is often possible to identify the impressions of the claws in front of the toes.

With another wildlife clearing on your left at 4.9 miles, cross over the ridgeline and begin to descend, passing through an eye-pleasing hardwood forest whose intermediate layer is made up of unusually large striped maple trees. Like all its North American relatives in the maple family, the striped maple's fruit develops as a seed pod that resembles brown helicopter blades late in the fall.

The route rises for a while at 6.1 miles, but resumes its descent at 6.6 miles, passing by more striped maples that have attained unusually large proportions. When not facing any competition, they can grow to be 30 feet tall with a diameter of more than 8 inches, but most striped maples within deep forests rarely become more than 8 feet high, with a trunk not much thicker than your thumb.

Be alert at 7.5 miles! When a wildlife clearing appears in front of you, bear right onto the (possibly) unsigned but orange-blazed Jerrys Creek Trail {FS 165}. Now a footpath instead of an old road, your way is lined by Indian pipe, crow's foot, and the pungent leaves of galax. Rhododendron and hemlock reappear as you descend along a pathway made soft by decades of decaying leaves.

The descent becomes steeper after you cross a small rock field at 8.0 miles, but by 8.4 miles you are almost level with Jerrys Creek. It would be a shame not to be doing this hike in June or early July, when thousands upon thousands of white great rhododendron blossoms cover nearly early foot along the steep gorge walls and narrow, flat bottomland. Many branches reach out over the water, reflecting upon its mirrored surface.

Cross the creek at 8.8 miles; do not follow the pathway that continues downstream! You will know you are on the correct route if it widens into FDR 845 within the next few yards. Pass a small wildlife clearing at 8.9 miles and a larger one with sassafras and poplar beside the road at 9.0 miles.

Crest a spur ridge at 9.2 miles and descend for a short distance before resuming the upward trend. The ferns growing along the road bank help stabilize the disturbed soil, while the wintergreen beside the route at 9.4 miles is dotted with tiny white flowers in July. Begin the final descent at 10.3 miles. The old, tall hemlocks in the bottomland to the right of the trail at 11.1 miles are evidence that this part of the forest is older than most. The large leaves of the Fraser magnolia do their part in providing shade to the forest floor, while milkweed takes advantage of the bits of sunlight in small, open spots next to the road.

Pass through a gate at 11.7 miles and turn right onto VA 643, returning to your parked automobile at 11.8 miles. Driving home, you may ponder whether you should tell a friend about the falls of Rowlands Creek—or should you be selfish and keep the secret of this Virginia beauty spot all to yourself?

25

Hungry Mother State Park

Total distance (circuit): 5.9 miles

Hiking time: 3 hours, 20 minutes

Vertical rise: 1,760 feet

Maps: USGS 7½' Marion; USGS 7½' Chatham Hill; park map

With the possible exception of "How do I get to the rest rooms?", the question employees of Hungry Mother State Park hear most often is, "How did the park get its name?"

There are a number of stories and variations on them, but historians generally agree the name derived from the legend of Molly Marley, who escaped with her child from their Indian captors. Wandering through the forest with only berries to eat, Molly eventually collapsed. The child wandered off, following a creek and coming to a frontier home, where the only words she could sputter were, "hungry mother." Sadly, when the search party finally found her mother, Molly was already dead.

One of the first state parks to be established in Virginia, most of Hungry Mother's network of pathways—some of which may retrace Molly's route—was built by members of the Civilian Conservation Corps in the 1930s. The park is easily reached by taking I-81 to Exit 47 near Marion, driving south on US 11 for 1.3 miles, and turning right onto VA 16 (Park Boulevard). Continue for an additional 4.0 miles into the park and turn right onto VA 348, which you will drive along for 0.6 miles before making a right onto the road marked for hiking trails. Bypassing any intersecting routes, continue to the end of this road and leave your car in the small parking area on the left.

Begin the hike by ascending the gated service road for 250 feet and making a right turn onto white-blazed Molly's Knob Trail. According to the legend, Molly's body was found somewhere around the base of this

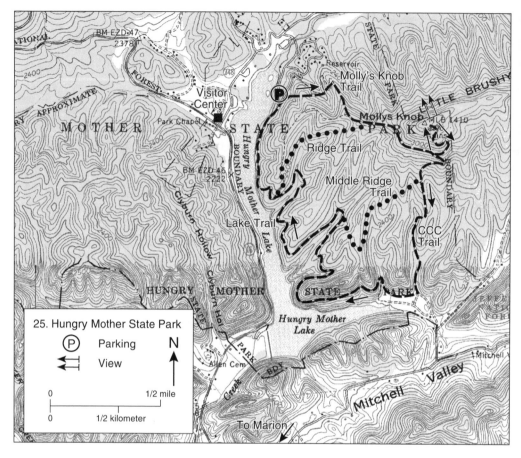

25. Hungry Mother State Park

(P) Parking   N

View

0 _____ 1/2 mile

0 _____ 1/2 kilometer

mountain. Use a footbridge to cross a small gully at 0.25 mile.

Switchback to the right at 0.4 mile, making sure to stay on Molly's Knob Trail as the ascent becomes a bit steeper. The gold-blazed Ridge Trail descends to the right at 0.8 mile. Keep left and continue to ascend along Molly's Knob Trail, which is now lined with pipsissewa, greenbrier, and fire pink. One of the brightest and most conspicuous of wildflowers found in the Appalachian Mountains, fire pink is also one of the longest lasting, blooming from some time in April to well into June. The pink in its name does not refer to the color of the flower (even though its petals are deep pink to crimson), but

rather to the notch at the end of each petal, which resembles the jagged or serrated edge of material cut by pinking shears.

Although your legs and lungs know that you have been gaining elevation, you may not realize how much—until a small break in the vegetation at 1.2 miles shows that you have already attained a height greater than that of many of the surrounding ridgelines.

Come to an intersection at 1.3 miles, bear left, and ascend steeply to Molly's Knob. Views begin to open up as you climb, while sassafras, striped maple, black co-hosh, and mayapple rise up from the forest floor. Identifying sassafras can sometimes be difficult. Its leaves may be any of three different shapes: three lobed, two lobed (resembling a mitten), or single lobed. Only one, or all three types may be present on any given tree.

At 1.7 miles, reach the summit of Molly's Knob (3,270 feet), the highest point accessible by trail in the park. It is surely time for a rest break, so take a few minutes to enjoy the vista stretching out before you. Round Top Mountain and the long, level ridgeline of Walker Mountain are to the right. Forming a backdrop to the town of Marion on your left are the lofty summits of Whitetop Mountain (see Hike 19) and Mount Rogers (see Hike 18).

Retrace your steps back to the intersection and bear left onto the orange-blazed CCC Trail, beginning a somewhat quick descent. There is a T intersection 2.4 miles into the hike where the yellow-blazed Middle Ridge Trail goes off to the right. You need to stay left on CCC Trail, continuing to descend and feasting on the abundant blueberries that ripen to delicious perfection in late July and early August.

Switchback into one of the loveliest sections of the hike at 2.7 miles, where a small mountain stream is bordered by a lush corridor of rhododendron and hemlock. Come to a Y intersection at 3.1 miles; the left route leads to a few picnic tables in a boat launch area. Bear right onto the navy blue-blazed Lake Trail.

The pathway emerges into an open area next to the boat ramp at 3.3 miles (chemical toilets are available) and swings to the right along the lakeshore. Cattails and poison ivy grow in this backwater area, and the dam, constructed in the 1930s, is visible directly across the lake.

The roots of a cattail are thin and fibrous, ideally suited to threading into the mud of marshy soils and gaining a foothold. It is one of the pioneer plants found along the edges of ponds and lakes that, through the years, will slowly dry out the area in which it lives, leading the way for plants that would not have been able to survive in a more moist environment.

Swing away from the lake at 3.5 miles, rise for a few feet, and level out in a grove of hemlocks and rhododendron. The yellow-blazed Middle Ridge Trail comes in from the right at 3.9 miles; stay left on the rhododendron-lined Lake Trail. Reach the head of a dark hollow at 4.3 miles and bend back toward the lake, rising at a gradual rate. The sound of traffic along the road on the other side of the lake becomes audible as you begin a gradual descent beside galax at 4.6 miles; cross a small stream at 5.1 miles and ascend. At dawn or dusk you might see a raccoon searching for a meal along the shoreline.

There is a comfortable resting spot at 5.3 miles that looks out across the lake. A few feet later, the gold-blazed Ridge Trail comes in from the right; keep left. A small beach at 5.6 miles provides one last spot to rest and enjoy the beauty of your surroundings before returning to your automobile at 5.9 miles.

In addition to hiking its miles of pathways, you should possibly consider making the park a destination unto itself. Using the campground or rental cabins as a base of operations, you could rent a rowboat or paddleboat to explore the lake's 6 miles of shoreline. If you are an angler, you may be pleasantly surprised by the quality and quantity of muskie, walleye, and smallmouth bass. When all of this activity raises your body temperature, take a swim in the lake and follow it up with a meal in the air-conditioned restaurant. If you run out of ideas, there is an innovative interpretive program that brings in noted authorities on various subjects. Depending on when you visit the park, you may have your choice of guided

The view from Molly's Knob

canoe trips, nature walks, night hikes, and presentations ranging from Native American dance to memorabilia of the Civil War.

A fun and interesting, albeit crowded, time to visit the park is on the third weekend of July for the annual Hungry Mother Arts and Crafts Festival. More than 100 artisans and craftspeople from the eastern U.S. display their paintings, photographs, woodworking, handmade clothing, and more to 20,000 potential customers. If you don't happen to find something to strike your fancy here, drive back to Marion, where other vendors gather along the town's sidewalks.

26

Burke's Garden and the Appalachian Trail

Total distance (round trip): 12.6 miles

Hiking time: 7 hours, 20 minutes

Vertical rise: 3,320 feet

*Maps: USGS 7½' Garden Mountain;
USGS 7½' Hutchinson Rock*

As with many discoveries, it was purely by accident that James Burke stumbled upon the land that would come to bear his name. The year was 1748, and Burke was a member of a party surveying the western frontier. Pursuing an elk in hopes of obtaining meat for the party, he tracked it over the mountains and into a valley that Native Americans referred to as the Great Swamp. He returned to the others with glowing reports, declaring that he had found the Garden of Eden, with "blue grass as tall as I ever did see," and "every kind of animal I know."

With curiosities piqued, the other men ventured into the valley, but before they could explore much, a winter storm forced them to break camp. Just as they were leaving, Burke buried some potato peels under a bit of dirt and brush so to keep the party's presence, and retreat, hidden from the Indians. When they returned the following year to complete the survey, the men found a large patch of potatoes had grown up on the spot where the peels had been buried. Amused by the incident, they jocularly referred to the place as "Burke's Garden."

This yarn about the potatoes has many of the elements of a tall tale, but there is no doubt that Burke's Garden is some of the most fertile land to be found within the commonwealth. Surrounded by high ridgelines, looking like a volcano crater's floor, the 9-mile-long valley sits atop a bedrock of limestone whose porous quality and mineral composition produce high-crop yields. Spared the disturbances of modern development, it remains one of the state's largest rural areas.

This out-and-back hike along a section of the Appalachian Trail does not go into Burke's Garden, but stays high above it on Garden Mountain, providing a number of views onto the fields below. With minor changes in elevation, except for one long uphill, the journey can be a nice day hike or, making use of a shelter situated atop the "crater's" rim, an excellent overnighter.

The drive to the trailhead is almost as scenic and pleasurable as the hike. Take I-77 to Exit 52 in Bland (a few miles north of Wytheville) and drive west on US 52/21/VA 42. The highway splits 4.0 miles later and you want to stay to the right on VA 42, following it for an additional 7.1 miles through a bucolic valley shadowed by Walker and Brushy Mountains. Make a right turn onto VA 623. Using the gravel road, cross over Brushy Mountain and descend into Hunting Camp Creek Valley. If it were not for the roadway, this quiet and peaceful place would show no signs of human disturbance. Situated as it is on Forest Service land, you may be tempted to leave the car and explore it on foot. Continuing the drive, however, you will gain elevation via long switchbacks and reach the AT parking area on the crest of Garden Mountain, about 7.5 miles after turning off VA 42.

Walk into the woodlands on the south side of the road and ascend steadily along the AT {FS 1} to a high point (4,052 feet) in 0.2 mile. About 30 feet to the right of the trail is an outcrop that provides your first glimpse onto Burke's Garden's long, rolling croplands as they gradually rise to the forested hillsides.

Continuing along the trail, the pathway is bordered on the right by a nearly continuous wall of sandstone that is 40 to 50 feet

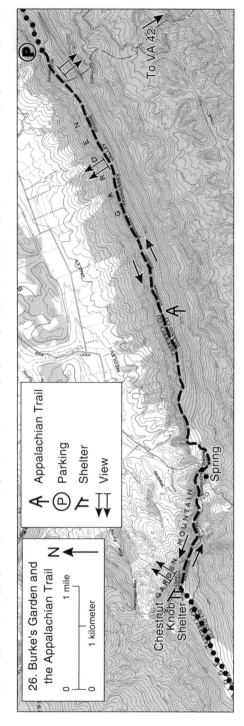

Appalachian Trail

Parking

Shelter

View

26. Burke's Garden and the Appalachian Trail

N

1 mile

1 kilometer

0

0

Mountain laurel

high in some places. As with so many portions of the AT in the Southern Appalachians, tall bushes of mountain laurel and rhododendron arch over the trail.

Rock outcrops on the high point at 1.0 mile furnish the excuse to take a rest and enjoy another view into Burke's Garden. Besides surveying the scene in front of you, take a look at the rocks you are sitting on (and others you pass along the way) and you might see the fossilized bore holes of wormlike creatures believed to have lived well over 400 million years ago. You can also see the distinct shapes of seashells outlined in the stones, reminding you that the Appalachian Mountains were at the bottom of an ancient ocean ages ago.

The AT continues its up-and-down roll, going over high points such as the knob at 2.2 miles and descending into small gaps like the one around 3.1 miles. Although other people had put forth similar ideas, Benton MacKaye's 1921 article, "An Ap-

palachian Trail: A Project in Regional Planning," is considered to have provided the impetus for creating the AT. MacKaye saw an America that was rapidly becoming urbanized, machine-driven, and removed from the positive aspects of the natural world. In addition to recreational opportunities, he envisioned the trail as connecting a series of permanent, self-sustaining workers' camps in which "cooperation replaces antagonism, trust replaces suspicion, emulation replaces competition."

The natural sandstone wall comes to end at 3.9 miles; it is the remains of a human-built rock wall you pass on the right at 4.4 miles. Old stone boundaries such as this can be found along the AT all of the way from Tennessee into New England, remnants of the days when the ridgelines were once grazing and foraging lands for cattle and swine.

Step over a woods road and a small water run (which may be dry in summer) at

4.9 miles and make an abrupt turn to the right. You will soon come into Walker Gap and cross another dirt road. (If spending the night on the mountain, you might consider a side journey of a little more than 0.1 mile round trip along the blue-blazed route to the left to obtain water from a reliable spring. There is no good water source close to the shelter.)

You now begin the long ascent mentioned in the introduction to this hike, climbing close to 900 feet in a little more than a mile. A rest break may be in order when you cross a woods road at 5.3 miles, not only to catch your breath, but also to linger over the view of Big Walker Mountain to the southeast. Prior to being relocated in the 1980s, the AT used to follow its long, nearly level ridgeline for many miles.

You reap the reward for making the climb just as you break out of the woods and into open meadowlands at 6.3 miles. Standing on the 4,409-foot summit of Chestnut Knob, it is possible to take in the sweeping, grandstand view of the entire expanse of Burke's Garden, more than 1,300 feet below you. With the circular ridgeline of Garden Mountain surrounding this indentation in the landscape, it is easy to see why some people refer to it as God's thumbprint.

Once a fire warden's cabin, the stone Chestnut Knob Shelter is just beyond the viewpoint. One of the few enclosed shelters to be found along the entire AT, it makes for a dry and cozy place to escape the rain storms and high winds that often buffet the mountain. If you are staying here for the night, your day's hike is done. Unpack gear, spread your sleeping bag out on one of the bunks, and relax. There is hardly a better place to enjoy the sunset, the magnificent display of stars as they appear in the night sky, and, as an added bonus for spending another day on the trail, tomorrow's sunrise.

If this is just a day hike for you, grab the shelter register and go back to the viewpoint for your lunch or snack. Northbound AT thru-hikers have walked more than 500 miles by the time they reach this point, and their entries into the register—some humorous, some aphoristic, and some disillusioned—provide insight into what they are experiencing.

When you finally decide it is time to leave, simply retrace your steps, enjoying how the late afternoon light plays differently on the landscape than the light that accompanied you earlier. The outing comes to an end when you return to your car, after walking 12.6 miles today.

27

Little Wolf Creek

Total distance (circuit): 10.5 miles

Hiking time: 5 hours, 45 minutes

Vertical rise: 1,880 feet

Maps: USGS 7½' Big Bend

In response to the changing face of the eastern U.S., the route of the Appalachian Trail has been moved many times, in many places, since its completion in 1937. Often displaced by new highways, homes, or commercial construction, it has also been relocated off private property and onto public lands in order to protect it from future intrusions.

Sometimes it becomes necessary to relocate the relocations, which was the case with the AT's displacement by the Blue Ridge Parkway in the 1950s. After spending decades building hundreds of miles of new trail to the west of the parkway, volunteers found themselves called upon again to move the route even farther west in the 1970s and 1980s; minor relocations continue to this day. By making use of former routes or connecting side trails, you can complete circuit hikes that would not have been possible before the relocations.

When it was moved from Big Walker Mountain to Garden Mountain (see Hike 26) in the early 1980s, the AT was routed along scenic Little Wolf Creek for nearly 3.0 miles. Although it is an appealing walk in an isolated valley, trail maintainers soon found out it was prone to dangerous stream crossings in times of heavy rains. As a result, they constructed an alternate route for such occasions. Just north of that, a separate relocation designed to put the AT on the optimal course created another short circuit with great views.

You will park your car in the middle of these two loops for the hike described

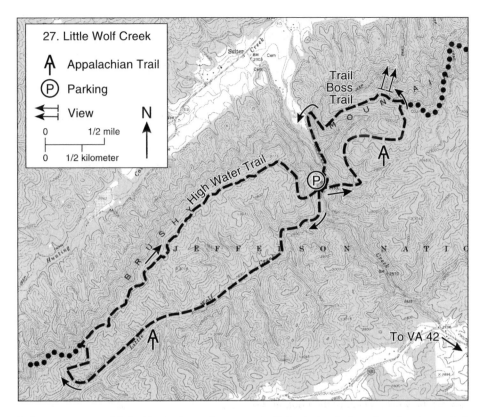

27. Little Wolf Creek

↑ Appalachian Trail

Ⓟ Parking

⇄ View

N

0   1/2 mile

0   1/2 kilometer

below, so you could decide to do each on separate occasions if you don't have the time or inclination to do the entire outing all at once. As both loops are on Forest Service lands, there is also the option of making this an overnighter by setting up camp wherever you wish.

The trailheads may be reached by taking I-77 to Exit 52 at Bland (a few miles north of Wytheville), driving to the southwest on US 52/21/VA 42 and making a right turn onto VA 615 in 3.2 miles. About a mile later, the roadway becomes unpaved as it enters Forest Service property. Watch for the AT footbridge and the small pullout on the left in another 1.5 miles.

Take the AT {FS 1} on the north side of the road, walking into a mixed hardwood forest, with an understory that includes great rhododendron and a floor carpeted with running cedar. Within a few feet of rising along a stream, the branches of the rhododendron rise high above and arch over the pathway to form a tunnel.

Switchback to the left at 0.3 mile, rising out of the tunnel. With more sunlight reaching the ground to nourish vegetation, the pathway is now lined with galax, wintergreen, and small blueberry bushes. Many people use the names huckleberry and blueberry interchangeably, but they are two distinct plants. The branches of blueberries always have small warts and each berry will have more than 100 seeds. A huckleberry contains fewer than a dozen seeds and its twigs are wart-free.

Attain the crest of the ridgeline at 1.4 miles, continuing to follow the AT over slight

---

Little Wolf Creek

ups and downs. Come to a T intersection at 2.0 miles, where you will take your leave of the Appalachian Trail and turn left onto the blue-blazed Trail Boss Trail. Members of the Outing Club of Virginia Tech gave the path its name to honor Keith Smith, a former official of their organization and a leader of one of the Appalachian Trail Conservancy's volunteer Konnarock trail crews.

Small breaks in the vegetation along this old woods road furnish the compensation for having gained more than 500 feet in elevation since leaving your car. From varying angles, you can look upon pastoral Hunting Camp Creek Valley, the small village of Bastion, tractor trailers moving along the winding route of I-77, and the southeastern slopes of Round, Rich, and Buckhorn Mountains.

Striped maple lines the trail as you begin to descend along the left side of the ridgeline at 2.3 miles. Leave the roadbed you have been following and veer to the left at 2.9 miles, continuing to descend. Swing around the western side of the ridge at 3.0 miles and you will have limited views into the valley below. About 500 feet later, switchback to the left and descend into a narrow defile at 3.4 miles to cross a small water run. Soon afterward, the gurgling of Laurel Creek becomes audible.

Cross Laurel Creek on a footbridge at 3.8 miles, turn left onto VA 615, and return to your car at 4.0 miles. If this is all the time you have, drive home with plans to do the rest of this outing another day. If not, take a short break and enjoy the snacks and drinks you left stashed in the car. It might even be time to cool off by wading into the pool at the base of Laurel Creek's small cascade.

When ready to resume, cross over the bridge (constructed of native materials by volunteers without the aid of modern tools) and follow the AT uphill to its intersection with the High Water Trail {FS 6507} at 4.1 miles. Stay to the left along the AT, the trail here lined with a variety of ferns, and swing right in a few hundred feet to begin paralleling Little Wolf Creek, your companion for the next several miles.

With the trail hemmed in by an abundance of rhododendron, cross the stream for the first time at 4.3 miles. This pattern is firmly established as you cross the stream again at 4.4 miles, 4.5 miles, 4.6 miles, and 4.7 miles. Although it may not be obvious, the route you are following is the bed of a railroad used to extract timber from the area in the early 1900s. The valley begins to widen as you rock-hop across the creek for the sixth time at 4.8 miles.

Swing away from Little Wolf Creek at 5.1 miles. However, you immediately need to cross one of its tributaries and, as you rise on hillside trail, several other small side streams. From mid- to late July, the rhododendron bushes drop so many blossoms onto the ground that it appears as if the flower girl from a wedding has come by, tossing white petals to prepare for the arrival of the bride.

Return to Little Wolf Creek, which is much narrower now, and cross it for the seventh time at 6.9 miles. Repeat the earlier pattern by crossing the stream again at 7.0 miles, 7.2 miles, 7.4 miles, 7.6 miles, and 7.65 miles. Soon after crossing for the twelfth and final time, the trail takes its leave of the creek and begins to make a switchbacked ascent.

It is time to say farewell to the AT when it intersects an old woods road at 8.5 miles. Turn right onto the blue-blazed Highwater Trail, with its abundance of tulip poplars and wintertime views to the northeast. If here in the early evening, the sudden *who-who* cry of a great horned owl might startle you out of your daydreams.

Playing in Laurel Creek

It might be possible to find a small tent site on the spur ridge you cross over at **8.8** miles; here flame azalea bursts forth in spring to fill the air with its sweet perfume. Be alert at 9.5 miles! The blue-blazed High Water Trail, the one you want to follow, stays to the right fork at a Y intersection. The way to the left is a former route of the High Water Trail—even side trails get relocated.

Your route soon becomes a footpath, descending via switchbacks, which returns you to the AT at 10.4 miles. Make a left onto the white-blazed pathway, cross Laurel Creek, and bring this outing to a close by returning to your car at 10.5 miles.

28

Dismal Creek and Sugar Run Mountain

Total distance (circuit): 9.6 miles

Hiking time: 5 hours, 40 minutes

Vertical rise: 1,980 feet

Maps: USGS 7½' White Gate

An agreeable saunter into a stream valley, a stiff climb of a bit more than a mile to provide a cardiovascular workout, an easy ridgeline walk with a superb viewpoint, and a quick, but rather gentle descent back to the car. What more could you ask for in a day hike?

Well, in addition to the above, there are an abundance of level tent sites or a trailside shelter you could use to turn this into an overnighter; the route is lined with more than its fair share of spring and summer wildflowers; you can have a history lesson in the origin of place names; and you have the option of making the journey a combination hiking/fly-fishing outing by casting a line into the trout-stocked waters of Dismal Creek. To top it all off, it's possible to stop on the drive in or out to visit an extremely picturesque waterfall and cool off in the pool at the bottom.

The beginning of the hike can be reached by taking I-81 to Exit 118 and driving US 460 west for approximately 30.0 miles to Pearisburg. (Watch for the many twists and turns on US 460 as you go by Christiansburg and Blacksburg.) Leave US 460 and follow Business US 460 for a little more than 5.0 miles to the center of Pearisburg, where you will make a left onto VA 100 South. Continue for an additional 10.5 miles, turn right onto VA 42 and, in another 10.5 miles, bear right onto VA 606. Only 0.9 mile later—just beyond a gas station/convenience store—turn right onto VA 671, which soon becomes dirt FDR 201. For the

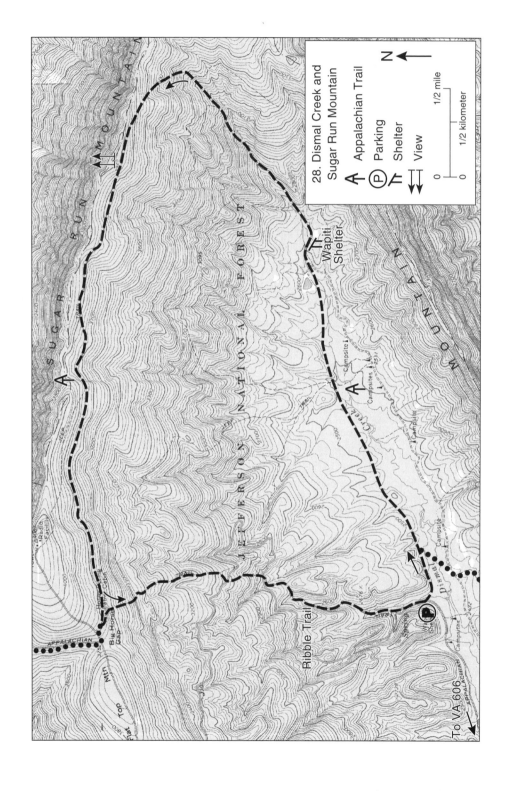

N

28. Dismal Creek and Sugar Run Mountain

— Appalachian Trail
Ⓟ Parking
⊓⊓ Shelter
⇊ View

0 _____ 1/2 mile
0 _____ 1/2 kilometer

SUGAR RUN MOUNTAIN

JEFFERSON NATIONAL FOREST

MOUNTAIN

Wapiti Shelter

Campsite
Campsites
Campsite
Campsite

Dismal Creek Trail

Campsite

Dismal

Radar
Facility

Big Horse Gap

Flat Top Mtn

APPALACHIAN

Ribble Trail

Spring
Sh.

Campsite

APPALACHIAN

To VA 606

waterfall side trip, be watching for a small parking area on the right about 0.9 mile after turning off VA 606. A short, unimproved trail will drop you down to the impressive Falls of Dismal Creek, whose base pool is a favorite local swimming hole.

The Forest Service's Walnut Flats Campground, developed with a water pump, picnic tables, and pit toilets, is 0.8 mile beyond the falls. A little more than 2.0 miles later, FDR 201 makes a 90-degree turn to the left. Park your car in a turnout on the right.

Begin the hike by taking the trail to the right of a gated, grassy road and enter a deep rhododendron thicket. Step across a small stream and swing to the right as the rhododendron gives way to lush thickets of mountain laurel. Avoid the faint trail to the right at 0.3 mile, but do bear right onto a woods road 0.4 mile after leaving your car. Take the right fork of a Y intersection at 0.6 mile and turn left onto the white-blazed AT {FS 1} less than 200 feet later.

Walk upon relatively level terrain, with Dismal Creek off to your right, and step over small water runs at 1.0 mile, 1.1 miles, 1.3 miles, and 1.6 miles. Pass through a couple of open areas and ascend along a woods road at 1.8 miles, only to turn off it at 1.9 miles to follow a footpath to the right, descending to the northern bank of Dismal Creek. According to local lore, the name of the creek and its narrow valley comes from the black shale present in the soil, making it a hard place in which to grow any crops and a dismal place to live.

After crossing another small stream at 2.0 miles, step over a constructed ditch at 2.3 miles, following the trail's white blazes along the embankment of a pond. Cross the main branch of Dismal Creek at 2.5 miles, bear to the right, and follow a blue-blazed side trail to the Wapiti Shelter. Erected by

the Forest Service in 1980, it replaced a shelter of the same name in a different spot that attracted large throngs of weekend partyers due to its accessible location next to FDR 201.

As you sit here taking a break and reading the trail register to find out how many AT thru-hikers have passed this way in the last few days, try to imagine yourself transported back a few hundred years to learn of the origin of the shelter's name. At that time, you could have caught sight of a herd of wapiti—the Native American name for elk (which, by the way, is also the British name for moose)—grazing about in the forest in front of you. Although they were extirpated from Virginia more than a century ago, a few wild elk have recently been seen in the Cumberland Gap area of far southwest Virginia (see Hike 50).

You will leave level terrain behind once you return to the AT and, with increasing steepness, continue your upstream journey of Dismal Creek, crossing two of its tributaries, the first at 2.9 miles, and the next at 3.3 miles. After gaining well over 1,000 feet in elevation since leaving the shelter, the route makes a sharp left onto a narrower footpath at 4.0 miles as you begin to traverse the main ridgeline of Sugar Run Mountain.

Having left the moistness of the stream valley, you may notice that the undergrowth is not as lush and the trees, primarily oaks, are shorter and more gnarled. The elevation gain is only gradual now, and another rest break is in order when you come to a rock outcrop at 5.1 miles. Almost due north is Pearis Mountain, serving as a backdrop for the green fields of Wilburn Valley, which are nourished by the waters of Sugar Run, below you. Turn a little more to the east to gaze across the tranquil rolling lands of the New River Valley.

Great rhododendron

AT. You do, however, want to leave the AT at 7.3 miles so that you can begin the descent back to your starting point; turn left onto the blue-blazed Ribble Trail {FS 62}, which starts out as a grassy road peppered with the crimson petals of fire pinks.

Walk by the remains of a cabin and descend to the right at 7.4 miles. After crossing a small boulder field and passing through a stand of evergreens at 7.7 miles, make a left turn onto an old woods road. The mountain laurel is so thick here that, when it begins to drop its petals in late June, it almost looks like snow has fallen on the branches of the sassafras trees and blueberry bushes and covered the ground with a flecked raiment of white.

Step across FDR 201 at 8.4 miles and continue to descend. From June into August, waxy white pipsissewa flowers droop over the dead leaves from the previous fall. Cross FDR 201 again at 8.7 miles and pass by a small campsite and a stream that is nearly hidden by the great rhododendron tunnel arching over it. The pink to purple blossoms of the Catawba rhododendron begin to bloom in May, but the pinkish-white clusters of the great rhododendron do not make an appearance until June.

Running cedar helps anchor the soil around the small stream you step across at 9.2 miles. Be sure to stay to the right when you come to a Y intersection 200 feet later. Cross the final stream of the hike at 9.4 miles, bringing the journey to an end when you return to your car at 9.6 miles.

Dropping a bit off the main crest of Sugar Run Mountain, turn right onto a woods road at 5.4 miles. Bloodroot, trillium, bluets, spring beauty, and mayapples push aside clumps of soil and small pebbles to emerge from the ground and into the sunlight in early spring; the crest of Flat Top Mountain is visible in the cooler months through the leafless branches to the right of the trail.

Be alert at 6.7 miles! The roadbed continues straight for 0.1 mile to the summit of Flat Top Mountain, but you need to make a hard left in order stay along the route of the

The Blue Ridge Region

29

Huckleberry Ridge Loop

Total distance (circuit): 9.0 miles

Hiking time: 6 hours, 15 minutes

Vertical rise: 2,280 feet

Maps: USGS 7½' Interior

More square than circular, the Huckleberry Ridge Loop Trail {FS 52} has been referred to by a succession of different names through the years. When the network of pathways was first being constructed, each side of the square had its own moniker—Kelly Flats, Dismal Branch, Dixon Branch, and North Branch. Not long after its completion, the four names were replaced by one, the Flat Peter Trail, reflecting the fact that the route rose from the lowlands of Kelly Flats to the upper reaches of Peters Mountain. Some time around 1980 it received the title it has now. Who knows? It could be called something else by the time you hike here.

However, no matter what its designation might be, the Huckleberry Ridge Loop is a great resource for taking a walk across the southeastern slope of Peters Mountain and exploring a number of its most wild, remote, and least-visited watersheds. Beginning in a young forest, the hike soon ascends into hidden valleys choked by entangling rhododendron thickets, coves of hardwood forest rich with poplar, oak, and hickory, and stands of old-growth hemlock trees. The wildlife, including white-tailed deer, black bears, wild turkeys, and bobcats, is abundant, so keep a watchful eye. Suitable campsites can be few and far between, but those that you may find have a truly isolated feel about them.

Be aware that there is one very major warning concerning this outing: Unless it has been worked on recently, the route ascending Dismal Branch has not been

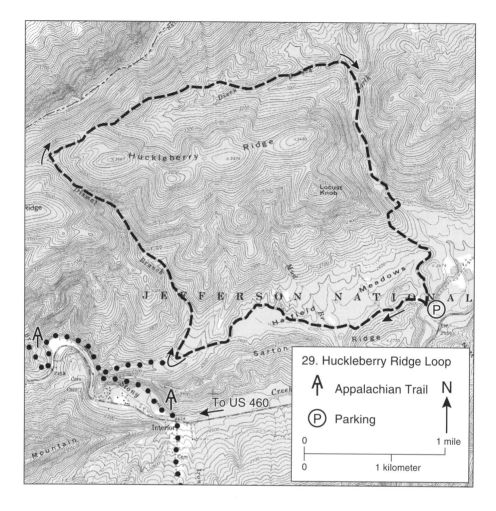

29. Huckleberry Ridge Loop

⚡ Appalachian Trail   N

Ⓟ Parking

0 ————————————— 1 mile

0 ————————————— 1 kilometer

maintained for so many years that it has become almost nonexistent along much of its length. This is not the journey for you if you are uncomfortable about having to find your own way. There will be many times when it will be necessary to bully your way through unyielding rhododendron branches, sometimes having to get on hands and knees to crawl under them. In addition, be ready to climb over countless blowdowns and wade into the middle of the creek. None of this is easy when you are wearing a day pack, and it can become positively frustrating when carrying a full backpack. If, however, you are up to the challenge, you will find that there is no greater sense of satisfaction than negotiating an obstacle course such as this and then emerging from it exactly where you had intended.

The Huckleberry Ridge Loop Trail may be reached by taking I-81 to Exit 118 and driving US 460 west for approximately 28.0 miles to pass through the small settlement of Pembroke. (Watch for the many twists and turns on US 460 as you go by Christiansburg and Blacksburg.) Make a right turn onto VA 635, continue for another 13.5 miles, and make a left onto FDR 772 (Glen Alton Road). Cross the bridge, keep to the left on the road signed as leading to Kelly Flats, then take the right fork and immediately park in the small space on the left.

Walk back the few feet to the intersection, turn right, pass through the gate, and begin to follow the route of Kelly Flats Road through a miles-long wildlife clearing and a few pine plantations. During the warmer months, a multitude of butterflies flitter from one umbel of Queen Anne's lace to another. Closer to the ground, the tiny Deptford pink blossoms add their own color to the field.

Just as the Virginia Department of Game and Inland Fisheries does on state wildlife management areas, the Forest Service creates these open areas in national forests in order to increase the diversity of habitat—primarily for game animals. Rabbits, quail, woodcock, and other birds are attracted to the thickets that grow up along the edges of the clearings, while wild turkeys have been seen using the meadows to rear their broods.

A small wetlands, with its own type of vegetation, is to the right of the pathway at 0.6 mile. The trail becomes little more than a couple of tire tracks through tall grass at 1.0 mile, a prime site for the hundreds of thousands of ticks that live here to latch on to you as you walk by.

Although it is most active in the spring and fall, the deer tick, the primary carrier of Lyme disease, is present throughout the summer and winter months, too. You may be able to recognize it by its orange-black body with a black spot near its head when it is an adult, but as a larva it is no larger than the period at the end of this sentence. Sometimes a bull's-eye-like rash—a ring with a center spot—will develop within 20 days of being bitten. Other symptoms may include fever, chills, headaches, fatigue, and stiffness in joints. In some cases there are no symptoms, so it is important for you to check yourself carefully after each venture into the outdoors. Most insect repellents don't appear to do much to repel ticks, but you can make it harder for them to reach your skin by wearing long pants and long-sleeved shirts when you go hiking and tucking your pants into your socks and boots.

Pass through a small pine plantation at 1.3 miles; just beyond, the openness of the fields provides an opportunity to gaze upon the upper slopes of Sarton Ridge and Potts Mountain, reaching toward the horizon on your left.

Be alert at 1.9 miles! Just as the wildlife clearings come to an end, you need to continue straight into the woods and avoid the grassy road heading off to the right. Be alert again at 2.1 miles! At this new intersection, you now want to make a right turn onto a grassy route that may have no sign and may be marked only by old, fading yellow blazes. As you ascend along this pathway lined with wintergreen, the drillings and calls of woodpeckers and other birds, along with the gurgling of the stream, drown out any noise of civilization.

Start paralleling rhododendron-crowded Dismal Branch at 2.6 miles. Soon, Indian pipe and galax line the pathway as it begins to narrow. By the time you rock-hop across Dismal Branch at 2.9 miles, you are walking into the deep shadow of thick, intertwining rhododendron branches. The pungent, earthy aroma of galax adds to the feeling of being inside a deep cave or tunnel.

Recross the stream at 3.0 miles, and again 200 feet later, as the route becomes much rougher and harder to follow. At this point the path is essentially nonexistent. Your route-finding skills will be put to the test here. Look for very faint paint blazes or old logs that were cut years ago to help you

A footbridge across North Branch stream

identify the trail. Step across Dismal Creek again at 3.6 miles.

Just when it looks like the trail comes to a dead end in a mass of gnarled rhododendron bushes, cross the creek and find the faint pathway continuing upstream. Cross Dismal Branch again at 3.9 miles, 4.0 miles, and for the last time at 4.3 miles. Watch for the trail to swing to the right just beyond a small, established campsite. Your struggle with rhododendron branches has come to an end; now it is the thriving thickets of mountain laurel that may slow your forward progress.

Pass over the height of Huckleberry Ridge at 4.7 miles, begin to descend, walk out of the wilderness area, and cross the headwaters of Dixon Branch at 5.0 miles—and again only 150 feet later. Swing left and cross the stream an additional time at 5.2 miles. Growing up from the roots of the oak trees, the yellowish-brown squawroot is sometimes called cancer root. Do not, however, confuse it with other parasitic plants of the same name, such as one-flowered cancer root or yellow cancer root, which more closely resemble Indian pipe. To confound things even further, black cohosh is sometimes referred to as squawroot, because it, too, was used to alleviate the pains of menstruation.

Cross a small water run at 5.4 miles, and another with a campsite beneath the shade of hemlocks just 200 feet later. Although there is some question as to whether or not the hemlocks along the headwaters of Dixon Branch are a virgin stand, some individual trees have been positively dated at more than 250 years old. Cross the creek seven more times within the next 0.75 mile.

Be alert at 7.0 miles! Do not ford the large stream directly in front of you (called North Branch), but turn left to cross a smaller watercourse and come to an established campsite. Here you will turn right to take a footbridge across North Branch.

The Blue Ridge Region

Walking downstream along this main drainage course may just be the prettiest portion of the hike. You are on a relatively easy path, the water gurgles as it drops down small riffles into wading pools, and the copious leaves of mountain laurel and rhododendron ensure that the forest understory will appear to be green at any time of the year.

The feel and vegetation of the forest begin to change about the time you ford the stream for the last time at 7.8 miles. Less than 300 feet later, the pathway ascends to the right, only to drop back to the stream within a short distance.

Be very alert at 8.0 miles! Although there is a pathway continuing downstream, the route you want to follow makes a sudden turn to the right for a steep, switchbacked ascent. Begin to descend upon reaching the ridgeline at 8.2 miles, swinging around a parcel of private land. The tall, white flower, spikes of the black cohosh grow along the Forest Service road you turn left onto at 8.6 miles, which will bring you back to your automobile at 9.0 miles.

30

Barneys Wall and
The Cascades

Total distance (one way): 4.9 miles

Hiking time: 2 hours, 15 minutes

Vertical rise: 220 feet

Maps: USGS 7½' Eggleston

Without a doubt, The Cascades is one of the most popular destinations in all of southern Virginia. In addition to locals flocking here in droves, the outing has almost become a right of passage for freshman students of nearby Virginia Tech. After coming here once, many people are drawn back time and time again, much like pilgrims who feel compelled to repeat the sacred journey to a holy site.

With land purchased by the Forest Service in 1965, The Cascades Trail {FS 70} was declared a National Recreation Trail in 1979. Following a massive flood in 1996 that wiped out just about every vestige of the pathway, the Forest Service spent several hundred thousand dollars and 3 years reconstructing the route and building a picnic/recreation area and large parking lot next to the lower trailhead.

Most visitors to The Cascades simply do an out-and-back hike from the lower trailhead. While this saves the time and hassle of a car shuttle, it precludes the all-downhill walk along the Nature Conservancy Trail {FS 7013} and the opportunity to experience one of Jefferson National Forest's most imposing vistas from atop the 1,000-foot rock cliff of Barneys Wall.

Since the hike described below takes in these extra attractions as a one-way hike, a car shuttle will be necessary. You can drive to the lower trailhead by taking I-81 to Exit 118 and driving US 460 west for approximately 25.0 miles to the small settlement of Pembroke. (Watch for the many twists and turns on US 460 as you go by Christiansburg and Blacksburg.) Make a right turn onto VA 623 and leave one car in The Cascades

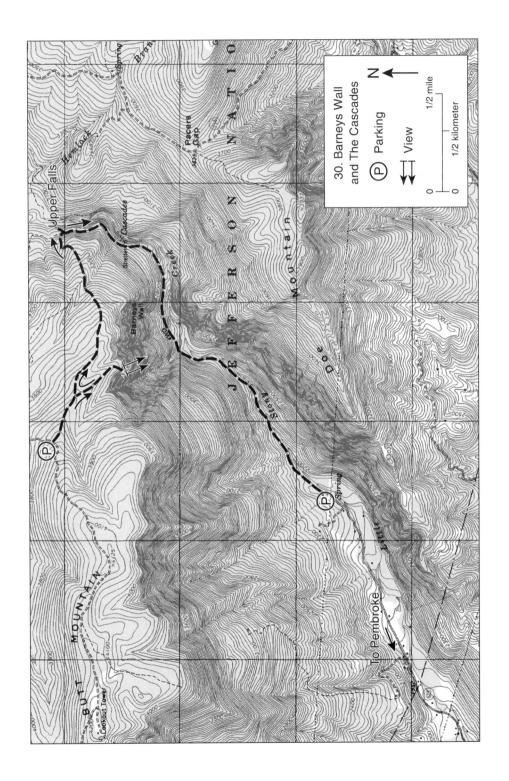

30. Barneys Wall
and The Cascades

N

ⓟ Parking

↓↓ View

0   1/2 kilometer

0   1/2 mile

Recreation Area parking lot 3.5 miles later. The area has picnic tables that are accessible to those whose mobility is impaired, flush toilets, water fountains, and garbage containers.

Return to US 460, turn left, follow it eastward for 2.0 miles, and make another left onto VA 613. Bear left onto VA 714 (Little Meadow Road) in an additional 4.0 miles, watching for the unsigned intersection 4.6 miles later, where you need to make the final left turn. A small turnout on the right only 1.0 mile later provides parking for the upper trailhead.

Walk across the road, enter a forest of white and scarlet oak, white pine, and chestnut, and descend along the wide, yellow-blazed pathway. Avoid the trail to the right at 0.15 mile. Although it is blazed and would lead to a spectacular view in several miles, sadly, it has been unmaintained for so many years that it has essentially disappeared. You do, however, want to take the next trail to the right at 0.3 mile to descend to an equally-inspiring vista. When the trail comes to a sort of cul-de-sac at 0.6 mile, take the fainter pathway to the right, arriving at the viewpoint less than 200 feet later.

And what a view it is. You are standing upon the upper edge of Barneys Wall, a sheer rock cliff that drops straight down for close to 1,000 feet, coming to an end where it meets Little Stony Creek, the stream that forms The Cascades. You don't need to wait until you descend all of that elevation to enjoy a waterfall, though. Just look a bit to your right and you will be treated to one of Little Stony's tributaries tumbling and rolling down the rock face and into the gorge. As you gaze out, your eyes will be drawn to the New River Valley and dozens of ridgelines—such as Rich Hill, Spruce Run Mountain, and Walker Mountain—receding far off to the south.

Return to the main trail and turn right onto the yellow-blazed route, descending among bluets, purple and yellow violets, and the coiled shoots of ferns—known as fiddleheads—early in the spring. If picked when young enough, fiddleheads can be cooked as a delicious alternative to asparagus or other green vegetables.

The descent steepens and crosses a creek through a thicket of rhododendron at 1.8 miles. Stay to the right here, as an old road comes in from the left. If hiking in the winter, you can use the leaves of the rhododendron to determine the temperature. In order to protect their soft undersides from the desiccating effects of cool breezes, the leaves begin to droop and curl under as the weather gets colder. The tighter the curl, the colder it is. When the leaves are wrapped around themselves to about the size of a choice cigar, the temperature is hovering around freezing; the diameter of a cheap cigar means that it is getting into the twenties and the teens. If you are out here when the leaves have become no larger than a cigarette, you better be wearing lots of layers—the temperature is mighty close to zero.

Come to a T intersection at 2.2 miles, bear right, and then make an almost immediate left to arrive at the Upper Cascades at 2.3 miles. Not as tall as The Cascades, it is still worth the walk to enjoy this stream dropping into a small pool (and it is a much quieter spot, since most people only visit the lower falls).

Return to the previous intersection, keep to the left, and head downstream. Bear left once again at 2.8 miles and drop down wooden steps and platforms to look at The Cascades. Now that you are here, you can understand why this is such a popular destination at any time of year. In spring, snowmelt and seasonal rains swell the stream, sending it roaring down the 66 feet

The view from Barneys Wall

over various rock layers; warm summer temperatures and a gentler cascade might invite you to take a dip in the wide, circular pool at the base of the falls. (There is a ledge you can sit on to let the splashing falls bounce off your body.) The volume of water is diminished in autumn, but it sparkles and shines because more sunlight pierces the canopy. Snapshots of the falls frozen in winter have graced countless Christmas cards mailed home by Virginia Tech students.

After wandering up and down all of the wooden steps and onto the numerous observation platforms, return to the main pathway and head downstream through more rhododendron and hemlock on an old woods road. (Another pathway runs along the edge of Little Stony Creek and, although it is rougher and rockier, you are welcome to make use of it; both routes are about equidistant. The creek is reported to be one of the best wild trout streams in the area.)

Stay to the right along the woods road at 3.3 miles, passing beside a huge over-hanging rock at 3.5 miles with star chickweed clinging to life in its small cracks and upon the ground. Like the rhododendron leaves, you can use the star chickweed as a weather gauge. According to folklore, if the blossoms are spread out to their fullest, the sun will be shining bright. However, if they begin to close up, you had better get out the rain gear, as precipitation will begin to fall within the next few hours.

At 3.8 miles, the purple blossoms of geranium line the pathway to the left that leads to the stream-edge trail. Yellowish-brown squawroot becomes quite prevalent at 4.1 miles, where Little Stony Creek creates small riffles and falls over large boulders within its bed. Phlox is the prominent flower on the forest floor when a bridge veers off to the lower trail at 4.7 miles.

You will reach your shuttled automobile and the end of the hike when you come to the lower trailhead parking lot at 4.9 miles. See Hikes 21, 23, 24, 28, 39, 41, 47, and 48 for other waterfall hikes within southern Virginia.

31

Mountain Lake

Total distance (circuit): 6.4 miles

Hiking time: 3 hours, 40 minutes

Vertical rise: 1,440 feet

Maps: USGS 7½' Eggleston; Mountain Lake trail map

"On a mountaintop in Virginia, there's a mountain lake whose waters beckon with the promise of extraordinary delights." As a general rule, you should take such words, written by a public relations firm, with a grain of salt, but this is not so in the case of Mountain Lake.

The resort, which has been in continuous operation for more than a century and a half, sits within a natural bowl surrounded by lofty Allegheny Mountain ridgelines. Its scenery is so picturesque that Hollywood producers chose it to be the setting for the 1986 movie *Dirty Dancing*. Just like Patrick Swayze, you can spend your time here in either the native stone hotel or one of the small cabins overlooking the lake. In addition to a network of hiking trails, you can go mountain biking, fishing, swimming, or boating.

Unlike most similar places throughout the world, the resort is operated as a nonprofit branch of a private foundation whose mandate is to maintain "the natural environment in perpetuity for the benefit and pleasure of people for generations to come." One of the most pleasant benefits of this philosophy is that nonguests are permitted to make use of the property's hiking trails upon paying a small parking fee.

Mountain Lake may be reached by taking I-81 to Exit 118 and driving US 460 west for approximately 20.0 miles (watch for its many twists and turns as you go by Christiansburg and Blacksburg). Make a right turn onto VA 700 and follow this winding mountain roadway as it gains elevation,

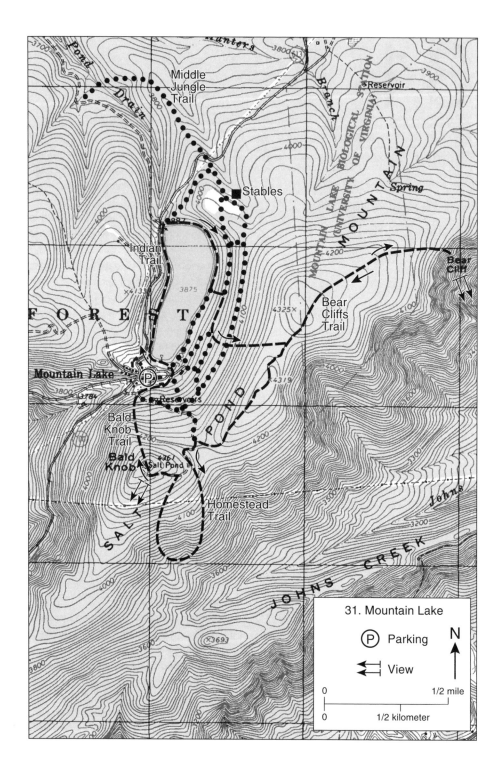

31. Mountain Lake

Ⓟ Parking
⬅ View
N

0 — 1/2 mile
0 — 1/2 kilometer

coming to Mountain Lake Resort in an additional 6.8 miles.

After obtaining the required permit, take the stairs toward the lake, making a left turn onto the gravel service road next to the gazebo. In 0.1 mile, bear right onto the Indian Trail, walk below a guest cottage, and enter the woods. Around the turn of the 20th century, individuals were invited to build these cabins around the lake and received discounts for meals and maid service from the hotel. After 15 years, title was required to be turned over to the resort, which continues to rent them out.

Fire pink and rhododendron are part of the forest understory, while openings in the vegetation provide one view after another of the lake. The display of mountain laurel in June along this portion of the hike is some of the most lush you are likely to find anywhere in Virginia. In addition, be watching for the jug-shaped leaf bracts of the jack-in-the-pulpit rising up to a foot off the forest floor from April into June. Later in the fall, the bracts wither away, revealing bright red seed clusters.

Walk behind a guest cottage, originally constructed in 1925 and rebuilt and redesigned in the late 1900s, at 0.7 mile and swing around the north end of the lake. Be alert and make sure that you stay on the Indian Trail—do not turn left onto the route leading to the horse barn. Hemlock, rhododendron, and mountain laurel provide deep shade as the pathway winds below an area of interesting rock formations known as the Garden of the Gods. Mountain Lake is one of only two natural lakes in Virginia (see Hike 4 for the other one) and was formed about 6,000 years ago, when an earthquake caused some of these sandstone boulders to fall, lodge together, and create a dam.

The pathway rises along the hillside at 1.0 mile before switchbacking down to a bench overlooking the lake. Shortly after is a wonderful forest of twisted rhododendron branches and towering hemlocks, both benefiting from the fact that the resort has been here as long as it has and there has been no timbering on this property for well over 100 years. Some hemlocks around the lake are estimated to be more than 350 years old.

Be alert at 1.3 miles! Turn left onto what may be a poorly defined pathway and rise for less than 200 feet to intersect the Lower Jungle Trail. Turn right on this graveled carriage road, walking through a forest of ferns, striped maple, hemlock, birch, oak, and both Catawba and great rhododendron.

Be alert again at 1.5 miles. Turn left and ascend along the pathway signed as leading to Bear Cliffs, Bald Knob, and Old Turnpike. (The hotel is 0.2 mile straight ahead from this intersection.) Come to a Y intersection about 300 feet later and keep to the left; you will soon cross over the Old Turnpike Trail and continue the ascent to Bear Cliffs.

Attain the ridgeline at 1.8 miles and turn left onto the Bear Cliffs Trail. Note that, due to the harsher weather conditions on this mountain crest, the trees are stunted and much shorter than their relatives at lower elevations. After rising through a jumble of rocks at 1.9 miles, begin a slight descent.

Those of you who have had the pleasure of walking through a field of beargrass in the northern Rocky Mountains may be surprised to see a similar-looking plant scattered throughout the forest here. While it does not grow quite as tall as its western relative, the fly poison's tiny cluster of white flowers at the top of its stem can be almost as large and impressive. As its name implies, all parts of the plant (especially the rootstock) contain toxic alkaloids that have been known to be fatal to grazing livestock. Consumption by humans may lead to vomiting, dizziness, heart problems, and possibly, death. The toxin is so strong that some authorities caution you to refrain from even touching the plant and advise washing your hands immediately if you do so.

Where the descent quickens at 2.2 miles, the flame azalea is so abundant that its Creamsicle-orange color can brighten even the dreariest of damp and foggy days.

Come to an intersection at 2.4 miles where the Spring Trail goes off to the left to the University of Virginia Biological Station. You want to stay to the right, still headed toward Bear Cliffs. Just over 200 feet later, swing to the left—being cautious of the deep crevices just in front of you—and almost immediately afterward make a swing to the right. Although it may be faint here, the correct route is marked by yellow blazes.

You will suddenly break out into the open upon reaching Bear Cliffs at 2.5 miles. From a height of 4,000 feet above sea level, you are now gazing out across Johns Creek Valley and Johns Creek Mountain onto a succession of ridgelines fading off to the south. If your eyesight is good, you may be able to make out the cattle roaming on the patchwork of farmlands below you. To enjoy this vista to its fullest, walk around the top of the cliffs; every few feet there's a different angle or perspective on the landscape. When you are ready to leave, return to the Spring Trail intersection and keep left on Bear Cliffs Trail.

The trail to the right at 3.2 miles is the one you arrived on from the lake; you should again keep left on Bear Cliffs Trail. The song of the wood thrush, which thrives in the deep woodlands of this high elevation, almost sounds as if the notes have been funneled through a long tube. Numerous bits of scat deposited upon the flat rocks in the trail are a reminder that you are not the only one to make use of these pathways.

Turn left onto the Bald Knob Road at 3.7 miles, where a stone bench could provide a few moments' rest. In order to extend your time in the woods as long as possible, be alert 200 feet later, as you want to turn left onto the Homestead Trail. (If desired, however, you could bypass this route and continue rising along Bald Knob Road for 0.2 mile and rejoin the hike description at the 5.6 milepoint.)

Cross under a power line at 4.0 miles; views are of the valley. Once it reenters the woods, the path becomes colorful with mountain laurel, fire pink, fly poison, and yellow star grass. White-tailed deer have also been spotted along this trail on a frequent basis. The descent steepens for a short distance just before you begin to rise and pass by the lower homestead site at 4.5 miles. Be sure to avoid the Johns Creek Trail descending to the left.

Swing right onto an old woods road at 4.9 miles, possibly stepping over one of the box turtles that inhabit the mountainside. Pass by the upper homestead site at 5.1 miles. During the spring, a female grouse may startle you by bursting out of the brush and running down the trail, pretending she has a broken wing. This act is designed to lead a potential predator away from a nest or nearby chicks. If the display fails, she may turn around and come charging toward you, hissing loudly.

Avoid the Homestead Connector Trail coming in from the left at 5.5 miles, swing right for a few feet, cross under some power lines, and continue to ascend along the Homestead Trail as it reenters the woods on a dirt road. Turn left at 5.6 miles and ascend the Bald Knob Road.

Keep to the left to avoid communications towers at 5.7 miles and attain the summit of

Flame azalea

Bald Knob (4,365 feet). With even better views than Bear Cliffs, you can now watch turkey vultures ride rising thermals while you look at the rolling countryside of the New River Valley. Along the southwestern horizon, Pearis Mountain stands above Pearisburg and the obvious gap that the New River has cut through mountains. Farther west are the ridgelines of West Virginia's Allegheny Mountains. Closest to you is Big Butt Mountain, from which flows Little Stony Creek (see Hike 30).

When you are ready to leave this aerie, take the pathway behind the stone bench and descend steeply on rock steps, which can be extremely slippery when wet. Losing elevation quickly, cross the Bald Knob Road at 6.2 miles, walk behind the main part of the hotel, descend wooden steps, and turn right toward the Activity Barn, where you descend to the left to return to your car at 6.4 miles.

If you have not had enough hiking here, there is another network of trails coursing their way through the western portion of the property. The Mountain Lake Trail map sketches out their routes and provides brief descriptions.

32

Wind Rock

Total distance (round trip): 0.6 mile

Hiking time: 20 minutes

Vertical rise: 140 feet

Maps: USGS 7½' Interior

The walk to Wind Rock is so brief it was almost not included in this hiking guide. Yet there are very few places in southern Virginia where you can reap such a marvelous and rewarding payback for expending such a small amount of energy. It is such an easy stroll that even those who are out of shape can handle it if they just take their time. This is also an excellent introduction for someone you are taking out on a hike for the first time. If you find the jaunt too short, you can always combine it with a walk on the trails of Mountain Lake (see Hike 31).

The trailhead may be reached by taking I-81 to Exit 118 and driving US 460 west for approximately 20.0 miles. (Watch for its many twists and turns as you go by Christiansburg and Blacksburg.) Make a right turn onto VA 700 and follow this winding mountain roadway as it gains elevation, coming to Mountain Lake Resort in an additional 6.8 miles. Do not take the road that goes into resort property, but keep slightly to the left on the main road, which is designated as VA 613. Stay left on VA 613 at a Y intersection in an additional 1.5 miles and pass by the trailhead parking for the War Spur Trail {FS 68} 2.7 miles later. Driving 2.2 more miles brings you to the Wind Rock parking area on the left.

The mountain you have been ascending is Salt Pond Mountain, so called because farmers used to bring their cattle to a salt lick near its summit. According to local legend, the cattle trampled the ground so much that they closed an outlet for the water, thereby forming Mountain Lake. (But

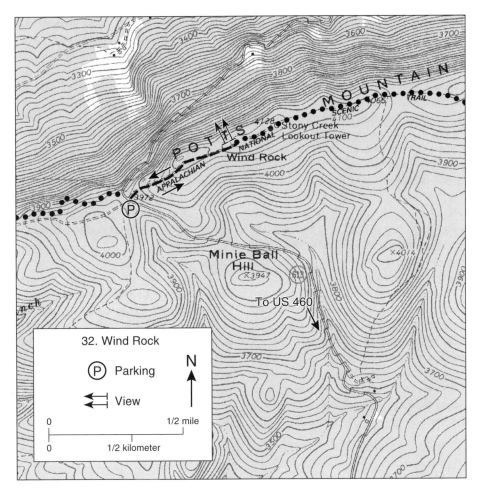

32. Wind Rock

P Parking

N

View

```
0                              1/2 mile
0           1/2 kilometer
```

see Hike 31 for the true story of the lake's creation.) The road you have been driving, VA 613, is also known as Salt Sulphur Turnpike, and was once the main carriage route over the mountains into West Virginia.

Cross the road and ascend the white-blazed Appalachian Trail {FS 1}, lined by striped maple and the unmistakable tall, white flower spikes of the black cohosh. Also known as bugbane, cohosh's unpleasant odor is said to repel insects. Native Americans made an elixir from the plant's boiled roots to treat kidney problems and rheumatism, while early settlers drank the

tea to ease the pain of sore throats and childbirth, or as an antidote for snakebite.

Less than 300 feet into the walk, the AT swings to the right, enters Mountain Lake Wilderness, and ascends steadily, becoming ablaze with the orange-yellow petals of flame azalea at eye level and the deep crimson blossoms of fire pinks upon the forest floor. As you are close to the edge of the woodlands, with the open areas of the parking lot nearby—prime rabbit habitat—keep an eye out for one or two to go hopping by.

The eastern cottontail is the most prevalent of the several species of rabbits and hares that are found in the Southern Appalachians. The female is larger than the male—the reverse of most mammals. It is just as well, for she needs all the strength she can get: Female cottontails may breed as much as 4 times a year, producing litters of 4 to 7 young less than 30 days after mating.

The AT swings to the right when you come to a small clearing at 0.25 mile. However, you want to bear left, rising to the open vista from Wind Rock a little more than 200 feet later. Nearly 2,000 feet below you, Stony Creek has carved out a narrow valley as it courses its way between the mountain you are standing on—Potts Mountain—and the rising hulk of Peters Mountain (see Hike 29) to the west.

Every time I have been here, I have been treated to some kind of special natural-world manifestation. On one trip, the early morning fog had not yet risen from the valley and still covered everything around me in a cottony white, softly shifting blanket. Only the tips of the highest knobs jutted out above the fog, looking like small islands in the sky. On an excursion in the fall, several hundred broad-winged hawks went gliding by me on their way south for the winter. Late one evening, the yipping of a pack of coyotes emanating from the valley floor ascended into the air to echo off the mountainsides. And I have lost count of the number of shimmering sunsets I have been privileged to experience here.

My advice is to linger on Wind Rock as long as possible. Make a full morning or afternoon of it; fill the day pack with munchies and lots of liquids and bring along a good adventure or outdoors book. Maybe stretch out on the sun-warmed rocks and take a nap, or just enjoy the silent passage of the clouds overhead.

Sadly, you will eventually have to leave. That, though, is an easy matter of retracing your steps back to the car at 0.6 mile. Of course, you could just continue walking southward on the AT, arriving at its terminus on Springer Mountain in Georgia a little more than 600 miles later. If you do not have the time or inclination to walk that far, Barneys Wall and The Cascades (see Hike 30) are just a short drive away.

33

Virginia's Triple Crown

Total distance (circuit): 35.9 miles

Hiking time: 20 hours, 50 minutes; 3-day backpack

Vertical rise: 7,760 feet

Maps: USGS 7½' Looney; USGS 7½' Glenvar; USGS 7½' Salem; USGS 7½' Catawba; USGS 7½' Daleville; Appalachian Trail Glenwood–New Castle Ranger Districts map

Most of us know about horse racing's Triple Crown. Well, Virginia has its own triple crown—of viewpoints. Many locals invest the time of several day hikes in order to reach these points, but on just a single, multi-day backpack journey you can visit all three of them, considered by many to be some of the best vistas within the Old Dominion. Dragon's Tooth is a monolithic formation rising vertically above the treetops; McAfee Knob juts horizontally into space; and Tinker Cliffs is a half mile of sheer rock walls running along the crest of a ridge.

A moderately strenuous but not entirely difficult hike, this outing makes use of the Appalachian Trail and several side routes. Water sources are few and far between, so be sure to fill up whenever you encounter one. Although you can make use of trailside shelters, it would still be a wise idea to carry a tent, as the shelters often fill up quickly on the weekends.

The trailhead may be reached by taking I-81 to Exit 141 near Roanoke and driving VA 419 to the north for less than 0.5 mile. Make a right turn at the stoplight and follow VA 311 north for 10.5 miles. The parking lot for the Dragon's Tooth Trail is clearly marked on the left side of the road.

First Day
Total distance: 13.1 miles
Hiking time: 7 hours, 30 minutes
Vertical rise: 2,700 feet
Enter the woods on the blue-blazed Dragon's Tooth Trail {FS 5009}, cross a

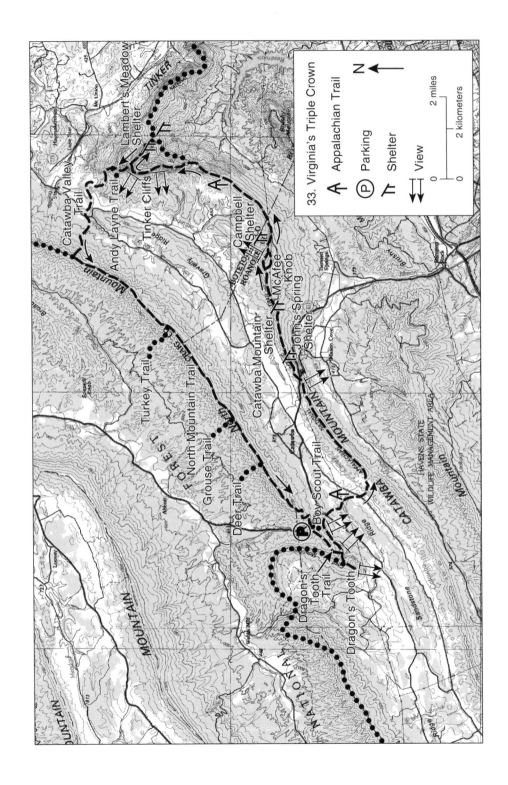

33. Virginia's Triple Crown

Symbol	Description
N ←	(north arrow)
A	Appalachian Trail
Ⓟ	Parking
⊤⊤	Shelter
↓↓	View

Scale: 0 — 2 miles; 0 — 2 kilometers

TINKER

Lambert's Meadow Shelter

Catawba Valley Trail

Andy Layne Trail

Tinker Cliffs

Campbell Shelter

BOTETOURT
ROANOKE

McAfee Knob

John's Spring Shelter

Catawba Mountain Shelter

CATAWBA MOUNTAIN

FOREST

Turkey Trail

Grouse Trail

North Mountain Trail

Deer Trail

Ⓟ Boy Scout Trail

Dragon's Tooth Trail

Dragon's Tooth

NATIONAL

MOUNTAIN

CATAWBA

HAVENS STATE WILDLIFE MANAGEMENT AREA

MOUNTAIN

Sandstone

couple of footbridges, rock-hop a stream, and come to a junction at 0.2 mile. The Boy Scout Trail goes left; you need to turn to the right, beginning your ascent along a water drainage route. This portion of the pathway was slightly relocated in the late 1990s, avoiding some of the wetter and more eroded areas, but adding about 0.2 mile to the overall length of the trail. As you climb, the pine trees become less prevalent and are replaced by hardwoods, such as oak and maple.

A series of switchbacks deliver you to the intersection with the AT {FS 1} in Lost Spectacles Gap at 1.7 miles. Tom Campbell, a member of the Roanoke Appalachian Trail Club (RATC) who was a pioneer in relocating the AT west of the Blue Ridge in the 1950s, gave this place its name after misplacing his glasses here during a hike to scout out a new trail route.

The initial, easy portion of your outing is over once you turn right onto the AT and start the climb across the eastern side of Cove Mountain. Occasional views of the Catawba Valley to the east may distract you from watching where you should place your feet along this rocky route. Volunteers with the Appalachian Trail Conservancy and RATC have devoted many hours to working on this trail, moving huge boulders, constructing rock steps, and defining the correct route. However, the steep and craggy terrain ensures that this will continue to be a rugged hike.

After negotiating the rocks and boulders, you will reach the crest of Cove Mountain (3,020 feet) at 2.7 miles, take your leave of the AT, and turn left onto the blue-blazed pathway leading just a few hundred feet to the Dragon's Tooth. Although you can obtain the same grand view of Catawba Valley, McAfee Knob, Tinker Mountain, and the Peaks of Otter from its lower portions, those of you who are adventurous can climb to the tooth's crown via a crack in the rock. (*Note:* Please use caution if you do so; a number of people have fallen here and sustained serious injuries.)

Retrace your steps back down to Lost Spectacles Gap at 3.7 miles, bypass the blue-blazed Dragon's Tooth Trail, and ascend along the white-blazed AT. Devil's Seat, a rocky outcrop to the right at 3.9 miles, grants an additional view of the Catawba Valley. The deep cleft along Sawtooth Ridge that you see almost directly in front of you is Beckner Gap, which you will be walking next to in just a few more miles.

The rocky ridgeline descends and begins to narrow at 4.0 miles, where Viewpoint Rock looks onto VA 311, snaking its way between Cove and North Mountains. The ridgecrest becomes even narrower where it courses its way through the sandstone rocks of Rawies Rest at 4.3 miles. More than 400 million years old, the boulders are believed to have been formed during momentous volcanic eruptions.

Continue your gradual descent, stopping occasionally to admire the vistas, and you will come to an intersection at 4.9 miles. The blue-blazed Boy Scout Trail heads off to the left; you want to keep right along the AT, descend into a stand of pines, and cross VA 624 at 5.3 miles. (Camping is permitted only at designated sites and shelters from here to the 3.0 milepoint in the Third Day itinerary. Please observe this rule and refrain from using any unauthorized sites you may find along the way. Usage is heavy along this section of the AT and authorities are trying to prevent any additional erosion and destruction of vegetation.)

Immediately begin to rise on a switchbacked route which, in early spring, passes through a veritable garden of wildflowers. Columbine, gaywing, and trout lily grow so abundantly that many of them spring up from the soil in the middle of the trail.

Trout lily originally got its common name from its leaves, which are speckled like the sides of a trout. Later on, people also pointed out that it blooms during the trout-fishing season. The leaves gave rise to another common name, fawn lily, because they stand straight up like the legs of a young deer and are spotted like a fawn's flanks. The protruding stamens of the flower caused some people to call it adder's tongue, and, although not a true violet, the plant's pointed, white corm is responsible for one more common name, dog-tooth violet.

Upon attaining the top of Sandstone Ridge at 5.8 miles, descend into a young forest on the mountain's eastern face. This land was primarily open fields when the AT was relocated onto it in the 1980s, but it is now on its way to becoming a mature forest. Join an old woods road and use a wooden bridge at 6.2 miles to step over a stream. Stop for just a moment and appreciate your surroundings. Because so few people, other than thru-hikers, traverse this section of the AT, this fetchingly serene, narrow valley is a hidden gem—one that you have now been lucky enough to experience.

Break out into an open cattle pasture at 6.5 miles, being mindful of where you step. Watch for the white blazes painted on posts and fence lines to direct you through the field, over a couple of stiles, and onto a crossing of VA 785 at 6.8 miles.

Step over another stile on the opposite side of VA 785, walk through a meadow, cross a footbridge over Catawba Creek at 6.9 miles, and make use of yet another stile a few feet later. After negotiating an additional stile at 7.1 miles, cross a small stream and ascend into an open meadow with Beckner Gap rising to your right. It might be time to take another break just before entering the woods at 7.3 miles. Turn around to let your eyes gaze across everything you have traversed so far—the two meadows, Sandstone Ridge, the eastern flank of Cove Mountain, and, towering above it all, the distinct, uplifted rock of Dragon's Tooth.

Enter the woods, continue to rise toward the ridgeline via switchbacks lined by trout lily, and cross the final stile of today's hike at 7.5 miles. Amidst white pine and Virginia pine, attain the crest of Sawtooth Ridge at 7.8 miles and begin to traverse the undulating terrain, which its name so aptly describes. Although there are many ups and downs for the next several miles, they rarely involve much more than 100 feet of elevation change. As you progress from one knoll to the next, you should thank volunteers of the RATC who spent many hours digging sidehill trail to eliminate a large percentage of the formerly steep ascents and descents.

Be on the lookout for jack-in-the-pulpit all along this route, but especially in the low point you walk into at 9.1 miles. Once you begin the final downhill on Sawtooth Ridge, there will be an excellent view of Mason Cove and Fort Lewis Mountain from an outcropping to the right at 10.8 miles. The traffic zooms by at high speed, so use caution crossing VA 311 at 11.1 miles.

By way of a couple of switchbacks, you will reach the ridgeline of Catawba Mountain at 11.3 miles and continue to ascend along its rocky crest. Upon reaching a trailhead bulletin board at 11.4 miles (and a nice view of Mason Cove and Fort Lewis Mountain on the right), the route becomes sidehill trail, running a few hundred feet below the main ridgeline. Serviceberry, iris, Bowman's root, fire pink, Indian pipe, chickweed, buttercup, and violets are just a few of the scores of plants that make this section of the AT a particular favorite of wildflower enthusiasts.

An outhouse and the John's Spring Shelter are just to the right of the trail at 12.1 miles. The shelter is a replacement for a previous one that used a tree trunk as a support for one of its sides. Although this arrangement made for a sound structure, the tree swayed back and forth in the slightest of breezes, causing the shelter's sheet metal to move and creak along with it. So you can imagine what kind of night a couple from Texas must have endured on their first visit to the AT, when the tail end of a hurricane assaulted the slopes of Catawba Mountain. Although they had hiked only one mile of a planned 30-mile outing, in the morning they walked back to their car at VA 311 and vowed never to return to the AT!

A series of ups and downs brings the trail onto a descending woods road at 13.0 miles, which, in turn, goes by a developed spring just a few hundred feet later. Cross a small stream and come to your home for the evening, the Catawba Mountain Shelter, at 13.1 miles. (A designated campsite is just a few hundred feet beyond the shelter.)

Second Day

Total distance: 8.1 miles
Hiking time: 4 hours, 45 minutes
Vertical rise: 1,800 feet

Awake and rise before the dawn! Although you probably won't make it to McAfee Knob before the sun appears over the Blue Ridge Mountains to the east, you do want to be there early enough to enjoy this spectacular view as it becomes bathed in the day's first few hours of light.

Cross a dirt fire road within 0.3 mile of leaving the shelter, pass under a power line (with views south along Catawba Mountain and Sawtooth Ridge), and begin to climb in earnest. The rocks to the left of the trail at 0.6 mile look out upon Catawba Valley, Gravelly Ridge, and your first good view of North Mountain.

After making a slight dip, the pathway resumes the climb and turns left onto a woods road at 1.3 miles. Local old-timers reminisce about driving their cars all the way to the top of McAfee Knob, one of their favorite "romancing" spots.

The trail splits at 1.4 miles; to get the most enjoyment from McAfee Knob, take the blue-blazed side trail to the left. Within 100 feet you will break out of the woods and come to what many AT thru-hikers believe to be the best view in all of Virginia. To the west are the Catawba Valley, North Mountain, and distant Potts Mountain (see Hike 34). Directly in front is the ridgeline you will be walking on to Tinker Cliffs, and to the northeast you can trace the route of the Appalachian Trail all the way to the Peaks of Otter and Apple Orchard Mountain, nearly 60 miles away. On very clear days you can make out the bulk of House Mountain (see Hike 37), almost due north.

Walk by the Anvil (it juts out into space) along the rock outcropping and come to its end with a view of the city of Roanoke nestled within the Great Valley of Virginia. Rejoin the AT and continue northward by descending into the Devil's Kitchen, a jumble of cracked and broken giant sandstone formations.

Lousewort grows in abundance along the switchbacks you use to descend the north side of the knob. One of the oddest looking flowers found in the woods, lousewort could almost remind you of a plant from a primeval forest. Its strangely shaped flower petals are arranged above a supporting pad of small leaf bracts, and its spreading basal leaves emulate the giant ferns of prehistoric times. Adding to this feel of being more of a primitive entity, several authorities point out that lousewort is somewhat parasitic, as it derives much of its

Tinker Cliffs

sustenance by stealing bits of nourishment from the roots of other plants. Other reference books conclude that the lousewort has entered into a symbiotic relationship with a fungus that grows on its roots and provides it with various nutrients.

The Pig Farm Campsite is to the right of the trail at 2.1 miles. Swine were raised near here until as late as 1982. In fact, much of the land you have traversed on Catawba Mountain was open farmland; it only began to grow back to forest once it was purchased for the AT.

The Campbell Shelter is to the right of the trail at 2.2 miles, and lily of the valley and spiderwort line the path as you continue northward. Turn left onto a woods road at 2.9 miles, only to leave it at 3.6 miles and ascend to the left. Pass between two large rocks, known as Snack Bar Rock, at 3.9 miles, and walk beside an overhanging slab—Rock Haven—at 4.2 miles. The outcropping at 4.5 miles provides an excuse to take a rest break and enjoy the views of Carvin's Cove (a water supply for Roanoke), Tinker Mountain, Peaks of Otter, and Apple Orchard Mountain. Turn your gaze back toward the way you came and look up to McAfee Knob.

Descending into Brickey Gap at 5.1 miles, a blue-blazed trail leads right to Lamberts Meadow; you want to stay on the AT and begin the final climb to Tinker Cliffs. Fringetree, one of the last trees to bear flowers and leaves late in spring, occupies much of the understory along this section of the hike. Its genus name, *Chionanthus,* means snow flower and justly describes its blossoms.

Walk onto the southern end of Tinker Cliffs at 6.4 miles, the last of the Triple Crown views. Stretching for half a mile, the rock cliffs overlook the Catawba Valley, Gravelly Ridge, and North Mountain. Once again, you can gaze upon McAfee Knob to the south. Use caution—especially if it has been raining or snowing—as you proceed along the narrow edge, which has bluets and stonecrop growing out of its small nooks and cracks.

Upon reaching the north end of the cliffs at 6.9 miles, make a quick descent on switchbacks, watching for the yellowish-brown spikes of squawroot. Bypass the Andy Layne Trail going off to the left in Scorched Earth Gap at 7.4 miles and continue to descend to the Lamberts Meadow Shelter at 8.1 miles. Although it is deep forest now, this area was open for the first half of the 20th century, when local farmers used it to winter their cattle.

Third Day

Total distance: 14.7 miles
Hiking time: 8 hours, 30 minutes
Vertical rise: 3,260 feet

After stocking up on a full day's supply of water (there are no more reliable sources), begin the last day of your outing by walking back to Scorched Earth Gap at 0.7 mile. Tom Campbell is also credited with naming this spot. According to the RATC lore, he and fellow hikers were on another scouting trip and had just climbed Tinker Mountain via what is now the Andy Layne Trail. A female participant, known to be quite religious, surprised everyone with her anger at the steepness of the route. She let loose such a volatile succession of expletives that Campbell said she had scorched the earth.

You want to descend westward along the blue-blazed Andy Layne Trail, now not quite as steep as it once was thanks to a relocation that was dedicated in 2001. The pathway is named in memory of one of the hardest working and most jovial volunteer trail workers in the history of the Appalachian Trail Conservancy. The route at first descends along a narrow waterway and then down the crest of a spur ridge to cross Catawba Creek on a footbridge at

2.9 miles. Walk downstream, where black-eyed Susans dot the meadow from mid-summer to late fall.

Use the bridge over Little Catawba Creek at 3.2 miles and pass through more cattle pastures before traversing a young forest to cross VA 779 at 3.8 miles.

Begin an immediate ascent on the yellow-blazed Catawba Valley Trail, the climb much easier than it once was thanks to a relocation completed in the late 1990s. However, the route does become rockier, rougher, and steeper as you get closer to the crest of North Mountain. Once upon the ridgeline at 5.2 miles, turn left to follow the yellow-blazed North Mountain Trail {FS 263}. This route may not be as well maintained as the AT, so be prepared for possible blowdowns and entangling vegetation.

A faint trail at 6.8 miles, which may or may not be marked, descends left more than 0.1 mile to an unreliable spring.

The Turkey Trail {FS 187}—again, possibly not marked—heads off to the right at 8.0 miles and descends 1.5 miles to FDR 224. Continue along the route of the North Mountain Trail, which negotiates the typical minor ups and downs of a ridgeline. Dogwood and redbud add bright spots to the understory in early spring. One of the showiest of trees, the redbud is a member of the pea family. Long before its leaves appear, its branches and twigs become festooned with thick accumulations of dark pink to purple blossoms. In days past, the flowers were often used in salads or fried and mixed with meat dishes.

The Grouse Trail {FS 188} comes in from the right at 10.8 miles, having climbed almost 1.0 mile from FDR 224. The Deer Trail {FS 186}, which makes its departure from the ridgeline at 11.8 miles, is also a 1.0-mile connector to the Forest Service road. Both of these routes are popular with mountain bikers, so be ready for some to zip by you as you walk between these two side trails.

Unless you have been hiking North Mountain when the leaves are off the trees and you can see the winter vistas, you will be happy to come to the outcrop at 13.0 miles for a view of Sinking Creek Mountain, Craig Creek Valley, and Cove Mountain.

Begin the final descent of the hike at 13.3 miles, making use of gently graded switchbacks at some spots. The North Mountain Trail comes to an end where you diagonally cross VA 311 to the right at 14.5 miles. Ascend the entrance road to the Dragon's Tooth Trail parking lot and return to your car at 14.7 miles, one of the few people to have achieved Virginia's Triple Crown in a single outing.

34

Potts Mountain

Total distance (one way): 5.8 miles

Hiking time: 2 hours, 45 minutes

Vertical rise: 490 feet

Maps: USGS 7½' New Castle; USGS 7½' Potts Creek

McAfee Knob (see Hike 33) and Potts Mountain are equally blessed with awe-inspiring, far-reaching vistas. Yet, while the first may host hundreds of visitors in a single weekend, the latter sometimes goes for weeks without one person setting foot upon its pathways. In addition to the experience of solitude, you are not restricted as to where you may set up camp as you are on McAfee, and your chances of seeing wildlife are greatly increased because fewer people are present to disturb local birds and animals. The hike is much easier, too. The trailhead for McAfee Knob is at about 2,000 feet, with a rise to nearly 3,200 feet at the high point. The starting point for the trail along Potts Mountain is already at 3,200 feet and you never attain a height of more than 3,690 feet.

As this is a one-way hike, a car shuttle will be necessary. The lower trailhead may be reached by taking I-81 to Exit 141 near Roanoke and driving VA 419 to the north for less than 0.5 mile. Make a right turn at the stoplight and follow VA 311 north for a little more than 20.0 miles to the small town of New Castle. Make a right turn onto VA 615 and follow that route for an additional 2.5 miles before making a left onto VA 609, which you drive for another 2.0 miles. Bear left onto VA 611 and continue for almost 3.0 more miles, where you need to stay to the right to get onto VA 617. The signed trailhead is on the left in another 5.5 miles.

(Just beyond the trailhead parking lot on VA 617 is a Forest Service campground, the Pines, with pit toilets and drinking water.)

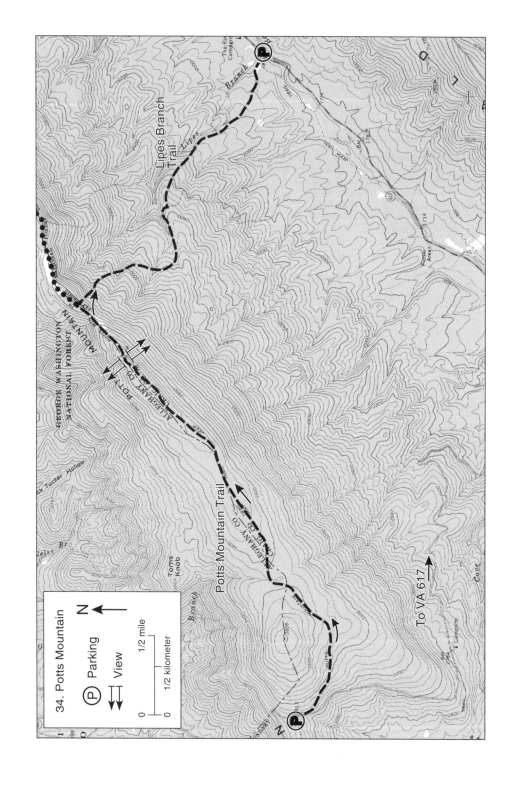

34. Potts Mountain

P Parking

View

0   1/2 mile
0   1/2 kilometer

N

Lipes Branch Trail

Lipes Branch

GEORGE WASHINGTON NATIONAL FOREST

MOUNTAIN

POTTS

ALLEGHANY CO

Potts Mountain Trail

ALLEGHANY CO

Toms Knob

Tucker Hollow

Welch Br

Branch

To VA 617

Leave one car in the trailhead parking lot and turn right onto VA 617. After retracing your route for approximately 4.0 miles, make a right turn and ascend FDR 176. Unless new signs have been erected, the Potts Mountain trailhead may be difficult to locate. Probably the easiest way to find it is to follow FDR 176 all the way to Potts Mountain's ridgeline and the intersection with FDR 177.1; turn around and go back the way you came for about 0.1 mile, looking for a dirt road that goes off to the left—the Potts Mountain East Trail.

As you begin to walk along this route you will notice that it is an official off-road vehicle trail that is also open to mountain bikes. Do not worry, though, for within the first 2.0 miles the roadbed begins to narrow and deteriorate so much that most ORV travelers don't use it. However, you may encounter a mountain biker or two. At 0.2 mile, the trail makes a gradual ascent, with mountain laurel alongside it; at 0.7 mile galax and wintergreen become the dominant groundcover. Growing upon low, 2- to 5-inch stems, wintergreen holds its shiny, deep green leaves throughout the coldest months of the year, giving rise to its common name. Chewing on one of the leaves will freshen your mouth and give your taste buds a treat as you walk on down the trail. Boiling the wintergreen's leaves and small red berries (which develop from the egg-shaped white flowers that bloom in July and August) makes a stimulating herbal tea.

At 1.0 mile you will begin a gradual descent and soon pass through a clearing where, if you do a bit of investigating, you will find a true rarity in Virginia—a naturally occurring pond. Although in many ways it looks like the ponds created by the Forest Service in some of their wildlife clearings, soil samples have shown this pond to be of ancient origin. The pond is located on a small private inholding in the national forest, so if you want to camp while on this hike please go just a bit farther before setting up your tent.

Continuing through mixed hardwoods, where black locust is one of the more numerous trees, you will come into a wonderfully green area of the forest that is festooned with hundreds of waving fern fronds at 1.6 miles. At 2.0 miles, a small, open, and grassy campsite appears on the left, just before your route gradually rises into an old orchard site.

Be watching through the vegetation at 2.5 miles because, by wandering just a few feet off of the trail to the right, you will be rewarded with one of the Olympian views for which you have been walking this trail. To the southeast, on the crest of Catawba Mountain and looking like a wave just about to break, is McAfee Knob. Further south is the bending ridgeline of Fort Lewis Mountain and the multitude of communications towers on Poor Mountain. Northward, and visible through a gap in North Mountain, is Tinker Mountain. More than 25 miles away from where you are now standing are Flat Top and Sharp Top at the Peaks of Otter (see Hike 39) along the Blue Ridge Parkway.

As you continue along your way, be sure to pay attention once again. This time be watching for the roadbed to begin a quick descent at 2.9 miles. When it does, you want to walk backward several yards and leave the trail. Wander through the vegetation to the east for an even better view of the Peaks of Otter than you had just a few minutes before. After you have enjoyed this grand vista for as long as you like, walk back to the trail, cross it, and push your way through vegetation to come to a large rock outcrop—sort of a miniature Tinker Cliffs (see Hike 33). This time the view is to the west, with lush green Potts Creek Valley

The westward-facing viewpoint

stretched out below you and framed by ridge upon ridge of the Allegheny Mountains along the Virginia/West Virginia border. Situated as you are along the Craig/Allegheny County line, there is no better spot in either county to watch the sunset from.

Back on the trail, you will drop into an overgrowing orchard at 3.2 miles that provides additional limited views of McAfee Knob, other points to the east, and a possible campsite or two. Whereas the previous viewpoint was a good place to be for sunset, this old orchard is the place to be for sunrise. If you are here in the fall, you could also enjoy one of the apples that the old trees still produce.

Just as you enter the woods at 3.3 miles, leave the Potts Mountain Trail, enter the 5,700-acre Barbours Creek Wilderness, and descend to the right along the yellow-blazed Lipes Branch Trail {FS 146}. Make a switchback to the left at 3.5 miles, crossing an often dry water run at 4.2 miles.

The forest floor is quite open at 4.9 miles; the blueberry bushes that have accompanied you along much of this hike are conspicuously absent. Begin to parallel Lipes Branch on an old woods road. If you are an astute observer, you have probably seen quite a bit of black bear scat on this journey. Pay close attention now and you might find a paw print or two pressed into some of the muddier spots of the roadbed. A few other signs that may be a little harder to find but will also let you know that bears have been around include logs and stumps turned over or destroyed in the search for grubs and insects, patches of squawroot (a parasitic plant that usually grows on the roots of oak trees) scattered and partially consumed, and branches broken by large animals climbing into the trees to obtain fruits or nuts.

Avoid side trails—one to the left at 5.6 miles and another to the right at 5.7 miles—and continue along the main route. The hike comes to an end when you return to your shuttled car, 5.8 miles after leaving your other automobile more than 1,400 feet higher up on Potts Mountain.

35

Patterson and Price Mountains

Total distance (circuit): 15.7 miles

Hiking time: 9 hours, 40 minutes

Vertical rise: 4,120 feet

Maps: USGS 7½' Oriskany; New Castle Ranger District map

Save this outing for that weekend when things in your life have built up to a point where you need a release from work responsibilities and a reprieve from human interactions; a weekend when you want to be alone with your thoughts or a close friend. Except during hunting season, the Forest Service trails on Patterson and Price Mountains receive very little foot traffic. In addition, I believe that many a year goes by with very few people, if any, setting up camp on either of these parallel ridgelines. So, even if you do happen to see a day hiker or two, you are nearly guaranteed to have the mountain all to yourself in the evening.

The hike could be accomplished as a long day trip, but to best appreciate it, you should make it an overnighter. In the spirit of keeping the area looking as pristine as possible—and of letting you meet this challenge on your own—I am not going to recommend any particular camping spot but will point out some general areas.

While this is a great hike, you should not underestimate the ruggedness of the terrain. In addition, unless they have been maintained recently, the trails barely exist in some places and blazing is spotty at best, absent at worst. Although you need to be sure you feel comfortable with such conditions, they do add to the overall sense of isolation and adventure that you may be looking for.

To get to the trailhead, take I-81 to Exit 150 (a few miles north of Roanoke), drive west on US 220 for about 7.0 miles to Fin-

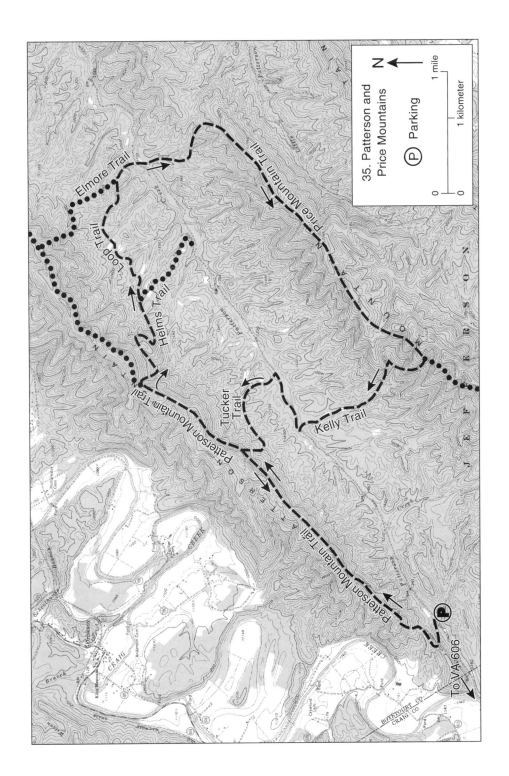

35. Patterson and Price Mountains

Parking

N

0 ____ 1 mile
0 ____ 1 kilometer

Elmore Trail

Loop Trail

Helms Trail

Price Mountain Trail

Tucker Trail

Kelly Trail

Patterson Mountain Trail

Patterson Mountain Trail

To VA 606

castle, and turn left onto VA 630. Make a right turn onto VA 606 only 0.3 mile later and follow it for 8.7 miles before turning right onto FDR 184. Keep to the right when the road forks 0.3 mile later, watching for the yellow blazes of the Patterson Mountain Trail (there may be no sign) on the left side of the road in an additional 1.7 miles. Park your car in the small pullout to the right, making sure to not block the gated road.

Cross FDR 184 and rise into the forest on the yellow-blazed Patterson Mountain Trail {FS 148}. Take the left fork when you come to a Y intersection at 0.1 mile, watching for your route to veer left, away from the gully. From late fall and throughout the winter, the red berries of the dogwood trees, a food source for many woodland creatures, add a bit of bright color to an otherwise brown and gray forest.

Come up against a private property line at 0.25 mile and switchback to the right onto a narrow sidehill trail. Descend into a gap at 0.6 mile and rise onto the ridgeline, beginning the ups and downs involved in following the crest of a typical Southern Appalachian mountain.

In the harsh growing environment of these ridgelines, the oaks become some of the most dominant trees. Thriving in open sunshine, they are among the first trees to become reestablished (from both seeds and stump sprouts) when a woodland has been destroyed by fire or cut for timber. Some species, such as northern red oak, chestnut oak, and white oak, are also quite tolerant of shade. So, even if a sapling happens to have sprouted underneath already standing timber, it will probably survive long enough to take the place of the older trees when they die. Also, the leaves of a sapling are larger and less indented than those of mature oaks, thereby providing the younger tree with more surface area to use to gather nourishment from the sun.

Rise onto a knob at 0.7 mile, whose soil might have disturbed patches in it indicating that turkeys have been scratching in search of tasty morsels. Descend into a gap at 0.8 mile and begin a long, switchbacked rise to a higher knoll. The winter views to the west of cattle dotting the open meadows of pastoral Craig Creek Valley are reminders of what much of Virginia looked like not all that long ago.

You will finally reach the knoll at 1.4 miles, only to immediately descend to a low point at 2.25 miles and rise to the next knob at 2.5 miles. The yellow-blazed Tucker Trail {FS 191} descends to the right from the gap at 2.8 miles (you will be returning via this route). The Patterson Mountain ridgeline alternates from being more than 50 yards wide to less than 30 feet wide; the land within this gap is relatively flat and broad, so you should be able to find a suitable tent site, if you wish.

Resume the ups and downs by rising to a knob at 2.9 miles, descending into another gap at 3.0 miles, and climbing to yet one more knob at 3.2 miles. Be very alert within 300 feet of beginning to descend off this high point! The trail makes a sudden (and possibly poorly marked) switchback to the right. Additionally, only 200 feet later it makes a switchback to the left and descends into a low point at 3.5 miles. The leaves of the low-growing rattlesnake plantain keep the top of the next knob, at 3.75 miles, green even in winter.

Be alert when you walk into the gap festooned by the white blossoms of mountain fetterbush at 3.9 miles. The Patterson Mountain Trail continues to the left, following the crest of the main ridgeline. You, however, want to turn right and descend along

Along the Patterson Mountain Trail

the (possibly faintly) yellow-blazed Helms Trail {FS 181}.

Be alert again at 4.3 miles, when the route makes a sudden switchback to the right, providing stunning winter views of Patterson Creek Valley and Price Mountain, with the high summit of Crawford Mountain rising above everything to the northeast. Cross a spur ridge at 4.6 miles, soon making a switchback to the left (it may not be clearly marked) and recrossing the spur ridge at 4.8 miles.

Be paying attention as the trail makes a swing to the right (it may not be clearly marked) at 5.0 miles to descend along the crest of a spur ridge. Be observant less than 500 feet later: The Helms Trail continues to the right, but you want to make a left onto the yellow-blazed Loop Trail {FS 153}; the blazes may barely be visible, though. Even if you can find no discernible trail, all you have to do is descend through the forest to your left, coming to a well-defined woods road less than 600 feet later. Do not follow the road uphill; keep to the left and descend to cross a small creek just a few hundred feet later. Beech trees, absent on the ridgeline, grow well in this lower elevation.

The wildlife clearing to the right at 5.3 miles would make a nice campsite; in fact, there are several good spots for the next half mile. After passing by a constructed pond, a fainter road will come in from the right at 5.6 miles. Keep left and ascend for 150 feet before dropping back down to cross another creek near a wildlife clearing at 5.7 miles.

The road you have been following comes to an end at a wildlife clearing at 5.8 miles. Pay close attention to the following directions, as the blazes and the route of the trail on the ground may be barely recognizable.

Turn right onto a lesser-used woods road just before you would walk into the wildlife clearing. No more than 50 steps later, you need to turn left into the woods. There may or may not be any blazes or a discernible pathway at this point. (There may or may not be a crude rock cairn here also.)

Walk through the woods for no more than 50 additional steps and, just before you would descend into the draw directly in front of you, swing to the left, hopefully locating the narrow pathway dug into the hillside.

Follow this trail as it tends to your left and drops into a narrow creek valley at 5.9 miles. Turn right and walk downstream. However, you must be very alert less that 200 feet later! The trail makes a sudden left turn (once again, it may be poorly marked) to ascend a side draw. (There may be an old deer-hunting stand at about the point where you should make the left turn.)

Rise to cross a low ridge at 6.0 miles and descend into a new drainage, following the water downstream. Cross the creek three times before intersecting the Elmore Trail {FS 151} at 6.3 miles. Turn right and follow this new route downstream through a narrow defile.

Ford Patterson Creek at 6.6 miles (a few hundred feet downstream may be easier), cross FDR 184 at 6.7 miles, and immediately begin ascending the yellow-blazed Price Mountain Trail {FS 334}.

This route looks like it is going to go into the wildlife clearing to the left, but watch for the blazes to take you to the right. Also, be alert after crossing a rivulet at 6.9 miles; the trail leaves the woods road and ascends to the left on a route marked by tiny yellow diamonds and an occasional yellow blaze. The pathway steepens a bit at 7.2 miles and becomes lined with wintergreen, partridgeberry, and rattlesnake plantain, all of which have evergreen leaves.

Attain the Price Mountain ridgeline at 7.7 miles, but continue to rise. The trail may become a bit faint at times, but just continue uphill. Crest a knob at 8.0 miles, with winter views of Patterson and Potts Mountains to the west and Switzer Mountain to the east. Gradually descend to begin a series of ups and downs reminiscent of those you negotiated on Patterson Mountain. After descending into a gap at 9.6 miles, rise toward a knob at a steeper grade than any other you have encountered so far on Price Mountain. Be very alert when you begin to descend, as the trail makes an indistinct turn to the right at 10.0 miles.

Dropping into a gap off of the main crest at 10.3 miles, the Price Mountain Trail bears left to regain the top of the mountain, but you need to turn right and descend a spur ridge along the (possibly) yellow-blazed Kelly Trail {FS 182}. There are winter views of Patterson Creek Valley as the pathway alternates from steep inclines to gradually descending sidehill trail.

Come into a bottomland at 11.3 miles, cross a small gully to your left, and follow the creek downstream. Cross the creek again at 11.5, rock-hop over Patterson Creek, and turn right onto FDR 184 at 11.6 miles.

Follow this dirt and gravel road for 700 feet, turn left, pass through a Forest Service gate, and follow the yellow-blazed Tucker Trail as it rises along this service road. Be alert at 12.0 miles as the trail leaves the road to ascend along a spur ridge. Also be watching for a couple of switchbacks when the terrain begins to steepen at 12.5 miles.

The crest of the ridgeline at 12.8 miles should look familiar to you. Here you need to turn left and retrace your steps along the Patterson Mountain Trail, returning to your car at 15.7 miles.

36

Lake Robertson

Total distance (circuit): 5.1 miles

Hiking time: 3 hours

Vertical rise: 1,100 feet

Maps: USGS 7½' Collierstown; Lake Robertson map

The list of amenities and things to do in the Lake Robertson State Recreation Area (LRSRA) are so extensive that it is more like a commercially-run, one-stop, never-need-to-leave-the-premises resort than the usual state-operated facility. After pitching the tent or leveling the RV in the campground (complete with water, electricity, dump station, sink waste pumps, hot showers, and individual dressing rooms), the whole family could spend an entire vacation here, each member being able to engage in his or her favorite outdoor activities.

There is the 31-acre lake (named after the late senator A. Willis Robertson) that anglers can cast a line into, either from the shore or a boat. If you don't own a watercraft but still want to get out onto the water, you can rent one. Although you are not permitted to take a dip in the lake, there is a swimming pool to cool off in on hot summer days—you might want to make use of it after playing tennis, volleyball, badminton, or softball. Even the little ones can have fun, frolicking about in the two tot-lot play fields. If you are unable to spend your whole vacation here and just want to get away for a day, there are picnic grounds with fireplaces and tables.

There is an extensive system of trails for hikers. Along the paths you can circle the lake, wander into narrow valleys, walk beside small mountain streams, and explore the higher ridgelines of the recreation area's 581 acres. Lightly traveled, they are the means to escape the liveliness of the main

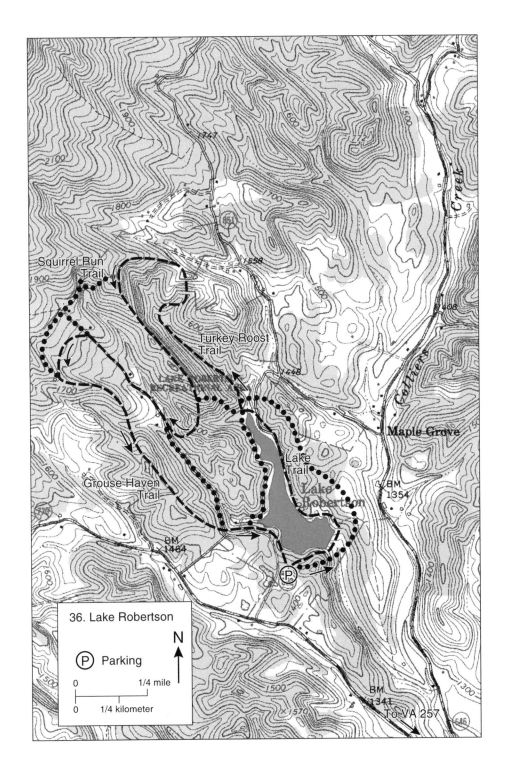

Squirrel Run
Trail

Turkey Roost
Trail

LAKE
RECREA

Grouse Haven
Trail

BM
1484

Lake
Trail

Maple Grove

Lake
Robertson

BM
1354

Creek

Colliers

36. Lake Robertson

N

(P) Parking

0   1/4 mile

0   1/4 kilometer

BM
1341

To VA 257

recreation area and explore its more natural side. Deer, bears, snakes, turtles, opossums, skunks, beavers, raccoons, bobcats, rabbits, chipmunks, and squirrels have all been seen, at one time or another, by trail users.

The LRSRA can be reached from I-81 Exit 188 near Lexington. Drive US 60 west for 1.9 miles, turn south onto US 11, and continue for an additional 0.8 mile to arrive at the US 11/US Business 11/VA 251 intersection. Go straight through the traffic light, drive southward on VA 251 for 4.4 miles, and make a left onto VA 770. Be sure to stay on VA 770 for 1.4 miles, through several twists, turns, and intersections. Make a right turn onto VA 652 and follow it for 0.2 mile as you enter the recreation area and leave your car in the large parking area to the right.

Start the excursion by rising along the signed Lake Trail into a forest of dogwood, eastern white pine, and red maple. Within a few feet, you must be sure to stay to the left on the Lake Trail and not go to the right along the Nature Trail. Although you have just begun walking, you might want to take a few moments' rest on the bench at 0.5 mile to enjoy the sunlight on the lake and survey the mountainous terrain you will soon be traversing.

Walk across the lake's earthen dam, which supports chicory, Queen Anne's lace, red clover, and thistle. Rise above the dam to a Y intersection at 0.25 mile where you want to stay to the left (the Turkey Roost Trail rises to the right) and drop back down to the lake. Eastern red cedar, which thrives in bright sunshine, lines the pathway and the shoreline. The cedar's blue berries are a favorite food for many birds, including the cedar waxwing, which is named for the tree.

At 0.5 mile, you can take any number of short fishermen's pathways to bring you down to the water's edge as you swing around a portion of the lake you have not yet seen.

Veer left into the woods along the Lake Trail at 0.8 mile and walk by the upper end of the lake. Beavers have made a small, separate pond of their own by damming the inlet. Like humans, beavers actually alter the landscape to suit their needs. By flooding a portion of this narrow valley, these industrious rodents have created an environment that suits their needs and permits a number of other animals and plants, such as the cattails you see along the pond's edge, to live in an area that was previously unsuited to them.

Cross the small inlet stream lined by jewelweed at 0.9 mile and bear right to rise along the Turkey Roost Connector Trail. Less than 500 feet later, make a left turn onto the Turkey Roost Trail, heading upstream along a minor waterway. Cross this small creek at 1.0 mile and rise into a narrow defile. It is interesting to note how the lay of the land on one side of the creek has captured the fallen leaves, giving the hillside a brown countenance, while on the other side there are no leaves, just the lush green of fresh grass and other low-growing vegetation.

Cross the creek on a culvert next to a silted-in pond at 1.4 miles and make two quick switchbacks to rise beside the pinkish blossoms of bergamot, a member of the mint family. From mid- to late summer, you could pause for a few moments to pick some blackberries where you turn left onto the Squirrel Run Trail at 1.8 miles.

Leave that pathway when you come to a four-way intersection at 1.9 miles and turn left onto the Deer Lick Trail. (To the right is private property.) Pass by a small shelter, not designed for overnight camping but as a resting point, and descend quickly into a gap at 2.1 miles. Rise for a short distance before

Lake Robertson

resuming the descent through redbud and dogwood trees. In the spring, the dogwood's white leaf bracts are accentuated and set off nicely by the rich purple blossoms covering almost every inch of the redbud's branches.

Stay to the right when the Opossum Trail heads off to the left at 2.4 miles. Be alert after crossing the creek at 2.9 miles; it may be unsigned, but you want to turn right and rise along the Hawk Creek Trail. (The path to the left leads to the main recreation area complex.)

Cross the creek on an old concrete culvert at 3.1 miles and pass through a wildlife clearing at 3.2 miles, where dozens of butterflies gather nourishment from goldenrod, Queen Anne's lace, bergamot, and black-eyed Susans. This small open space allows you to look up onto the higher ridges surrounding Lake Robertson.

Make a left turn onto the Fox Path at 3.5 miles, soon make a switchback to the left, and continue to rise. There is another small shelter close to the next intersection, at 3.8 miles. The Grouse Haven Trail goes both left and right; you want to make a left turn

and descend into a narrow creek defile. Be careful where you step if you are wearing shorts—long stems of stinging nettle arch over the pathway. Brushing up against the plant will give its tiny stiff hairs an opportunity to scratch your skin and deposit an irritant that may itch for the rest of the day. Early in the spring, before the hairs have developed, nettle shoots can be cooked as a tasty substitute for kale or other greens.

Cross a footbridge at 4.1 miles and rise to follow the undulations of the ridge beside a fence line. The thin tree trunks indicate that this is a younger forest than most of what you have been hiking through. An old stone wall runs along the fence line just before you begin to descend at 4.5 miles. Merge onto a woods road less than 500 feet later and continue the downward trend.

Do not cross the gate into the campground nor turn left onto the Hawk Creek Trail at 4.8 miles. Rather, stay more or less straight and continue the descent along a grassy route. Bypass the steps dropping off to the left less than 500 feet later, turn right onto the paved recreation area road at 4.9 miles, and return to your waiting automobile at 5.1 miles.

37

House Mountain

Total distance (round trip): 6.4 miles

Hiking time: 3.5 hours

Vertical rise: 1,800 feet

Maps: USGS 7½' Collierstown

House Mountain is familiar and unmistakable to those who drive along I-64. Approaching it from the east, the mountain stands alone, disassociated from any nearby ridgelines, and rising abruptly from the lowland valleys that surround it. As travelers continue westward, their attention is drawn again to the mountain as it takes on an entirely different look. No longer appearing as one large mass, one can see that it has two distinct summits, each towering hundreds of feet above the U-shaped saddle that separates them.

While doing the research for this guidebook, I became impressed by how many open spaces in Virginia have been preserved through the initiative of concerned individuals. House Mountain is one of those. When more than 900 acres were put on the real estate market in 1988, volunteer members of the Rockbridge Area Conservation Council and the Virginia Outdoor Foundation joined together to explore ways of protecting the land from development. A campaign, begun in the spring of 1989 to obtain funding, proved successful, and the upper portion of House Mountain is now preserved for all to enjoy.

The first part of this journey rises at a gentle rate along a woods road, making it a perfect trip to bring the kids on or to introduce friends to the pleasures of backcountry backpacking without subjecting them to the rigors of a more rugged terrain. A shelter, located in the saddle, makes spending a night on the mountain more comfortable. With superb views, multitudes of wildflowers,

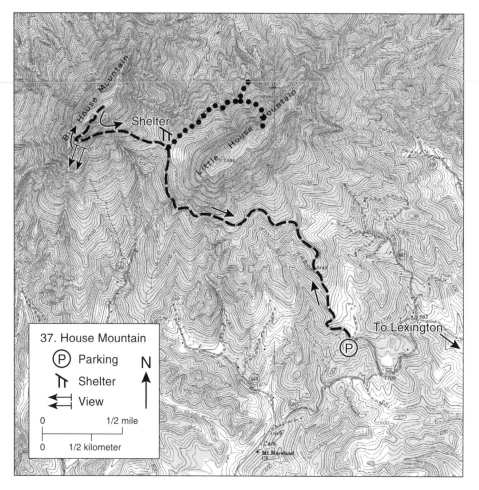

37. House Mountain

Ⓟ Parking
Ⓣ Shelter
View

N

0   1/2 mile

0   1/2 kilometer

and the chance of glimpsing an array of wildlife, House Mountain offers a rewarding outing—even if you never make it to the summit. An article in *Blue Ridge Outdoors* magazine proclaims the mountain to have "without a doubt, one of the best views to be had in Virginia."

To arrive at the trailhead, drive US 60 west from downtown Lexington for approximately 2.0 miles, turn left onto VA 641 (Jacktown Road), continue for another 3.5 miles, and turn right onto VA 643 (Saddle Ridge Road). There is a small pullout on the left side of the road in an additional 0.3 mile

that serves as the trailhead parking area. (You might be able to continue driving for another 0.5 mile, but the road is recommended for high-axle vehicles only.)

Begin the hike by walking the road from the parking area and veering onto the lesser-used road to the right in less than 300 feet. The open farm meadow on the right at 0.2 mile furnishes a slight hint of the views you are going to be treated to once you rise higher onto the mountain. Upon coming to the final parking area at 0.5 mile, take the left fork and continue to gain elevation as you walk by blueberry bushes.

At one time, much more of the mountain was inhabited than it is today; plantings of decorative flowers, including periwinkle, mark an old homesite at 0.8 mile. An imported plant (which causes concern that it is replacing some native species), periwinkle forms extensive carpets, its intertwining roots forming a thick mat underground that holds on to and stabilizes the soil. Its name probably comes from the Latin word vincio, which translates as "to bind," reflecting this trait.

The gated road to the right at 1.0 mile leads onto private property; stay left and continue to rise along the road, which is now lined with mountain laurel. A profusion of raspberries and blackberries appear 1.1 miles after you leave your car and may tempt you to tarry if you happen to be taking this hike in mid- to late summer. Starry campion, jewelweed, and tall bellflower are also a part of the undergrowth. Don't be confused by bellflower's name; its purple-blue blossoms more closely resemble a star than a bell. Descend for a short distance at 1.6 miles before resuming the climb.

Although you have been seeing it sporadically since the beginning of the hike, wild bergamot, with its clusters of light purple, tubular flowers, becomes more prevalent at about 2.0 miles. This is a member of the mint family, so consider picking some of its leaves to make a refreshing cup of tea at camp later this evening. In addition to identifying it by its distinctive blossoms, you can ensure that you have the correct plant by feeling its main stem, which, like that of most mints, is square.

Come to an intersection of roads when you reach the mountain's saddle at 2.2 miles. For the moment, instead of continuing the climb, wander around the meadow, exploring its many hidden charms. Daisies and asters grow tall; snakes and turtles

creep through the lush grasses; and foxes, deer, and even bears have been seen here. Take a rest break, lie back, and enjoy the wisps of clouds drifting across the patch of blue sky visible between the mountain's two peaks. Although it surely must have been a struggle to live here in times past, you can't help but envy the beauty those folks were privileged to experience every day. (If you are feeling particularly energetic, you could take a side round-trip journey of about 1.5 miles by following the pathway to the summit of Little House Mountain at 3,386 feet above sea level.)

Return to the roadway intersection and turn right, making another right onto the shelter's side trail at 2.3 miles. Close to the shelter is a spring. If this is going to be your home for the night, you can leave the bulk of your heavy equipment here and just take a jacket and some drinking water when you return to the main route and continue the climb.

The ascent steepens, but you are compensated for your exertion by breaks in the vegetation that allow you to watch the valley floor drop farther away from you. The climb becomes even steeper as the road makes a switchback to the right at 2.8 miles (do not take the narrow pathway to the left), but the views get even better. More than a thousand feet below you is a mosaic of rectangular farm fields stretching across the floor of the Shenandoah Valley. Like the scenic backdrop of a theatrical production, the main crest of the Blue Ridge Mountains sweep upward to the eastern horizon.

The trail levels out a bit below some cliffs at 3.0 miles, where beardtongue manages to grow in bits of soil within the tiny cracks and fissures. An old communications building announces that you have reached the summit of Big House Mountain (3,645 feet) at 3.2 miles. Although there is no view from

Along the Big House Mountain Trail

this particular point, consider wandering around a bit and perhaps you will discover some vistas from rock outcroppings hidden by the overgrown vegetation.

Eventually, it will be time to leave the mountain, and you can do so by simply retracing your steps and returning to your car at 6.4 miles.

38

The Maury River

Total distance (one way): 6.2 miles

Hiking time: 2 hours, 50 minutes

Vertical rise: 15 feet

Maps: USGS 7½' Lexington, USGS 7½' Glasgow, USGS 7½' Buena Vista

In springtime, when the vegetation along the mountainsides is that new, neon-green color and the seasonal rains have swollen the waterways, a walk along the Maury River may just be one the prettiest outings in all of Virginia. Formed by the meeting of the Cowpasture and Calfpasture Rivers north of Lexington, the Maury initially courses into a narrow gorge of vertical mountain walls as its whitewater tumbles over huge boulders. This Class II-IV section of the river is popular with canoeists and kayakers, while later in the year, when the water level has dropped, entire families float lazily downstream on inner tubes.

Becoming a bit more tame as it flows to the south and east, the river soon meanders along the northern edge of Lexington. Beyond the city, it widens a bit as it delivers its waters past the green meadows of the Shenandoah Valley, eventually coming to an end where it empties into the James River.

Like all navigable waterways, the Maury River corridor has long been a natural conduit for transportation. Small watercraft first used its route, giving way to larger boats upon completion of the James River and Kanawha Canal. Then came the Richmond and Allegheny Railroad (which was purchased by the Chesapeake and Ohio), and now modern roadways. After it suffered devastating infrastructure losses from Hurricane Camille in 1969, the C&O abandoned its line along the river.

Recognizing that a rare opportunity had presented itself, members of various organizations and interested individuals worked

The Blue Ridge Region

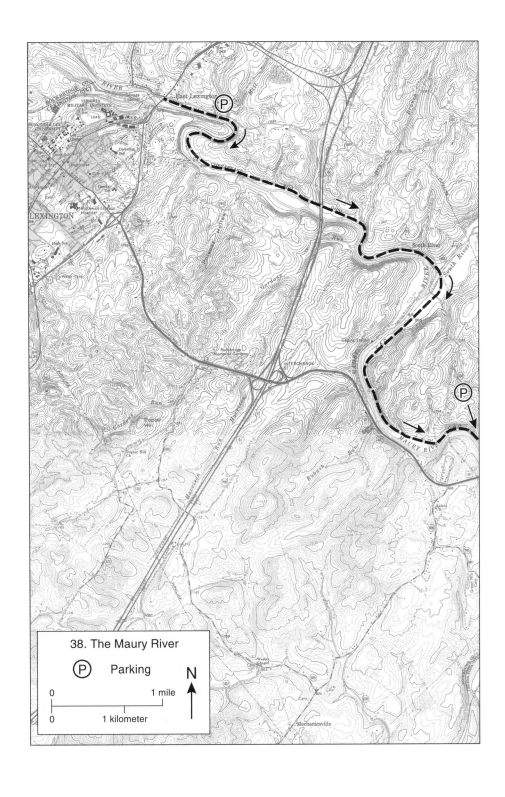

on obtaining the right-of-way and developing the old railbed into a trail. The Nature Conservancy acquired the property in 1978 and turned it over to the Virginia Military Institute Foundation in 1979.

The result of all of this hard work is the Chessie Nature Trail, a premium outdoor recreational resource that runs along a somewhat isolated length of the river from Lexington to Buena Vista. With the old railbed providing a flat surface, this is a hike that just about anyone can enjoy. When there is enough snow on the ground, the cross-country skiing is superb. Alternating woodlands and pastures guarantee a diversity of flora and fauna, and bird life is exceptionally rich at just about any time of the year. The remains of locks and other structures from the days of the canal give the hike an added historical dimension. Pleasantly, as this is one of the very few rail-trails in the entire country that is open to pedestrians only, your reverie will not be interrupted by any bicyclists suddenly zooming past you.

Since this is a one-way hike, a car shuttle will be necessary. The eastern trailhead may be reached by taking I-81 to Exit 188 at Lexington, driving US 60 east for 2.7 miles, and turning left onto VA 608 (Stuartsburg Road). There will be a large parking area on the left almost immediately, but continue for another 0.2 mile and leave one car in the small parking area next to the gated access for the nature trail.

Continue along VA 608 in the other car for 5.0 more miles, where you will cross over the South River and the road you are on magically becomes VA 703. Stay on VA 703 for an additional 1.7 miles, make a left onto VA 631 (Old Buena Vista Road), and go 1.8 more miles to a small parking area on the right side of the road, directly across from the Chessie Nature Trail side. (Offi-cially the trail begins on VMI Island in Lexington, but starting at the point described saves you almost a mile of walking by busy US 11 and next to a series of warehouses and industrial businesses.) Be aware that the trail is only open from dawn to dusk.

Walk a few feet down the access road and turn left onto the nature trail. The access road, known as the Wye for its Y shape, was actually a part of the railroad that provided a place for trains to turn around. As they came in from the east, the trains would back up the western leg of the Wye, pull back down into the eastern leg, and then travel in reverse all the way to the station, and the terminus of the rail line, in Lexington.

Pass though a gate at 0.2 mile, walking beside low cliffs and ailanthus and box elder trees. Also known as the tree of heaven, the ailanthus is an introduced species that was once planted as a landscaping ornamental. Sun tolerant and able to spread quickly, it often crowds out native vegetation. Because its roots are poisonous, it has sometimes caused water wells to be abandoned. Its male flowers produce a strong offensive odor, and some people have allergic reactions to its pollen. The tree's seed pods are winged (as are the box elder's) and are reminiscent of those of the maple tree, which children throw into the air so they will float back down, spinning like helicopter blades. Cedar and sassafras trees become part of the understory at 0.8 mile.

Pass under a utility line at 1.0 mile, where trumpet vine creeps over the rocks and other vegetation.

The site of Reid's lock and dam is at 1.3 miles. It was here that the livestock that had been pulling vessels from Lexington were ferried across the river so they could continue downstream along a towpath. Just beyond this is a side trail to the water's edge, which

Along the Chessie Nature Trail

enables you to obtain a different perspective on the lock and to watch ducks run the small riffles of the stream. This portion of the hike has much of the same look and feel as the C&O Canal Towpath along the Potomac River in Maryland (see *50 Hikes in Maryland*).

The river is split in two by a long island at 1.9 miles. Cross Warm Run on a footbridge at 2.0 miles, pass under I-81, and step through a gate and into an open meadow. Pass through another gate at 2.3 miles and walk under a utility line, where several species of daisy-like flowers are taking advantage of the bright sunshine.

Mimicking the river, the trail bends to the right at 2.6 miles. The 'BF 16' that is emblazoned on the post next to the trail marked the distance along the railroad from this point to Balcony Falls on the James River. The cliffs above you have exposed various types of limestone, whose formations date back more than 450 million years. Look closely and you will see veins of calcite and, to a lesser degree, some of quartz.

After passing though a gate at 2.8 miles, you could almost expect to see a horse and buggy come riding up the roadbed, inasmuch as the trail begins to resemble an old country lane with meadows on both sides of it. Along its south side, the river has cut into the bedrock, exposing the stratum. Also across the river are the remains of the South River Lock, where boats left the river and traveled along a canal, enabling them to skirt the Maury/South River confluence.

The slope of the Blue Ridge Mountains encompassed within the James River Face Wilderness (see Hike 40) is visible for the first time through a break in the trees at 3.1 miles. You will pass through a gate at 3.3 miles where VA 703 is next to the nature trail. There's also a tuft of Asiatic dayflower at 3.4 miles.

Pass through another gate at 3.5 miles,

come to a parking area, and cross the South River. The remains of an old trestle are visible in the woods to the left at 3.7 miles. Proceed to still another gate and into a cow pasture at 3.8 miles. Sadly, restful rural landscapes such as this are becoming increasingly rare, so slow down and enjoy all that it has to offer. Thistle and chicory spring forth from the ground, goldfinches perch on the wire fence, and turkey vultures soar on rising thermals.

The 'W' on the post at 4.1 miles was to remind the train engineer coming from Buena Vista to blow his whistle as he approached the upcoming road crossing (it's now the almost-abandoned dirt road you just stepped over). Pass through yet another gate where a number of sycamores—water-loving trees— grow along the riverbank.

The wires of an old cable car stretch across the stream at 4.5 miles. Some trails in the American West still make use of these to enable hikers to cross unbridged waterways. You will pass the 'BF 14' post 4.6 miles into the hike, where traffic is visible along US 60 on the south side of the river. Look closely at the cliffs on your left at 4.9 miles and you can see the holes that were drilled into the rock and into which explosives were loaded.

The Ben Salem Lock, possibly the best preserved along the Maury River, is on the opposite bank at 5.1 miles, as is the Ben Salem Wayside, where you may see people picnicking, swimming, and fishing. The large rocks, piles of gravel, and stretches of sand in the lower portion of the meadow you walk into after stepping through a gate at 5.2 miles mark it as being a part of the flood plain. Walk by more box elder trees and the 'BF 13' post at 5.6 miles. Zimmerman's Lock, at 6.0 miles, was constructed to provide boats a way around the swift currents in this part of the river.

The journey comes to an end as you pass through the final gate and return to your shuttled automobile at 6.2 miles. Other hikes within a short driving distance of Lexington include House Mountain (see Hike 37) and Lake Robertson (see Hike 36). Also nearby, and described in *50 Hikes in Northern Virginia,* are the Rich Hole Wilderness, Tuscarora Overlook, and Beards Mountain.

39

Fallingwater Cascades

Total distance (circuit): 1.6 miles

Hiking time: 1 hour

Vertical rise: 400 feet

Maps: USGS 7½' Peaks of Otter

The Peaks of Otter area on the Blue Ridge Parkway (BRP) is a place that can truly be enjoyed any time of the year. Spring arrives with hummingbirds, warblers, and woodpeckers seeking sustenance from the awaking natural world. In summer, an early evening stroll may be rewarded with the sighting of a raccoon beginning its nightly foraging or a quickly-moving bobcat dashing into the underbrush. The changing leaf colors of hickory, birch, oak, and maple brighten the hillsides, announcing cooler temperatures in the fall. In winter, the Peaks of Otter Lodge, with its picture-windowed sun room, is a pleasant place to sip a cup of coffee and warm yourself, perhaps after tracking a gray fox along one of the snow-covered trails.

In proximity to the lodge, a large network of pathways could keep you walking and exploring for several days. The strenuous 3.0-mile round-trip Sharp Top Trail has been delivering hikers to a grandstand view of the mountains and piedmont since the early 19th century. A companion route, the 4.5-mile Flat Top Trail climbs to a height of 4,001 feet above sea level. For an evening saunter to work off some of the calories of the lodge's popular Friday night buffets, there is an easy 1.0-mile route encircling Abbott Lake.

On the western side of the parkway, the Johnson Farm Loop and Harkening Hill Trails connect to take visitors through the forest and out to a mountain farm operated as a living history demonstration project. Less than a mile long, the Elk Run Self-Guiding Trail

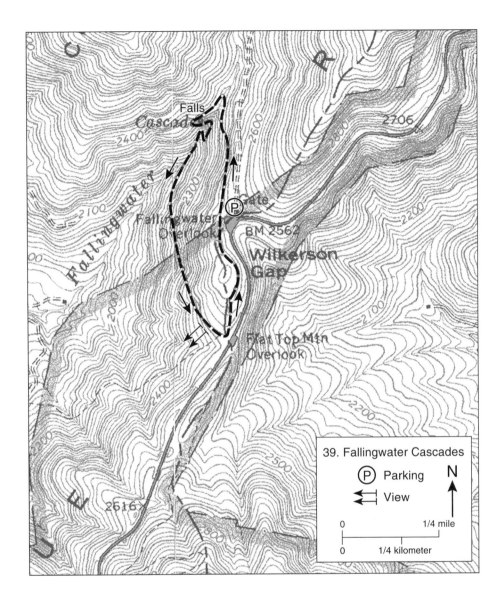

39. Fallingwater Cascades

Ⓟ Parking   N

⟵⟶ View

0   1/4 mile

0   1/4 kilometer

has signs identifying the plants and animals of the forest to help increase your awareness and understanding of your surroundings while on it and other trails.

In addition to the trails and the lodge (open year-round), the area contains a Park Service visitors center, picnic area, gift shop, and a campground with a store.

Although you are encouraged to seek out and hike each of the above-mentioned routes, the Fallingwater Cascades Trail just may be the premier hiking experience of the Peaks area. Snowmelt and spring rains swell the amount of water rushing over the falls, and the resulting sound is echoed within the narrow confines of the gorge.

Tunnels of mountain laurel and rhododendron provide welcome coolness and relief from summer heat, and intense leaf colors are pleasing to the eye in the fall. The stillness and isolation of a hike in winter is accented by snow-covered branches and 30-foot icicles growing on the rocks of the cascades.

The trailhead may be reached by taking I-81 to Exit 167 at Buchanan and driving US 11 south for close to 2.0 miles. Make a hard left on VA 43 and rise on a twisting route for 5.5 miles to the parkway. Drive northward on the BRP, passing the main Peaks of Otter complex in an additional 4.0 miles. The Fallingwater Cascades parking lot is on the left, 2.6 miles beyond the lodge.

If you are here in late summer, take a look into the treetops before beginning the hike and you might be lucky enough to spy a cerulean warbler or two. Like many of North America's songbirds, their numbers are diminishing as a result of rapid destruction of their winter homes in the tropical forests of Central and South America and the Caribbean. Fragmentation of the U.S.'s woodlands just exacerbates their plight. The male cerulean warbler has a powder blue back and head and black streaks on either side of its white chest. Females lack the black streaks and are a duller, blue-gray shade.

Descend from the parking lot, walking into tunnels of rhododendron and mountain laurel. A small viewpoint at 0.1 mile looks into the stream gorge and onto the slopes of the nearby mountains. Negotiate a steep set of rock steps, and the trail soon levels out on a rough and rocky pathway. In the spring and during periods of heavy rain, the sounds of crashing water can be heard.

Cross hemlock-lined Fallingwater Creek at 0.3 mile on a footbridge and come to the head of the falls. The stream races down many pathways on the bedrock, churning itself into a whitewater spectacle as it drops in a series of cascades. Sometimes swirling together into one course, other times spreading out to cover every inch of its channel with a thin veil of sun-dappled liquid, the water takes on a number of countenances on its hurried journey down the mountainside.

Mingling with other tributaries, Fallingwater Creek carries bits of Appalachian Mountain soil into the Shenandoah River, which delivers it to the Potomac River. Coursing its way eastward to the Chesapeake Bay and the Atlantic Ocean, the Potomac may deposit the soil on the shoreline. Just think about it: Someday, when you are vacationing at Virginia Beach, the grain of sand that gets caught between your toes may once have been part of a rock on the hillside you are now standing on.

After dropping steeply down natural stone steps at 0.4 mile and passing by a couple of benches, switchback to the left for the first really good view of the cascading water. Continue descending for an even better view at 0.5 mile—and a large, inviting pool at the base of the falls.

Cross the creek on another footbridge at 0.6 mile, enjoying the feeling of isolation here, for most people turn back once they have reached the bottom of the cascades. Begin the climb back up to the parkway, passing by an overlook into the steep, narrow confines of the gorge the creek has carved out for itself.

A rock slide opens up additional views through the vegetation at 0.9 mile. Bobcats are such elusive creatures that in all of my thousands of miles of hiking in the Appalachian Mountains I have caught glimpses of them on only two occasions. One of those times was near this area. Primarily nocturnal and highly secretive, bobcats usually spend daylight hours in hollow

Fallingwater Cascades

trees, under rocks, or hidden by heavy brush. Other than scat, tracks, or scratch marks, bobcats leave little sign of their existence. The scratch marks are evidence of perfunctory efforts to cover the scat, which is marked off in short segments by constrictions and almost always contains the hair of rabbits or small rodents.

This shy feline receives its name from its short, stubby tail. About 400 years ago, in the northern part of England, the word bob meant a bunch, as in a bob of flowers. Hair that had been gathered in a bunch, which made it appear shorter, was called bobbed hair. Eventually, bob came to mean anything that was cut short, such as a horse's tail—or a wild cat's.

Stay to the left when you come to an intersection at 1.1 miles. The trail to the right leads 200 feet to the parking area for the Flat Top Trail. In conjunction with that route, the Fallingwater Cascades trail was named a National Recreation Trail in 1982.

Upon reaching a knoll at 1.3 miles—the high point of the hike—begin to descend, returning to the parking lot at 1.6 miles.

More than 200 trails emanate from the Blue Ridge Parkway as it courses its way for more than 469 miles from Shenandoah National Park in Virginia to the Great Smoky Mountains in North Carolina, and all are worthy of some of your hiking time. If you want further information, *Walking the Blue Ridge: A Guide to the Trails of the Blue Ridge Parkway,* contains detailed descriptions of every one of the trails. It also includes information on where you may camp on Forest Service lands adjacent to the roadway, lodging, campgrounds, a parkway mileage log, and a roadside bloom calendar.

40

Devil's Marbleyard

Total distance (circuit): 8.2 miles

Hiking time: 4 hours, 45 minutes

Vertical rise: 2,200 feet

Maps: USGS 7½' Snowden; Glenwood Ranger District map

An old story tells of a native tribe that once lived near the James River. High upon the mountainside, they had an immense stone altar surrounded by lush, green grass, and on each full moon they would walk to it to praise the Great Spirit with song. One day an old man and young woman arrived in their village. Although old, the man had a commanding presence, and the woman possessed a beauty beyond compare. Never having seen such people, the tribe was willing to worship them as gods. The visitors, however, told the natives of a higher power and, after a time, the tribe came to worship the new god.

The next year a great drought caused all of the crops to fail, and the tribe blamed the new deity. Hoping to make amends to their old god, the natives burned the old man and young woman on the stone altar, but as their spirits rose into the sky and became bright stars, a horrendous storm appeared. Streaks of lightning crossed the sky and thunder crashed so loud that it shook the mountain, causing trees and giant boulders to come crashing down onto the altar, cracking it into the huge jumble of rocks that we now call Devil's Marbleyard.

Until the blazing of the Glenwood Horse Trail in the 1990s, it was not possible to visit the Marbleyard while doing a circuit hike. Now, however, you can make the climb to the site, enjoy its geological oddity and its vistas, follow a descending ridgeline to catch views into the Shenandoah Valley, and return to the starting point via the area's

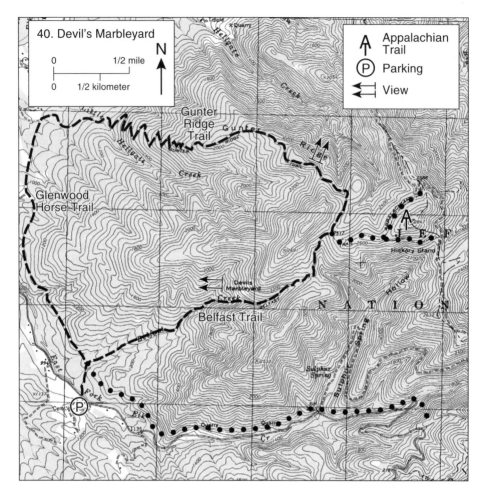

40. Devil's Marbleyard

N

0   1/2 mile

0   1/2 kilometer

Appalachian Trail

P Parking

View

Gunter Ridge Trail

Glenwood Horse Trail

Devils Marbleyard

Belfast Trail

lower slopes. Since all the land is on Forest Service property, you could make it an overnight journey, camping anywhere you wish. If you do not have the time to do the entire circuit, remember that you can always do a rewarding out-and-back just to the Marbleyard.

The trailhead may be reached by taking I-81 to Exit 175, driving north on US 11 for 1.8 miles, and turning right onto VA 130 east. Make a right onto VA 759 in another 3.1 miles and a left turn onto VA 781 in an additional 3.2 miles. Continue for 1.4 more miles to the marked parking area on the left.

Walk the footbridge over the East Fork of Elk Creek, following the Belfast Trail {FS 9} past the bulletin board, an intersection with the Glenwood Horse Trail {FS 3004}, and the remains of Camp Powhatan, an old Boy Scout facility. Cross Belfast Creek and bear right at 0.2 mile onto an old woods road, now the route of both the Glenwood Horse and Belfast Trails. Less than 200 feet later, the horse trail turns off to the left and you stay to the right, beginning to rise at a moderate rate.

Enter the James River Face Wilderness at 0.3 mile and cross Belfast Creek (twice) at 0.9 mile. The climb becomes steadily steeper and rockier as you ascend. Just as you come to the base of the Marbleyard at 1.3 miles, the creek drops over a large rock and, in winter, becomes a frozen waterfall, with 15-foot icicles sparkling in the sun.

The Belfast Trail does not take you right to the Marbleyard, but you could walk onto it at any time by taking a few steps to the left and enjoying the view into Arnold Valley. If you are feeling energetic, wander around the rocks, exploring (and being careful of) their many cracks and crevices. Maybe you will find tiny boreholes created by Skolithus, wormlike creatures that lived millions of years ago.

The old legend notwithstanding, Devil's Marbleyard had its origins about 600 million years ago, when it was on the shoreline of what would become North America's East Coast. As time progressed, geologic forces pressed the sand into sandstone, an extremely hard rock. When continents collided around 200 million years ago, the stone was forced upward, and it cracked into the large boulders you see today. Following the dictates of gravity, the large stone blocks have been slowly rolling downhill. While there are a number of such sights found through the Blue Ridge Mountains, Devil's Marbleyard is unique in that its rocks are still so large and the pile has stayed so high on the mountain.

Continuing along the Belfast Trail, the ascent levels out a bit, going past beech and striped maple trees and the holes drilled by pileated woodpeckers. Cross over a ridgeline at 2.0 miles and follow a sidehill trail as it gradually ascends to a gap with a trail intersection at 2.4 miles. The Belfast Trail continues to the right, but you want to bear left onto the Gunter Ridge Trail {FS 8}.

Cross another ridgeline at 2.7 miles, where the lack of leaves in the wintertime opens up some grand views. At times you can gaze so far north onto the rolling lands of the Shenandoah Valley that it seems like you can make out the curvature of the earth. Other times you can look up to a succession of peaks or out to the west to see the peculiar U shape of House Mountain (see Hike 37) near Lexington. When you swing to the left of a knob at 3.0 miles and begin a long descent, you can make out the cut of the Blue Ridge Parkway on the mountains to the south.

A score of switchbacks makes the downhill journey easy on the knees, and a smattering of mountain fetterbush becomes intermingled with the mountain laurel as you descend. A member of the heath family, the fetterbush's long clusters of tiny white blossoms bloom early in the spring, appearing about a month before the mountain laurel's does. Drying up later in the year, they almost look like small, brown peppercorns hanging from the tips of the branches.

You will have lost a lot of elevation by the time you have hiked 4.5 miles; galax, rattlesnake plantain, and crow's foot are part of the undergrowth. Leave the James River Face Wilderness at 5.4 miles and cross Little Hellgate Creek, the first water you will have encountered in almost 4.0 miles. Bear right onto an old woods road at 5.5 miles, coming to a T intersection with a dirt service road 1,100 feet later.

Turn left onto the road, which is part of the Glenwood Horse Trail, a cooperative effort of the U.S. Forest Service and local equestrian groups. With well over 50 miles of trails wandering beside rhododendron-lined brooks, along rocky ridgelines, and out to open viewpoints, it was developed in the late 1980s and early 1990s.

Continue along the route to the right of a wildlife clearing at 5.8 miles, walking through a forest much younger than the one

The Shenandoah Valley as seen from the Gunter Ridge Trail

you have been in. The road swings to the left at another wildlife clearing at 6.3 miles and soon passes by a private home.

Be alert at 6.7 miles! The Y intersection may be unmarked and confusing; do not take the route rising to the left, but rather the more worn one descending to the right. Stay to the right again when you come to a T intersection at 7.0 miles, and swing to the left at the next intersection just 300 feet later.

Your heart rate may accelerate a bit if one of the resident flocks of turkeys suddenly bursts out of the underbrush in front of you. Once considered creatures of mature forests only, wild turkeys have surprised biologists by adapting to a variety of environments. They roost in secure areas, may use open lands to rear their young, and will wander over miles of terrain in their search for food and cover. Researchers have found that they scrupulously avoid roads with motorized vehicles but will often make use of woods roads—such as the one you are following—as convenient routes through the forest.

At 7.4 miles, begin walking through an old timber sale area whose increased sunlight has nourished a thicker amount of undergrowth. Things should look familiar to you as you turn right onto the Belfast Trail at 7.9 miles and retrace your steps to the hike's starting point at 8.2 miles.

For an additional outdoor diversion before heading home, drive uphill from the parking area; paved VA 781 becomes dirt FDR 35 in just a few hundred feet. Follow this twisting road for several miles to make a right turn onto the Blue Ridge Parkway. Drive south on the parkway for 3.7 miles, pull into the Thunder Ridge Overlook, and take the short pathway through a mountaintop environment of hardwoods and rhododendrons to one of the loftiest views of the Shenandoah Valley found anywhere along the Blue Ridge. If you start at one end of the parking lot and follow the 0.1-mile trail around to the other end, you can brag to friends that you have walked a portion of the famous 2,100-mile Appalachian Trail.

Far Southwest Virginia

41

Pinnacle Natural Area Preserve

Total distance (round trip): 4.6 miles

Hiking time: 2 hours, 45 minutes

Vertical rise: 920 feet

Maps: USGS 7½' Lebanon

Situated west of I-81, far southwest Virginia is a world apart. Although it was the gateway through which Daniel Boone and early settlers passed on their way to the western frontier, it was the last area in Virginia to be settled. Isolated from the rest of the state, things are still a little rough around the edges—and that is its allure. Malls and supersized discount stores are few and far between, large luxury resorts occupying thousands of acres are nonexistent, home-style cooking is what you will find in the restaurants, and mom-and-pop enterprises are the norm. The mountains are more rugged than those east of I-81, rising more in jumbles than in long ridgelines. This is Virginia's coalfield, and while driving on the narrow roadways you may often look into the rearview mirror only to see the grill of an overloaded coal truck barreling down the mountain just inches from your rear bumper.

Much of this may change, as there are plans to open the region to "economic development," with the construction of a four-lane highway coming in from West Virginia and the upgrading of the entire length of US 58. The time to visit far southwest Virginia is now, before it loses its rough edges, and before its roadsides are littered with fast-food restaurants instead of being bordered by modest homesteads. Visit now, before other folks learn of its charms, and while the trails of national forest, national park, and state lands are not well visited. This might be your last chance to explore the region's open spaces in relative peace and quiet, rarely encountering another traveler.

Of all the places worthy of being protected from the encroachments of the modern world, it is hard to imagine one any lovelier than the Pinnacle Natural Area Preserve. In addition to sparkling cascades, towering hemlock and northern white-cedars, vertical cliffs, and vistas of rural countryside and distant mountains, the preserve contains interesting karst topography. The erosive effects of water created a landscape of odd rock formations, sinkholes, and caves. And as if this were not enough, the preserve is within the Clinch River watershed, which has the highest number of globally imperiled and threatened freshwater species in the U.S.

You can drive to the preserve by taking I-81 to Exit 17 at Abingdon, following US Alternate 58 west for 2.1 miles (it makes a couple of turns in town, so watch for signs), and turning right onto US Business 19 North. Come into the town of Lebanon 18.3 miles later and turn left onto VA 82 west. Continue an additional 1.1 miles to a right turn onto VA 640. After driving another 4.2 miles, make a left onto VA 721 and follow the gravel road for 0.8 mile to the parking area on the left.

Walk across Big Cedar Creek on a superbly constructed suspension bridge and follow the pathway to the gravel road and a low-water bridge at 0.15 mile. Bear left onto the roadbed and parallel the creek, enjoying its many small ripples and inviting wading pools. Chicory and Queen Anne's lace grow along the roadside, but make sure you avoid the wasps' nests that may be hanging from the lower branches of the trees.

Each nest is made of paper from bits of wood that the insects strip from old trees, boards, and fence posts. By chewing it and mixing it with their saliva, the wasps reduce the wood to a slurry pulp and use their jaws and front feet to pat down layer upon layer,

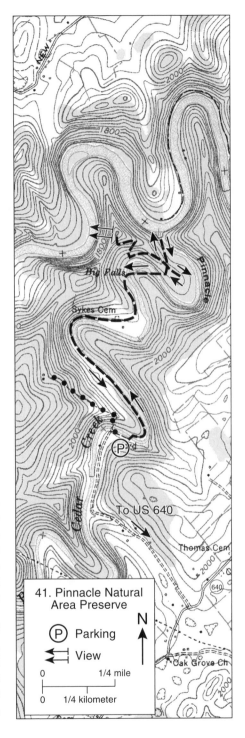

41. Pinnacle Natural Area Preserve

N

(P) Parking

View

0   1/4 mile

0   1/4 kilometer

The rock steps along the trail

shaping the nest as they go. Used as berths for larvae, the cells inside are also made of paper, unlike the wax cells that store honey inside a beehive. Also unlike those in a beehive, these cells hang downward, and females glue the immature wasps into place with more of the sticky pulp. These caretakers also chew prey into a nourishing mash to feed to the young.

The creek and the road both bend to the right at 0.9 mile, coming to the lower parking lot at 1.1 miles. Just as you enter this open area, bear left onto an old road and rise to pass a small cemetery in which many of the graves are identified only by simple rock markers, the oldest bearing an 1891 date. There are rest rooms to the right of the parking lot.

Descend beside redbud and stinging nettle at 1.2 miles, and turn right onto a side trail at 1.3 miles to stand at the base of Big Falls, a favorite local swimming hole. Although the water only drops 10 to 15 feet—very little compared to some mountain waterfalls—the creek is wide at this point and the volume of water crashing over the steps and layers of erosion-resistant sandstone makes for an impressive scene.

Return to the main route and continue downstream, now following a narrow footpath. Ascend a set of rock steps at 1.6 miles and come to a four-way intersection 200 feet later, where you want to continue straight ahead. This pathway delivers you to a mingling of waters—the confluence of Big Cedar Creek and the Clinch River—at 1.8 miles.

With their rich supply of dissolved calcium, a mineral needed for the formation of shells, these streams are home to a number of rare freshwater mussels. The bivalves anchor themselves to the riverbeds, gaining nourishment from the abundant microorganisms in the water. Because they are filter feeders, they are highly susceptible to pollution and are good indicators of water quality.

Retrace your steps to the intersection, turn right, and begin the climb to the Copper Ridge Overlook. Avoid the unauthorized trail to the right at 2.0 miles and ascend via a series of switchbacks, which become steadily steeper. You may need to hold on to the constructed handrails when you come to the overlook at 2.2 miles. Standing upon a narrow rock outcropping, the mountainside drops almost at a 90-degree angle, only coming to an end as it meets the rippling waters of the Clinch River hundreds of feet below. High on the mountain on the other side of the stream are sloping green cattle pastures. Looking at the livestock grazing upon this angled land, you might understand why farmers in this area joke that their cows have two legs shorter than the other two.

Descend back to the four-way intersection, this time continuing straight ahead to the Pinnacle Overlook at 2.8 miles. More than 500 million years ago, this region lay at the bottom of a shallow sea where the remains of calcium-rich corals, algae, and other marine organisms accumulated. Over time, these deposits—along with the sand on the ocean's floor—were compressed into layers of limestone and sandstone. Much of the limestone was chemically changed to a harder rock, dolomite, when it came in contact with magnesium.

The differing erosion rates of limestone, dolomite, and sandstone are responsible for the strange rock formations on the hillside in front of you. The largest is the Pinnacle, a tower of dolomite rising hundreds of feet above Big Cedar Creek. Continue to descend to the stream to obtain a different perspective of this natural phenomenon, which looks like it belongs more in the mountains of Italy than in those of Virginia.

The preserve's complex geological makeup creates conditions that are right for a number of rare species to survive. Look into the cracks and crevices of the limestone walls above you for two globally rare plants, Canby's mountain lover and Carolina saxifrage. Making its home in these plants is the Big Cedar Creek millipede, found nowhere else in the world. Growing along creek banks in the preserve is glade spurge, a plant whose flowers have no petals or sepals.

Return to the four-way intersection, turn left, and retrace your steps. Once again walk by Big Creek Falls, the cemetery, and the lower parking area; cross over the suspension bridge and return to your car at 4.6 miles.

42

Natural Tunnel

Total distance (circuit): 4.3 miles

Hiking time: 2 hours, 35 minutes

Vertical rise: 740 feet

Maps: USGS 7½' Clinchport; park map

Close to 850 feet long, 175 feet wide, and nearly 100 feet high, Natural Tunnel is one of far southwest Virginia's most impressive geological wonders. Although many theories have been proposed as to how it came to be, most geologists agree the tunnel's origins go back about 1 million years. Like in the limestone caverns of the Shenandoah Valley, water containing carbonic acid percolated through cracks and crevices and slowly dissolved the surrounding limestone and dolomitic bedrock. As the cracks widened, a cavern was formed, the water table dropped, and Stock Creek became rerouted into its existing valley. The erosive action of the stream enlarged the cavern into the tunnel you see today.

Established in 1967, Natural Tunnel State Park not only protects this fascinating feature, but also offers visitors the chance to hike its 850 acres, picnic, camp, and take a dip in a modern swimming pool. A chairlift delivers to the mouth of the tunnel those who are unable or unwilling to walk down the short path. The visitors center has a detailed array of exhibits covering the geology, history, plants, and animals of the area, while interpretive programs include nature walks, crafts demonstrations, campfire presentations, wild cave tours, and Clinch River canoe trips. Park personnel aid local schoolchildren in using the park for environmental studies.

With a minimum of backtracking, this hike makes use of almost all of the park's pathways. It takes you down to the tunnel, up to a number of viewpoints of its mouth

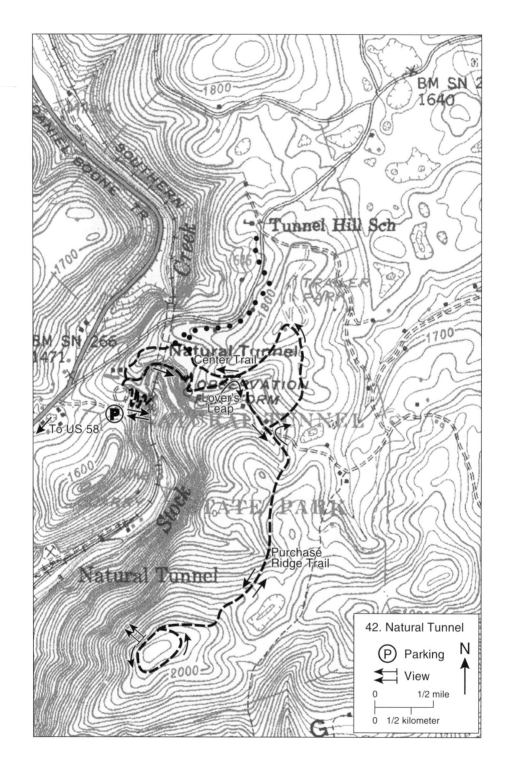

BM SN 2
1640

Tunnel Hill Sch

TRAILER
PARK

BM SN 266
1471

Natural Tunnel

Center Trail

OBSERVATION
Lover's
Leap

P

To US 58

NATURAL TUNNEL

STATE PARK

Stock
Creek

Natural Tunnel

Purchase
Ridge Trail

42. Natural Tunnel

P Parking

N

View

0   1/2 mile

0   1/2 kilometer

G

and gorge, and into woodlands removed from the developed areas. For such a small park, the wildlife is amazingly rich, so be on the lookout for fox and gray squirrels, raccoons, red and gray foxes, muskrats, deer, mockingbirds, eastern bluebirds, wild turkeys, and eastern phoebes. Plant life is just as interesting and contains spotted wintergreen, Deptford pink, eastern red cedar, devil's bit, and a globally rare plant, Canby's mountain lover.

You can drive to the state park by taking I-81 to Exit 1 in Bristol, following US 58 west for 39.0 miles, and turning right onto VA 871. Make another right into the park 1.3 miles later, continuing an additional 0.2 mile to the parking area.

Begin the outing by taking the sidewalk in front of the visitors center and descending quickly via switchbacks and scores of steps along the green-blazed Tunnel Trail. Lined in spring by columbine, jack-in-the-pulpit, and fire pink, the trail receives cooling shade from the large leaves of the tulip poplars later in the summer.

The narrow platform to the left at 0.25 mile provides a limited view of the tunnel; veer right and continue to descend onto the valley floor. Walk by the chairlift house, cross the railroad tracks, and arrive at the platform overlooking the tunnel at 0.35 mile. There could be no better example of the power of water than the one before you. While it is easy to see how water running on the surface of the ground can slowly erode it away, it is almost impossible to comprehend how it could have punched its way, centimeter by centimeter, through solid rock to create such a large hole under the ground.

With the boom of the coal industry in the late 1800s, railroad builders took advantage of the tunnel's easy passage to transport the coal to market. (The tunnel behind you is not natural but was blasted out of the hillside to permit a more direct route than the one permitted by the bends of the creek.) Passenger trains also went through the tunnel and sometimes stopped at its mouth to allow people to enjoy the scenery. In the early 1900s, a stage stood where you are now and was used for dances, weddings, and other social events. Trains full of coal continue to use the tunnel each day.

Return to the visitors center at 0.75 mile and walk past it to ascend the blue-blazed Lover's Leap Trail. Thanks to small signs placed on some of the trees—eastern hemlock, American sycamore, tulip poplar, black locust, post oak, red maple, sourwood, pignut hickory, sugar maple, and white oak—you won't have to carry a guidebook in order to learn each tree's identifying characteristics.

Turn right when you come to the intersection at 0.8 mile and enjoy a view of the Natural Tunnel and its amphitheater wall. Return to the intersection and continue the ascent, staying to the right on the Lover's Leap Trail when the Tunnel Hill Trail comes in from the left. Swinging around the head of the amphitheater, you can look straight through the constructed tunnel. With only a narrow strip of land to work with, the builders of this remarkable trail did a great job in providing you safe passage across the steep terrain.

Rise away from the gorge on a series of switchbacks and come to Lover's Leap at 1.1 miles, obtaining a new perspective on the tunnel gorge. There are a number of Lover's Leaps to be found throughout the Southern Appalachians, and they all seem to share a similar story. The local legend for this one tells about Winninoah, a Cherokee maiden, who fell in love with Cochessa, a Shawnee warrior. Forbidden to marry, they climbed to the top of this pinnacle and, as

Natural Tunnel's amphitheater wall

the rays of a new day spread over them, jumped to their deaths.

The Lover's Leap Trail comes to an end 200 feet later. Stay to the right, now following the yellow-blazed Gorge Ridge Trail, lined by a number of trailing vines, such as poison ivy, Virginia creeper, and greenbrier.

Turn right onto the brown-blazed Purchase Ridge Trail at 1.3 miles and descend into the quietest and most isolated portion of the park. About the only sounds you will hear are birds singing and, in late summer, the buzzing whir of katydids, locusts, and other insects. Arrive at a Y intersection at 1.6 miles and bear right, ascending along the trail lined by crow's foot and marked as leading to the overlook. With some ups and downs, come to the loop trail intersection at 2.2 miles. Turn right and continue to rise, noting that the forest to the left of the trail is younger than that to the right.

Turn right at 2.4 miles and follow the short pathway to the overlook; it provides a view of the upper portion of Natural Tunnel, the open meadows and farmlands on distant hillsides, and the park's prominent conference center, located close to the swimming pool.

Return to the intersection and stay on the loop trail, bypassing a service road that descends to the right at 2.6 miles. Less than 200 feet later, return to the loop trail intersection and retrace your steps. Having come back to the Y intersection at 3.3 miles, swing right toward the campground, walk by a small cemetery at 3.4 miles, and

rise to a wide grassy area where you need to turn left. Come into the group camping area and follow a narrow gravel road to the main campground.

Just as you come to the campground at 3.6 miles, swing to the left of the rest rooms, reenter the woods on the yellow-blazed Gorge Ridge Trail, and descend. The Purchase Ridge Trail comes in from the left at 3.8 miles; stay right. Make another right at 3.9 miles to stay on the Gorge Ridge Trail. A short distance later, stay left when a route heads right to the Picnic Area, making sure to stay to the left again at 4.1 miles to follow the orange-blazed Tunnel Hill Trail.

Be alert less than 200 feet later! Do not continue downhill on the dirt road to the right, but veer left to continue along the Tunnel Hill Trail. Bear right onto the Lover's Leap Trail at 4.2 miles, and return to your car at 4.3 miles.

If you happen to be in this area on a Saturday night, you can participate in a surviving mountain tradition by visiting the Carter Family Fold (276-386-6054). To get there, drive back to US 58, go east for 23.0 miles, turn left onto VA 709, and then follow VA 614 to Maces Spring. Close to the home of the famous Carter Family, the sounds of traditional acoustic music flow out of the auditorium. However, when the music starts, the seats do not get much use. Just about everyone—from old geezers to grade-schoolers—jump up to begin clogging or buck dancing. This is an old-time mountain music experience not to be missed.

43

Breaks

Total distance (circuit): 3.7 miles

Hiking time: 2 hours

Vertical rise: 420 feet

Maps: USGS 7½' Elkhorn City; park map

In many people's opinions, Breaks Interstate Park has the most beautiful and dramatic setting of all of the state-run recreational facilities within the commonwealth. Blessed with an abundance of hemlocks and rhododendron, it is perched along the edge of the Russell Fork Gorge, whose vertical walls drop 1,600 feet into the largest canyon east of the Mississippi River. Not only do the hiking trails lead to exciting vistas, but the restaurant and lodge rooms even have picture windows overlooking the 5-mile-long gorge. Without a doubt, this is far southwest Virginia's premier attraction; if your time in this region is limited, you should bypass everything else and spend your days here. If I had my way, I would spend my whole summer here.

Part of the park's allure is that it is not easy to reach. Far removed from any four-lane highways, it requires an investment of time, gasoline, and miles of driving on winding yet picturesque mountain roads. As with any destination, there are number of ways to drive to the park, but the most scenic is probably to head northward from Wise on US 23 (about 55.0 miles west of Abingdon via US Alternate 58). Approximately 15.0 miles later, take US Business 23 into the small town of Pound and drive eastward on VA 83. So that you can enjoy even more of what this area has to offer, bear left approximately 10.0 miles later onto VA 631 in Clintwood. Cross the Pound River 5.0 miles from Clintwood, make a right onto VA 611, and travel through woodlands, meadows, and farmlands perched high along the eastern flank of Cumberland Mountain, known

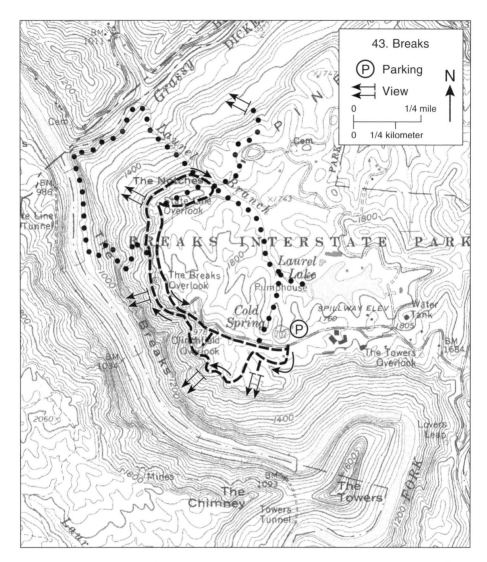

43. Breaks

Ⓟ Parking

◁═ View

N

0   1/4 mile

0   1/4 kilometer

locally as Pine Mountain. (For a diversion, look for the sign that will direct you down a 0.5-mile side road through hemlocks and hardwoods to the Branhams Farm Wildlife Area. At the end of the road is an easy walk of just a few minutes along a grassy route that brings you to pleasing views of the John W. Flannagan Reservoir.)

Continuing on VA 611 to Bartlick, you will come to a spot that is a favorite put-in for rafters and kayakers of the Russell Fork.

During the four weekends in October when the Flannagan Dam is releasing water, the river becomes the most technically challenging commercially rafted stream in the East. Descending at a record gradient of 200 feet per mile, with nearly 5 miles of continuous Class V+ whitewater, running its steep plunging drops has become a right of passage for the country's boldest paddlers.

When VA 611 comes to end, make a left onto VA 80, climbing uphill to Breaks

Interstate Park. Follow the park road past the main complex of lodge rooms and turn left into the Shelter #2 parking lot.

Begin this exploration by walking behind the shelter, following the green-blazed Loop Trail into an understory of rhododendron and mountain laurel, and crossing a footbridge at 0.1 mile. Stay to the left at 0.3 mile (right goes to the Tower Tunnel parking area), and come to another intersection less than 100 feet later. Make a left onto the yellow-blazed Tower Tunnel Trail, and come to your first overlook—at 0.5 mile—into what has been referred to as the Grand Canyon of the South. You can also see how Breaks came by its name—it refers to the break in the mountain created by the erosive action of the Russell Fork of the Big Sandy River.

The tracks of the old Clinchfield Railroad are far below you on the floor of the gorge; they are still used by CSX Transportation. You might even see a coal train chugging its way into the Towers Tunnel, which was cut through the mountain to save having to make the circuitous route around the Towers, the ½-mile-long and ⅓-mile-wide sandstone formation that stands high above everything else.

Return to the intersection, turn left onto the orange-blazed Prospector's Trail, and descend quickly, walking underneath a large overhanging rock at 0.7 mile. Swinging to the right at 0.8 mile, the trail passes through a small cave at the base of the cliffs and crosses a small boulder field at 1.3 miles.

Come to an intersection at 1.5 miles. (Although this hike stays to the right, you could opt to take a detour and rejoin the main hike a little later. If this is appealing, follow the intersecting path to the left and descend steeply on the blue-blazed River Trail, walking beside Russell Fork to its confluence with Grassy Creek. The route then becomes the green-blazed Grassy Creek Trail, which you follow for 0.5 mile before making a right turn onto the red-blazed Laurel Branch Trail and ascending steeply to rejoin the hike description at the 2.0 milepoint. These trails probably receive the least amount of traffic because of their steepness, so they are the ones to walk if you are looking for some solitude. Be aware that going this way will add 1.0 mile to the overall length of the hike, and you will lose and regain nearly 1,000 feet of elevation in a very short distance; it is definitely not suitable for small children or people with little stamina.)

Continuing to the right along the Prospector's Trail, rise to walk directly below the cliff, going under overhanging rocks and around huge boulders that have broken off from the main rock face. All of us have seen how even the tiniest clump of grass can crack the thick slab of a concrete sidewalk. In the same way, as tree and shrub roots grow and expand, they will actually pry apart large rocks, cracking them and causing them to break apart.

It is water, though, that plays the largest role by far in the process of eroding the mountains and sculpting them into the shapes you are presently hiking on. During colder weather, water that has seeped into the small cracks and openings will freeze and expand, splitting the rock apart in the same manner that plant roots do.

Pass between two large boulders, ascend, and make a right turn onto the red-blazed Laurel Branch Trail at 2.0 miles. You can hear an underground stream flowing through a quiet grove of hemlock and rhododendron. Less than 400 feet later, stay left on the Laurel Branch Trail when the white-blazed Geological Trail comes in from the right.

The Clinchfield Overlook

Leave the Laurel Branch Trail at 2.1 miles, bear right, and ascend along the blue-blazed Ridge Trail into a forest of hardwoods and mountain laurel, passing by what park personnel refer to as the mini canyon. Rising out of the hemlocks, come into an oak-hickory forest that also has several species of magnolias as part of the mix.

Continue straight across the parking lot at 2.4 miles to the State Line Overlook, possibly the most popular spot in the park. Far below you, the railroad tracks disappear into the State Line Tunnel near the Russell Fork/Grassy Creek confluence on the Virginia/Kentucky border. In the air, turkey vultures may be circling on rising thermals just a few yards above your head.

Walk back toward the parking lot for just a few feet and turn right onto the green-blazed Overlook Trail, which has occasional views into the gorge and across the Pine Mountain ridgeline. Swing by Pinnacle Rock at 2.8 miles, where skinks and other lizards warm themselves on bright sunny days. A rock outcrop provides a truly Olympian view of the gorge and the tunnel portal at 2.9 miles. Descend to the paved park road at 3.1 miles and rise to an intersection less than 500 feet later. Turn right to enjoy your final views from the Clinchfield Overlook; walk all around to obtain different perspectives.

Return to the parking lot and make a right turn onto the route marked 'FOOT TRAVEL ONLY'. Cross the Tower Tunnel Overlook parking area at 3.5 miles and return to your car at 3.7 miles.

After having seen a small part of the Breaks, you may want to experience more of what the 4,500-acre park has to offer. Just learning about the history of the area could keep you busy for a long time. The Shawnee and Cherokee Indians hunted the woodlands for hundreds of years, and there are stories of Daniel Boone spending time here on his way west. An Englishman, John Swift, is said to have hidden a treasure of silver close to the Towers, while the legendary Hatfield and McCoy feud had its origins near here, and some of the strife might have taken place on what are now park holdings.

Breaks Interstate Park was developed in the 1950s, just after the first two-lane, paved highway provided access to the area. Operated jointly by Virginia and Kentucky, its boundary encompasses land in Pike County, Kentucky, and Dickenson and Buchanan Counties in Virginia. In addition to the scenery, history, and hiking trails, the park offers horseback riding, a mountain-bike route, a swimming pool, fishing, boating on a lake (and paddleboat rentals), picnic areas, a hard-surfaced nature drive, a restaurant, gift shop, campground with camp store and modern facilities, rental cottages, and lodge rooms. (The newer rooms, constructed around the turn of the 21st century, are nice enough, but be sure to ask for one of the original rooms. Since they are built upon the very lip of the gorge, you could lay in bed and enjoy the spectacular scene outside the picture window—without ever having to move a muscle.)

In addition to the usual interpretive programs of guided hikes and evening presentations, there is an impressive calendar of events. Running from early spring to late fall is a succession of bluegrass concerts, gospel sings, and arts-and-crafts festivals.

Now you know why I said I would spend an entire summer here if I could.

44

Red Fox Trail

Total distance (round trip): 2.3 miles

Hiking time: 1 hour

Vertical rise: 450 feet

Maps: USGS 7½' Jenkins West

As hikers, we use the oldest routes of transportation employed by the human race—footpaths. When equines became domesticated, the routes became horse trails. With the invention of the wheel, the paths were widened into cart and carriage lanes. Upon its own railbed, the steam engine increased the speed of transportation of goods and people, while the first automobiles enabled individuals to cross the mountains on twisting, muddy, one-lane routes that several decades later became paved roads. Inside the powerful cars of today, we zip along four-lane superhighways, going from place to place at speeds unimagined by our ancestors.

On the way to, and during, this hike you will make use of or encounter evidence of all of these modes of transportation. Rising onto the upper slopes of Pine Mountain, the trail will also take you by an abundance of wildflowers and into a deep forest of hemlock and rhododendron. With the walking quite easy, and the route barely more than 2.0 miles round trip, it is a nice early morning or early evening stroll.

From the intersection of US 23 and US Business 23 at the south end of Wise (about 57 miles west of Abingdon via Alternate US 58), drive north on four-lane US 23—just completed in the late 1990s. Approximately 14.0 miles later, turn left onto VA 667—the old route of two-lane US 23. The trailhead parking, possibly only identified by a Forest Service gate, is on the left side of the road in an additional 0.6 mile.

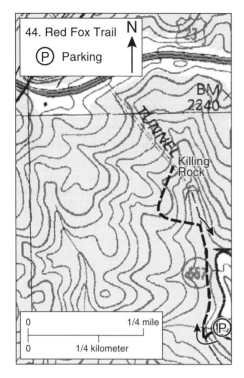

44. Red Fox Trail N

(P) Parking

BM
2240

TUNNEL

Killing
Rock

0   1/4 mile

0   1/4 kilometer

a plant quite different from *Daucus carota.* Yet going in the other direction, another investigator, in the space of three years, obtained from Queen Anne's lace roots that were as fleshy and large as those of the garden carrot.

Be alert in 0.2 mile where you will need to turn right onto the yellow-blazed Red Fox Trail {FS 205}, the original route travelers used to pass through Pound Gap and into Kentucky. Gradually ascend in an attractive forest of hemlock trees and twisting rhododendron bushes.

Go left for a few feet when you come to an intersection at 0.4 mile. This is the site of the station that a lumber cooperative constructed to help service its narrow-gauge railroad. There was also a Y in the tracks here that the trains used to change their direction.

Return to the main trail, turn left, and cross a creek that supplied travelers and their animals with drinking water. Mule teams traversed this road, hauling building materials across Pine Mountain to Kentucky to help construct the town of Jenkins. Rising higher onto a drier portion of the hillside at 0.6 mile, you may notice that the rhododendron and hemlocks cease to grow in such heavy concentrations. There are a couple of places along the road at about 0.7 mile that are so muddy they would have been impassable to carriages and automobiles. An enterprising local kept a team of mules stationed here and charged travelers $5.00 to be hauled across the quagmire.

Pass under a utility line at 1.0 mile, where the road is in a deep ditch with high banks on both sides.

Arrive at the Killing Rock and the end of the trail at 1.15 miles. On the morning of May 14, 1892, gunfire rang out from behind this rock, and five travelers were killed. For some reason, the thieves spared Jane Mullins's life, and 14-year-old John Mullins

Walk through the gate and swing left onto a gravel service road. Jewelweed, joe-pye weed, black-eyed Susans, chicory, Queen Anne's lace, and goldenrod take advantage of the openness and sunlight and make this part of the walk exceptionally colorful.

A controversy about Queen Anne's lace has kept botanists quibbling for years. Many sources, including the well-respected *National Audubon Society Field Guide to North American Wildflowers,* state that the plant was the ancestor of the garden carrot. This theory is further strengthened by the fact that the scientific name of Queen Anne's lace is *Daucus carota,* and the carrot we eat is *Daucus carota sativa,* which seems to imply that it is a subspecies of Queen Anne's lace. There is, however, a study that disputes this. By allowing a garden carrot to go uncultivated for several generations, it was found that it reverted to

The Killing Rock

managed to escape on foot. Jane identified the assailants as Cal and Henan Fleming and a locally familiar character who was a preacher and former revenue agent, "Doc" Taylor, also known as the Red Fox of the Mountains.

Cal was killed in a gunfight with a posse that captured Henan, while Taylor was apprehended getting off a train in Bluefield. Found guilty in a trial, Taylor was sentenced to hang. Insisting on sermonizing at his own funeral, the Red Fox arrived dressed completely in white and preached for two hours before he was put to death. He predicted he would rise from the dead, a prognostication which, so far, has not come true.

By the time Henan was brought to trial, Jane Mullins had passed away. Even though he had confessed to the murders, the court ruled that, since there was no living witness to identify him, he was not guilty and was set free.

The hike comes to an end when you retrace your steps and return to your automobile at 2.3 miles.

You can learn more about the Red Fox and the colorful history of this area by reading John Fox Jr.'s *The Trail of the Lonesome Pine*. Based in part on fact, the book was the first novel in America to sell a million copies and portrays the love story between a young local girl and a mining engineer from the East. Set it the boom days, it clearly depicts the drastic ways in which the advance of the modern world changed the lives of the mountain people.

If you are in this area during the usual tourist months, it is strongly suggested that you drive to Big Stone Gap (just a few miles west of Wise via US 23) for a visual depiction of the story. For many decades, *The Trail of the Lonesome Pine* has been presented as a summer outdoor drama by an ever-changing cast of local volunteers and actors. During the play, you will be introduced to characters such as the not-quite-right preacher Red Fox, family patriarch Devil Judd Tolliver, and mountain neighbors Uncle Billy and Old Hon Beam. Next door to the theater is the June Tolliver House, named for the story's heroine. Her character is based on a young girl who actually lived in the house when she came down from the mountains to attend school.

45

North Fork of Pound Reservoir

Total distance (round trip): 3.2 miles

Hiking time: 1 hour, 40 minutes

Vertical rise: 440 feet

Maps: USGS 7½' Jenkins, west;
USGS 7½' Flat Gap

There are very few places in all of Virginia where you can expend as small an amount of energy to reach a designated backcountry campsite as quiet and isolated as Laurel Branch. The site is located next to one of the northern arms of the North Fork of Pound Reservoir, and the hike to reach it is short and easy. The route crosses a small mountain stream and passes over just one low ridgeline. With the possible exception of a fisherman or two floating slowly by as they obey the no-wake rule in their watercraft, it is quite possible you could camp an entire week here without seeing another person.

Construction of the North Fork of Pound Reservoir and its dam was authorized by Congress in 1960 as part of a comprehensive plan for flood control in the Ohio River Basin, but the U.S. Army Corps of Engineers didn't begin work on the project until 1963. Soon after the completion of the 122-foot-high, 600-foot-long rock fill dam in 1966, the lake reached its present length of 5.4 miles and width (at its widest) of about 0.3 mile; it has a surface area of 154 acres and is enclosed by more than 13 miles of shoreline. The Corps retains the responsibility of managing flood control, water quality, and 90 acres at the dam, tailwater area, and an overlook, but the U.S. Forest Service administers the surrounding lands.

Spread around the lake are boat-launching ramps, a developed campground, and fishing access sites. Among other fish, the lake contains largemouth bass, muskie, bluegill, sunfish, catfish, and crappie. The

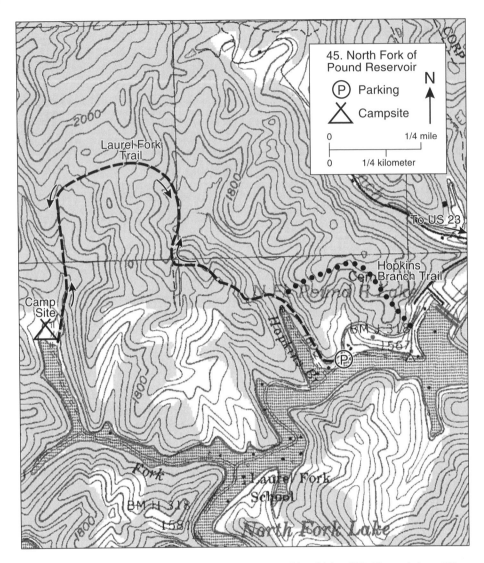

45. North Fork of
Pound Reservoir

Cane Patch Campground, at the head of the lake, is one of the most developed spots, with modern facilities, warm showers, a playground for the kids, and a dump station. Nearby is a sandy swimming beach, picnic shelters, and a 1.0-mile interpretive trail that loops past waterfalls, an old homesite, a railbed, and a spot where a whiskey still was once in operation.

The trailhead for this hike may be reached by driving US 23 north from Wise for approximately 15.0 miles. About 0.5 mile north of the intersection with US Business 23 going into Pound, turn left onto VA 630 and follow it all of the way to the Pound Launch and Picnicking Area, where you may leave your car.

Walk back up the road a few feet, turn left onto the yellow-blazed Laurel Fork Trail {FS 206}, and swing right along the edge of

Hopkin's Branch. The majority of visitors to the lake come for the fishing, boating, and swimming, which you also can enjoy, but by walking the trail you can explore the natural world at your feet, including plants like rattlesnake plantain, partridgeberry, crow's foot, and several kinds of ferns.

Shake the dust out of a fern and each spore, although too small to make out individually, has the potential to reproduce more ferns. Inside a hard outer shell, the spore can wait for years for the perfect growing conditions. As it develops into a heart-shaped structure, it grows roots that reach into the soil. On these are small round pockets that contain what could be compared to pollen in other plants. Longer pouches have the equivalent of the ovules of flowering plants. When water floats some of the pollen over to the ovules and they become fertilized, the fern begins to grow. Yet it may still be several years before the plant is strong enough to send out fronds of its own covered in spores.

Rhododendron becomes part of the forest as you approach the head of the inlet at 0.3 mile and cross a small water run at 0.4 mile. Merge onto an old roadbed for a few feet before crossing another small rivulet. The tracks you see in the soft mud that look like the prints of a dog's paws may actually be those of a coyote.

Coyotes are probably newcomers to the Appalachian Mountains. Although there have been reports of coyote-like animals in the eastern United States since the first colonists arrived, most experts conclude that the sightings were of gray wolves (which were quickly extirpated from the East). Coyotes were first confirmed in New York some time in the 1920s, and they have now spread far into the southern states. The theory is that they migrated from the west, moving northward and then eastward through southern Canada and dropping down into the U.S. once they were past the Great Lakes. Since tagged coyotes have been found to travel up to 400 miles, the theory could certainly be true.

Because eastern coyotes are larger than their western counterparts—averaging 35 to 40 pounds as opposed to 20 to 25 pounds—biologists thought they might be a new species or subspecies. In fact, recent research has shown them to have some wolf genes, possibly from having crossbred on the migration through Canada. However, there seems to be no consensus in the scientific community, so eastern coyotes are still given the same Latin name, *Canis latrins* ("barking dog"), as western coyotes. Its common name comes from the Nahuatl Indians of Mexico, who called it coyotl.

The unmaintained Hopkin's Branch Trail comes in from the right at 0.7 mile. Stay left, cross Hopkin's Branch 200 feet later, and rise through the heavy vegetation of an overgrown field. Unless the trail has been groomed lately, you may find yourself wading through shoulder-high thornbushes and copious amounts of poison ivy. Thankfully, this only lasts for 700 feet before you reenter a forest of dogwood and hickory and continue to rise.

Cross over a low ridgeline at 1.1 miles and descend quickly into a quiet and peaceful grove of hemlock trees. In winter, thickets such as this provide cover and food for wildlife, with deer browsing on the foliage and squirrels and birds breaking open the small cones to obtain nourishment from the seeds.

Come into the open field of the campsite at 1.5 miles and continue to the water's edge at 1.6 miles. Joe-pye weed and horse nettle flourish in the bright sunshine while cardinal flower is more attuned to the moist soil of the shoreline. Ducks float upon the lake's surface, and the water is so clear you

The North Fork of Pound Reservoir

can see small schools of fish darting about. You might even be able to make out the bowl-shaped depressions on the lake bottom that sunfish fashion to lay their eggs in.

As you are likely to be the only person here, you have the freedom to do what you wish; swim, sunbathe, fish—whatever comes naturally. If you are feeling energetic and are an adventurous type who does not mind striking out on routes that are neither marked nor maintained, there are dozens of miles of old logging roads, railbeds, and hunters' trails emanating from the campsite and coursing over the southeastern slopes of Pine Mountain. Or, you could just sit on the shoreline and watch the clouds drift by and become mirrored on the lake's surface.

Every once in a while you may see the contrail of a jet flying thousands of feet above you; you can use these artificially produced clouds to help predict the weather for the next couple of days. Short contrails indicate that conditions will be comfortable because the air is relatively dry and the ice crystals are quickly sublimating back into vapor. However, long streaks of white, which will only form in moist air, mean that precipitation might arrive in a day or two.

Unfortunately, no matter how lovely this spot is, you are eventually going to have to leave. It is, however, just as easy a walk back as it was on the way in. Simply retrace your steps, finishing this round-trip hike when you return to the parking area at 3.2 miles.

46

Chief Benge Scout Trail

Total distance (one way): 16.1 miles

Hiking time: 6 hours, 30 minutes

Vertical rise: 620 feet

Maps: USGS 7½' Coeburn; USGS 7½' Dungannon; USGS 7½' Fort Blackmore; USGS 7½' Wise; USGS 7½' Norton

The Chief Benge Scout Trail (CBST) is one of the best backpacking outings in southern Virginia at any time of year, but to get the most fun out of it, wait for a hot weekend in midsummer. Although it starts high atop Stone Mountain, the majority of the hike is along one creek or another, each with miles of small ripples and a profusion of wading holes. Even if you don't want to take advantage of these mountain streams to cool your feet, you will still need to cross them more than two dozen times, so it may be best to wait until the swell from the spring rains has subsided and summer weather has had a chance to raise the water temperature a few degrees.

If hiked in the direction described, the 16.1-mile journey is a descending route that lends itself to either a long day hike or an excellent overnight trek. You have the option of choosing your own backcountry site or of taking advantage of the modern amenities in the two developed Forest Service campgrounds that the trail passes. Actually, since there is road access at both ends and at the campgrounds, you could make this hike about as short or as long as you wish. In addition, many people combine this hike with the 2.9-mile Little Stony National Recreation Trail (LSNRT) (see Hike 47) in order to enjoy that route's many waterfalls and cascades.

Since this is a one-way hike, a car shuttle will be necessary; the shuttle involves many miles of driving, so allow ample time. From the intersection of US Alternate 58 and VA 72 in Coeburn, drive southward on

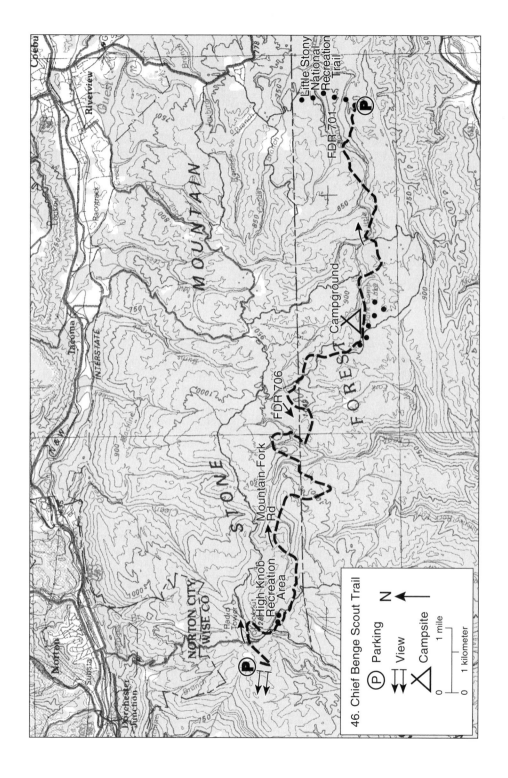

46. Chief Benge Scout Trail

P Parking

N

View

Campsite

0   1 mile

0   1 kilometer

Little Stony National Recreation Trail

FDR 701

Campground

FDR 706

Mountain Fork Rd

High Knob Recreation Area

NORTON CITY
WISE CO

Padgtt Tower

STONE

MOUNTAIN

FOREST

Norton

Dorchester Junction

Subusta

Coeburn

Riverview

Tacoma

Roclord

Exeland

VA 72 for more than 3.0 miles and make a right turn onto VA 664. Turn left onto FDR 700 1.2 miles later and left onto FDR 701 in 1.3 more miles. Leave one car in the large LSNRT parking lot on the left in an additional 0.8 mile.

Return to FDR 700, turn left, and follow it several miles to the intersection with VA 822. Bear right onto VA 822, passing by the entrance to the Bark Camp Campground and coming to another intersection, where you want to turn left onto FDR 238. Staying on this route through many twists, turns, and intersections for approximately 14.0 miles, pass by the High Knob Campground and Recreation Area, turn left onto the road to the High Knob Tower, and leave your car in the parking area. Before you officially begin the hike, you should climb the superbly constructed lookout tower on the top of the 4,162-foot summit for a spectacular 360-degree view across the surrounding mountains and valleys of Virginia, North Carolina, Tennessee, Kentucky, and West Virginia.

Enter the woods at the upper end of the parking lot, beside one of the most profuse displays of jewelweed you are likely to encounter anywhere, and gradually descend along the yellow-blazed Chief Benge Scout Trail {FS 401}, passing under a utility line in 0.6 mile.

Make a right turn onto the paved High Knob Campground road at 1.1 miles and stay on the main route to the picnic area, passing by a water fountain and rest rooms. Come to the road turnaround at 1.4 miles and take the trail to the lake, staying to the left at the picnic tables and to the left again 100 feet later. Bear left onto a service road at 1.5 miles, walking by a cabin and a view of the lake, before turning right across a log bridge to reenter the woods on the CBST.

The industrious work of beavers is evident in many places near the stream. Not only do these busy rodents gnaw trees down in order to build their dams and lodges, but they feed upon the cambium, the live layer of tissue just under the outer bark. Because they do not hibernate, their metabolic requirements are the same in winter as in summer, and in order to meet this need, they cut and store large amounts of limbs and branches on the muddy stream and pond bottoms.

Cross a creek at 1.8 miles and then a log bridge across Mountain Fork just below the dam. After rising to an overlook of the dam, stay to the right to continue on the CBST—which is now much less maintained or used. Cross Mountain Fork at 2.3 miles, 2.4 miles, and 2.5 miles, trying to avoid the copious amounts of stinging nettle along the narrow, rocky, and root-filled pathway. Since you need to keep your eyes on the ground to prevent tripping, it's nice that wood sorrel, false Solomon's seal, and black cohosh are there to add color to the undergrowth.

Somewhat resembling those of the spring beauty, the flowers of the wood sorrel have five white—or sometimes pale pink—petals that are marked with very noticeable dark pink to purple veins and are (usually) notched at the tips. Laura C. Martin, in her book *Wildflower Folklore,* writes that in the days before the Irish population was converted to Christianity, the wood sorrel leaf was used as a symbol by the Druids and had a place in the Celtic sun wheel. The plant does, in fact, have a strong relationship to Ireland in that a legend holds that it was the wood sorrel leaf, and not the shamrock, that St. Patrick used as a way to explain the Doctrine of the Trinity—that three separate entities could exist as one.

The valley widens some at 3.1 miles and your footing becomes a bit easier as you walk by rhododendron and tall hemlock trees. Diagonally cross Mountain Fork Road

High Knob Tower

at 3.9 miles, also stepping over Mountain Fork in the process. Cross the creek again at 4.1 miles; soon afterward a washout area forces you to walk on slippery creek rocks. Cross the creek once more at 4.4 miles on an old railbed lined by rattlesnake plantain and pass by aged, rusting equipment from the days when the railroad came through here at 4.8 miles.

Cross the creek for the final two times at 4.9 miles, rise away from it on the old railroad grade, and swing into another stream's drainage system. Cross side creeks at 5.7 miles, 5.9 miles, and a pipeline right-of-way at 6.0 miles, and you will soon ascend to traverse a level ridgeline.

Dropping off the crest, turn left onto a gravel road at 6.7 miles and then right onto a grassy route just 200 feet later. Be alert at 6.9 miles! The trail leaves the road and makes a sudden left turn into the woods, an area where hikers often see the red or orange of red efts—the terrestrial phase of the red-spotted newt—standing out in bright contrast to the green vegetation and brown leaves on the ground.

Almost anyone who has hiked in the woods after a rainy day is familiar with the red eft, with its red spots and long, thick tail. Existing for two to three years in this-land-dwelling form, the eft eventually matures into the red-spotted newt, whose flattened tail aids it as it swims in mountain streams.

Cross paved VA 706 at 7.6 miles and follow a (possibly faintly) blazed woods road. Be alert in the small overgrowing clearing at 7.8 miles where the trail swings to the left; it does the same thing again less than 500 feet later. Having come to the headwaters of Little Stony Creek at 8.1 miles, cross it and begin to parallel it downstream, crossing it twice more with the next half mile.

Be alert at 8.7 miles! The trail suddenly makes a left turn away from the creek and rises beside a small water run to attain a ridgeline at 8.8 miles and turn left onto a woods road. Merge onto a dirt road at 8.9 miles and follow it 200 feet to make a right turn onto a gravel road.

Barely 300 feet later (just before you would pass through a Forest Service gate), make a sudden left turn into the woods and descend quickly, walking beside squawroot and paralleling a stream. Cross the creek at 9.4 miles and soon head upstream along a different waterway. Within a few yards, begin following a (possibly faintly) blazed woods road.

Be alert at 10.2 miles! The trail leaves the road and enters the woods as a footpath, coming to an intersection at 10.3 miles. Officially, the CBST goes right, but in order to take advantage of the amenities at the Bark Camp Recreation Area, you want to bear left onto the Lakeshore Loop Trail {FS 211}. Although you are walking along the head of the lake, it is pretty much hidden by the lush growth of mountain laurel and rhododendron. The trail to the left at 11.1 miles heads to the upper portion of the campground. Pass by all other side trails and come into the picnic area (rest rooms and water are available) at 11.8 miles. If you are going to spend the night in the campground, walk uphill to its entrance; some of the nicest sites are #5 through #8.

Early morning fog drifts off the surface of the water as you continue along the Lake Shore Loop Trail, swinging right to cross the dam spillway at 12.0 miles and turning left into the woods on the CBST. Make a right onto a gravel road at 12.3 miles, only to turn left back into the woods less than 300 feet later on a path bordered by striped wintergreen.

Cross Little Stony Creek at 12.7 miles and 17 more times within the next 3.3 miles. Some of the fords could be intimidating in the spring, while others have some very inviting wading pools. At times you are following the straight and narrow route of an old railroad bed, often lined by galax, cardinal flower, and pinesap. The pinesap lacks chlorophyll, but unlike Indian pipe—the ghostly white relative it resembles—it can range in color from red to lavender to yellow depending on what time of year it blooms.

Walk onto FDR 701, turn right, and follow it several hundred feet to your parked car at 16.1 miles. If you are not going to have time to complete the entire Little Stony National Recreation Trail, you should at least walk down it for a few minutes to enjoy the first of its many waterfalls.

47

Little Stony Creek

Total distance (one way): 2.9 miles

Hiking time: 1 hour, 15 minutes

Vertical rise: 80 feet

*Maps: USGS 7½' Dungannon;
USGS 7½' Coeburn*

On land acquired by the federal government during the creation of the Jefferson National Forest in 1936, the pathway along Little Stony Creek was designated a National Recreation Trail in 1988—and deservedly so. Winding its way through a gorge 400 feet deep and 1,700 feet wide, the route goes by three major waterfalls and dozens of cascades. Numerous pools invite you to take dip after dip as you walk below towering cliffs and large, angular rock outcrops covered by mosses and lichens. A put-and-take stream, Little Stony Creek is stocked with trout by the Virginia Department of Game and Inland Fisheries. Last logged in the 1920s, the forest within the gorge has had many decades to regenerate into cool hardwood coves and thickets lush with rhododendron, mountain laurel, and lofty hemlocks.

If done in the direction described, the hike is a moderately easy one, following the route of an old narrow-gauge railroad that descends at a pleasant 4 percent to 8 percent grade. For an overnight hike of 19.0 miles, many people combine Little Stony with the Chief Benge Scout Trail {FS 401} (see Hike 46). Camping is permitted along Little Stony, but the terrain is such that you would be hard pressed to find a suitable site. The first, and certainly one of the best, falls is just a couple of minutes into the hike, so if you don't have time to complete the entire journey, you should at least do the short round-trip walk to it—and maybe whet your appetite for the rest of the trail.

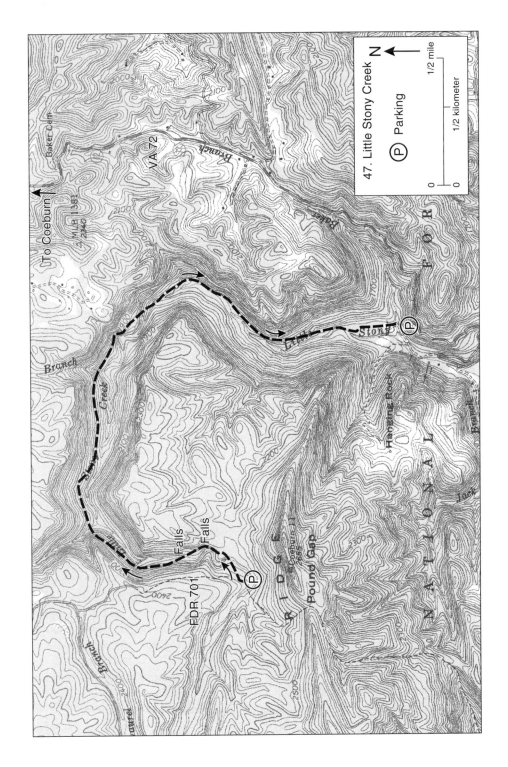

47. Little Stony Creek

Ⓟ Parking

N

0   1/2 kilometer
0   1/2 mile

To Coeburn

△ M.B. 1381
2340

VA 72

Baker Branch

Baker Cem

Branch

Creek

Branch

Stony

FOR

NATIONAL

Favorite Rock

Jack Branch

FDR 701

Falls

Falls

Branch

Laurel

RIDGE

Pound Gap

McCoeburn 11
2865

Since this is a one-way hike, a car shuttle will be necessary. From the intersection of US Alternate 58 and VA 72 in Coeburn, drive southward on VA 72 for nearly 10.0 miles, turn right into the Forest Service's Hanging Rock Picnic Area, and leave one car. Return to VA 72, turn left, and follow it for 5.8 miles. Turn left onto VA 664, making a left turn onto FDR 700 1.2 miles later, and another left onto FDR 701 in 1.3 more miles. The trailhead parking is on the left in an additional 0.8 mile.

Follow the yellow-blazed Little Stony National Recreation Trail {FS 331} into the woods, staying to the left at in intersection in just a couple of hundred feet; the beauty of the hike you are embarking upon is already apparent. Cross the footbridge over the creek at 0.15 mile, pausing to watch the water begin its tumble over the top of the falls.

Less than 200 feet later, take the steps down to the base of the falls, which drops 25 feet down a crescent moon-shaped grotto into a large circular basin. When the summer sun is perched directly over the narrow gorge the stream has worn into the mountain, warming rays of light fall onto the water and surrounding rocks.

On one of my hikes—a combination of the Chief Benge and Little Stony Trails—I was pleasantly surprised to find that the water was milder in temperature than I had expected. I felt so free during this solo journey, during which I had not seen even one other person, I decided to experience the ultimate liberation: I slipped my shorts off and enjoyed feeling the water encircling every inch of my unsuntanned skin.

Yet within a few moments, I began to experience a creeping paranoia. I was only a minute's walk from the parking lot and I began to imagine what would happen if a busload of first-graders suddenly appeared

with their teachers and chaperones. Screams, yells, maybe laughter, and possibly arrest would ensue after their exposure to more of nature than they had anticipated. To further dampen my enthusiasm for skinny-dipping, unseen creatures of the deep began to nibble on my toes and ankles. What was going to happen when they discovered my other body parts that, no longer encased in nylon, were also readily accessible to their teeth and tiny claws?

I spent the rest of the afternoon sunbathing on the rocks, reading a copy of Hilton's *Lost Horizon,* munching on handfuls of gorp, and taking a few more short dips into the water. All with my shorts on— and without another person ever appearing.

After taking your own swim, return to the main trail and continue downstream, crossing a second footbridge at 0.4 mile. Be sure to gaze back and enjoy a small but pleasing cascade. You could enjoy another dip if you wish at 0.6 mile by taking the side trail to the base of a third falls. Dropping down the face of a band of smooth bedrock, this one may be even prettier that the first.

Staying along the Little Stony National Recreation Trail, cross a third footbridge at 0.8 mile over a tributary lined by dozens of conspicuous cardinal flowers. The flat rocks in Little Stony at 0.9 mile are great platforms on which to sunbathe or study the partridgeberry and bluebead lilies clinging to life on the inclined terrain of the gorge.

Favoring cool, moist woods with an acidic soil, bluebead lily is most common in the evergreen forests of the Northeast. However, it does range throughout the Appalachian Mountains and can be found in abundant colonies in the forests of the South—such as those in the Great Smokys along the North Carolina/Tennessee border, or in higher elevations in Virginia. This penchant for chilly environments is reflected in

The first falls of Little Stony Creek

its species name, *borealis*. Its genus name, *Clintonia* (as well as another common name, yellow clintonia), honors DeWitt Clinton, a governor of New York and a noted amateur naturalist in his day.

Rise and descend along the hillside at around 1.2 miles in order to avoid a washout, and return to the creek next to yet one more tempting pool of cool water. Amidst the varied trees of a cove hardwood forest, step over another tributary at 1.5 miles. Covering sheltered slopes and extending into low-elevation coves and valleys, the Southern Appalachians' famous cove hardwood forests are encountered at elevations of approximately 4,000 feet and lower. Here is the most diverse forest of all. Some of the most prevalent trees here are hickory, beech, poplar, sugar maple, yellow birch, buckeye, magnolia, and eastern hemlock. Before the leafy canopy blocks out most of the sunlight in midspring, the floor of this forest will be dotted with the luxuriant growth of trillium, fringed phacelia, bloodroot, hepatica, rue anemone, Solomon's seal, bellwort, and lady's slippers. Existing within ¼ of an acre of a cove hardwood forest will be anywhere from 40 to 60 species of vascular plants, while an equal area of a spruce-fir forest will contain only seven or eight species.

Use footbridges to cross Little Stony Creek at 1.7 miles and 2.5 miles. You are now so deep into the gorge that the sound of the tumbling water bounces off the walls, creating small echoes and giving the impression that the stream is larger than it is. Those of you with a curiosity for geology may be interested to know that the gorge is within the Hunter Valley Fault, where middle Cambrian shales and limestones have been thrust onto younger Chattanooga shales. Both sedimentary rocks, shale is composed of clay and silt grains that have been compacted and undergone minor chemical changes, while limestone is primarily calcite (calcium carbonate). The latter usually forms in shallow waters as a chemical deposit or from an accumulation of shells from a variety of sea creatures.

Winding among huge boulders that have broken off from the cliffs above at 2.8 miles, rise away from the creek at a very gradual rate and return to the Hanging Rock Picnic Area at 2.9 miles. It is time to browse through this guidebook and begin to plan your next outing.

48

Stone Mountain

Total distance (one way): 14.2 miles

Hiking time: 9 hours

Vertical rise: 3,160 feet

Maps: USGS 7½' Appalachia; USGS 7½' Big Stone Gap; USGS 7½' Keokee

Little used, rarely maintained, and barely blazed, the Stone Mountain Trail can be a challenge—to body, mind, and spirit. Full of contrasts and contradictions, it can be physically demanding in its many ups and downs. The vigilance required to stay on the correct route will keep your mind working, and your spirit will soar from the many sights of nature's wonders, but it may also become heavy from witnessing the disrespectful acts some people commit. The rewards of tackling such an adventure are many; you will pass from moist lowlands to dry ridgeline and back, and the variety of environments, plants, and animals is greater on this outing than on many others of comparable length. It is a good workout for the body, you will obtain a real sense of satisfaction from completing a route that many people choose to skip, and you will certainly gain a deeper understanding of the human race's impact upon itself and upon the natural world.

Because of the difficulties you might encounter in negotiating the trail, I recommend that you do not try to accomplish it as a day hike but make it an overnight backpack that could easily be completed in two days. Water is scarce, so carry plenty.

As this is a linear, one-way trip, you will need a car shuttle. From the intersection of US Business 23 and US Alternate 58 in Big Stone Gap, drive north on US Business 23 for 1.4 miles to a small parking area on the left side of the road at the trailhead (which may only be identified by a yellow blaze on a rock or tree). Leave one car here, return to the intersection in Big Stone Gap, drive west on US Alternate 58 for 4.0 miles, and

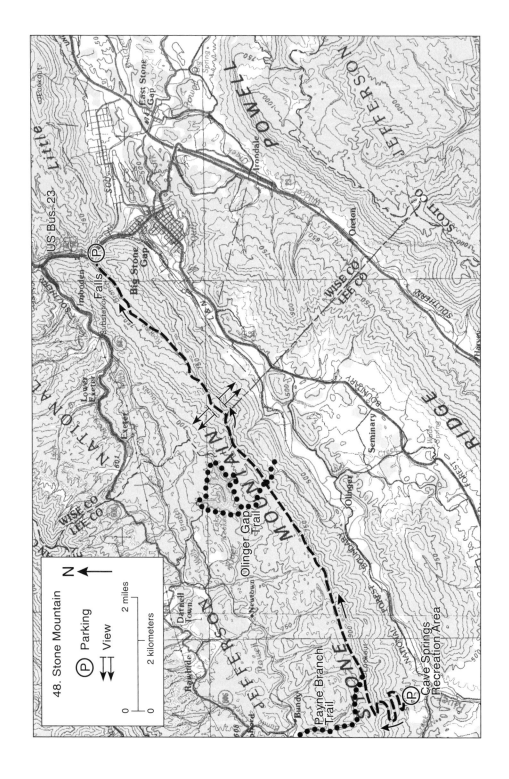

48. Stone Mountain

Parking
View

N

2 miles
2 kilometers

Stone Mountain

Olinger Gap Trail

Payne Branch Trail

Cave Springs Recreation Area

JEFFERSON

NATIONAL

POWELL

JEFFERSON

RIDGE

Big Stone Gap

East Stone Gap

Falls

US Bus. 23

Little

WISE CO
LEE CO

SCOTT

Trandale

Oceon

Olinger

Seminary

Newtown

Darnell Town

Raven de

Bundy

Lower Exeter

Exeter

make a right onto VA 621. Follow that route for an additional 6.7 miles and turn right into the Cave Springs Recreation Area on VA 845. Continue along the campground road to Campsite 21, where the hike begins.

Enter the woods and rise on a stone-lined route. Keep to the right at an intersection 300 feet later and arrive at aptly named Cave Springs. Within a dark, deep grotto, an underground stream breaks to the surface, sending gallons of subterraneanly-cooled water down the mountainside.

A few hundred feet later, bear right and ascend yellow-blazed Stone Mountain Trail {FS 207}. Although the route is nicely graded with long switchbacks, the ascent will take at least an hour, so pace yourself as you climb through the mixed-hardwood forest. Virginia creeper and poison ivy both line—and grow over—the trail in plentiful amounts, but there is an especially large patch of the toxic vine about 1.1 miles into the hike. Be aware that the blazes may become less obvious the longer you hike.

Walk beneath a rock wall and small cave after 2.3 miles of climbing. As you switchback to the right at 2.7 miles next to an impressively large rock wall, you will be walking underneath a rock overhang and weaving around giant chunks of stone that have broken off the wall. Attain a low ridgeline at 2.8 miles; unless the trail has been maintained recently, its route may be hard to identify. Blazes may be very infrequent, bushes and tree branches may have grown over the pathway (expect to be scratched), and there may be no discernible trail on the ground. It may sound difficult, but if you just stay along the gradually ascending ridgeline and look for the faded paint blazes, you will do fine.

Make an abrupt turn to the right upon reaching the main ridgeline at 3.7 miles. Unfortunately, the trail is now heavily used by all-terrain vehicles (ATVs), which have changed its character from a simple footpath to something more resembling a rutted and muddy roadway. Apparently, the Forest Service lacks the staff to enforce the no-motorized-vehicles policy on this isolated section of Stone Mountain, but at least there is a definite course to follow. The route to the left, which the ATVs use to attain the ridgeline, is the Payne Branch Trail {FS 213}; it descends along the west side of the mountain for about 1.5 miles to VA 625.

Stay to the right on the Stone Mountain Trail and ascend somewhat steeply to the top of a knob at 4.0 miles, the site of a former fire tower. Drop into a gap at 4.4 miles, where you will almost immediately begin to ascend again, a pattern that will be repeated quite a number of times as you follow the mountain's crest. Along the way is an exceptional variety of wildflowers: the low-growing rattlesnake plantain with its evergreen leaves; squawroot, which is totally devoid of chlorophyll and therefore of any green color; and the rose twisted-stalk, with its zigzagging stems. A plant sometimes mistaken for Solomon's seal, the rose twisted-stalk is found in abundance in New England, but only in scattered spots in the mountains of the South.

Drop into a gap at 5.6 miles; if you were to go several hundred feet down the left side of the mountain, you might find some water. Rise out of the gap and step up onto a rock ledge that has a narrow cave below. An outcrop at 5.8 miles provides your first good view, looking onto Wallen Ridge and Powell Mountain to the southeast. A break in the vegetation at 6.0 miles provides an even better panorama, which includes Powell Valley and shows just how quickly and dramatically Stone Mountain drops off from the ledge you have been walking upon.

The debris of an old clear-cut and a reemerging forest are on your left from 6.4

Formations along the Stone Mountain Trail

miles to 7.25 miles. As you walk along the border of the national forest, the trail is lined by galax, rhododendron, Solomon's seal, false Solomon's seal, and false foxglove. The woods road you step across at 8.2 miles is the Olinger Gap Trail {FS 327}, descending to the right for approximately 0.6 mile to VA 622, and to the left for less than 1.0 mile to the southern shore of Lake Keokee. Rise gradually out of the gap on the yellow-blazed Stone Mountain Trail.

ATV use comes to an end at 8.4 miles as the vehicles are unable to negotiate the narrow, rocky crest. The hike once again becomes a journey along a footpath that may be very overgrown. Continuing on, with numerous ups and downs, there are places where the sheets of rock on the spine of the ridge are so narrow and high above the surrounding land that it feels as if you are walking on an elevated concrete sidewalk.

Attain the summit of Big Butte at 10.0 miles for the best views of the hike. To the southeast is the Powell River meandering through its emerald valley, with Wallen Ridge and Powell Mountain forming a backdrop. Turn to the northeast and you will gain insight into life in a major coal-producing area.

Not quite the king it once was, coal and its impact are still very much a part of the daily life of this region. The large metal structure rising high into the air is an old, rusting coal tipple, part of the abandoned Bullit Mine Complex owned by the Westmoreland Coal Company. At its zenith, the company employed more than 55,000 miners, but they were all laid off in favor of mountaintop removal and surface mining. You can see the results of this mining practice by gazing a bit farther north, onto the scarred slopes of Black Mountain across the Kentucky border.

As you descend from this vantage point, you may feel thankful that the public land you are walking upon protects the striped wintergreen, bluebead lily, rhododendron, mountain laurel, pinesap, Fraser magnolia, rattlesnake plantain, and running cedar you will see growing in a moist mountain valley at 10.9 miles.

Enter a rhododendron tunnel at 11.5 miles, where you might as well resign yourself to getting your feet wet if it has been raining within the last few days—the headwaters of Roaring Branch doubles as the trail for a few hundred feet. Cross the creek at 12.1 miles and again at 12.4 miles. This may be the prettiest section of the hike, especially when you come into a spectacular grove of old-growth hemlock trees, some known to be more than 300 years old, at 13.0 miles.

Descend the first set of rock steps, constructed by the Youth Conservation Corps in the 1970s, at 13.5 miles. Within a narrow gorge, cross the creek as it rushes down small riffles and falls; there is so much water here that it seeps from the rock walls at 13.8 miles. Be sure to stop for a few moments to enjoy the stream's best waterfall just before you return to US 23 and your car at 14.2 miles.

Sadly, as you walked the last few hundred feet of the hike, you may have noticed some of the cast-off debris of uncaring or unthinking people. Paper plates and napkins might be blown about by the breeze, while beer cans or soda bottles lay beside the trail or next to the parking area. Instead of littering the woods, all of these items could be recycled to save precious resources. Recycling just one aluminum can saves enough energy to manufacture 19 more, one recycled glass bottle saves enough energy to light a 100-watt bulb for four hours, and every ton of paper recycled keeps 60 pounds of pollutants out of the air and saves enough energy to heat the average home for six months.

49

Cumberland Gap
National Historical Park

Total distance (circuit): 10.8 miles

Hiking time: 6 hours, 40 minutes

Vertical rise: 2,640 feet

Maps: USGS 7½' Middlesboro South; USGS 7½' Wheeler; USGS 7½' Varilla; USGS 7½' Middlesboro North, KY; park map

Just like water, transportation routes tend to follow the path of least resistance. Understanding this, when you look at a topographic map of Virginia, it will be obvious why Cumberland Gap became the most utilized and famous passageway across the Appalachian Mountains. As early settlers migrated to the southwest, through the Shenandoah Valley, and into the narrowing Great Valley of Virginia, there was no easy place to turn to pursue a westward course. In 1750, a surveying party headed by Thomas Walker came upon the gap and returned home to tell everyone of the natural portal they had found.

Of course, Walker and his companions were not the first to discover the Cumberland Gap. For centuries, buffalo, deer, and elk had migrated through the gap in their yearly searches for food. Native Americans used the gap to hunt for these animals, incorporating the gap into the Warrior's Path, which stretched from the Ohio River to the Potomac River near the Atlantic coast. In 1775, the most celebrated person associated with the gap, Daniel Boone, along with a group of 30 men, blazed the 208-mile Wilderness Trail from (present-day) Kingsport, Tennessee, across the gap, and into the lands beyond. By 1800, the route had become a bustling two-way road, with more than 300,000 people crossing it in the hopes of establishing new lives. Hundreds of thousands of cattle, sheep, hogs, and turkeys, among other livestock, were sent through the gap to the markets of the eastern seaboard.

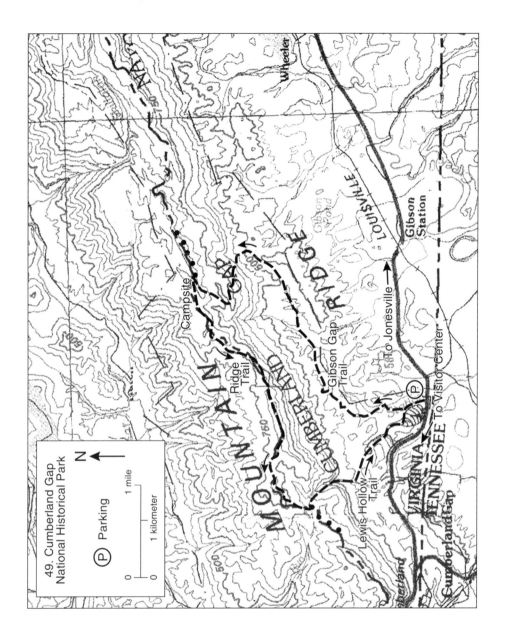

Cumberland Gap National Historical Park was authorized by Congress in 1940 to commemorate and preserve this pioneer passage to the western frontier. It opened to the public in 1955 and occupies land in Virginia, Kentucky, and Tennessee. Within its 20,000 acres are approximately 50 miles of trails, designated backcountry campsites, picnic areas, and a campground (open year-round) with hot showers and flush toilets. The visitors center, just across the Kentucky border, contains displays on the history of the area and sponsors a vast array of interpretive programs on the front lawn, at the campground, and in various places throughout the park.

This outing, a circuit hike from the lowlands to the mountain crest, takes you across the southeastern slope of Cumberland Mountain, across its ridgeline, through a dense oak-hickory forest rife with wildflowers, and past a small cave thought to have been used by Native Americans. The hike begins next to the Wilderness Road Campground, which is a nice base of operations, but there is also a designated backcountry campsite at about the halfway point, so you could make this an easy overnight journey if you wish. (If you intend to spend the night at the designated backcountry site, you need first to obtain the required permit at the visitors center.)

The trailhead may be reached from the US 58/US Alternate 58 intersection at Jonesville (about 65.0 miles west of Bristol via US 58). Drive US 58 west for approximately 35.0 miles to the small pullout on the right side of the highway next to a gated park service woods road. As it is not signed at the highway, it may be hard to identify. The easiest way to find it is to drive to the Wilderness Road Campground entrance, turn around to travel east on US 58, turn around at the first opportunity, and you will find the gated woods road about 0.5 mile before the campground entrance.

Walk through the gate, follow a woods road, and come to an intersection at 0.2 mile. The Wilderness Road Campground is to the left; you want to stay to the right, however, and soon you will have to avoid a different woods road that also comes in from the right. Be alert at 0.4 mile! You need to make a sudden turn to the right to stay on the Gibson Gap Trail and use a footbridge

to cross Station Creek, which is lined by jewelweed. Cross a second footbridge at 0.7 mile.

Be alert at 0.8 mile! You must veer left onto the pathway marked as leading to the Ridge Trail and begin to rise, passing by a register box and small magnolia trees. The magnolia's berries turn a bright red in the fall, attracting a variety of migrating birds to feast upon the lipid-rich, energy-providing fruits, which are 30 percent to 60 percent fat. The seeds will likely pass through the birds' bodies and be excreted a distance away from the mother tree—nature's way of ensuring propagation and dispersion.

Walk upon a bit of land between two branches of Station Creek and swing around the headwaters of one branch at 1.2 miles, where sassafras is a large part of the understory. Descend into a narrow, isolated valley, where the only reminder of the 21st century might be the sound of an occasional jet passing thousands of feet overhead. Hemlocks and rhododendrons thrive in the moist soil here.

Cross footbridges at 2.2 miles, 2.7 miles, and 3.1 miles. Rise to cross a spur ridge, leaving behind the drainage system you have been traversing and descending into another one. Come to a T intersection at 3.4 miles, bear left, and begin ascending a series of somewhat steep switchbacks. The trail finally levels out a bit at 4.4 miles when you come to a ridge populated by mountain laurel and star moss. Cross a rhododendron-crowded creek on a footbridge at 4.5 miles and continue to ascend. If you will be spending the night on the mountain, be sure to fill up with water here as there is no readily available source at the campsite.

Swing by large rock formations on the spine of the ridge at 4.8 miles, attain the ridgeline at 5.0 miles, and turn left onto the

Skylight Cave

Ridge Trail at 5.1 miles. Located on sloping ground, the designated Gibson Gap Campsite is to the right of the trail.

The smell of galax permeates the air as you enter a rhododendron tunnel at 5.5 miles. Again, sassafras is abundant. With cliffs and rock formations above you, descend quickly to the lichen-covered Table Rock at 5.9 miles. Actually an interesting marriage of algae and fungus, lichens are one of Earth's most widespread life-forms. With more than 20,000 species, lichens are found from the Arctic to the Tropics, growing at sea level, as well as on the rocks of the highest mountains. When conditions are right, lichens can live for very long periods of time—some in the Arctic are estimated to be more than 4,000 years old—yet, because they obtain all their nutrients directly from the air and rainwater, they are highly susceptible to pollution. Lots of lichens means a healthy environment; fewer of them indicates an area in trouble.

As you follow the ridgeline's undulations, you may well hear the cries of pileated woodpeckers near a small break in the vegetation at 6.5 miles; the area also offers a limited view of the Indian Creek Valley to the east. The tiny white flowers of pokeweed bloom on top of the plant's tall stems from July into September. As the days shorten and cooler temperatures become the norm, the flowers develop into drooping clusters of dark purple berries. Be alert at 8.6 miles! The Ridge Trail continues to the right for 1.7 miles to the Pinnacle parking area, but you should turn left and descend along the Lewis Hollow Trail. Negotiate a set of rock steps and cross a footbridge at 9.0 miles, taking a few steps uphill to explore the Skylight Cave.

As you continue to descend along the Lewis Hollow Trail, stinging nettle may make your legs itch if the trail has not been groomed recently. If you are the first person to pass this way in some time, you may find yourself running into the silk strands of one spider web after another. Because it is so thin, the silk may seem quite fragile, but research has shown that it has a breaking strength greater than steel. Spiders make a variety of silks, each produced from a different gland and with varying purposes, from wrapping prey and lining burrows, to anchoring webs. The arachnids may be the world's original recyclers—they eat the strands of old webs before building new ones.

A trail leading to the Wilderness Road Picnic Area comes in from the left at 9.4 miles; keep right and rise a short distance before resuming the descent. Cross the paved picnic area entrance road at 10.1 miles and continue along the pathway, which is now lined by another plant to avoid: poison ivy. Turn left onto the paved campground road at 10.4 miles, staying left at all intersections and bypassing the Green Leaf Nature Trail.

Be alert! Just after passing the sign for the amphitheater, turn left onto a woods road marked as leading to the Gibson Gap Trail. Turn right at the next intersection, at 10.6 miles, and return to your car at 10.8 miles.

50

Cumberland Mountain

Total distance (one way): 20.6 miles

Hiking time: 11 hours; 2-day backpack

Vertical rise: 2,040 feet

Maps: USGS 7½' Middlesboro; USGS 7½' Varilla; USGS 7½' Middlesboro South; USGS 7½' Ewing; park map

This is it. This is as far west as you can go for an overnight hike and still be in Virginia. You are so far west, in fact, that if you were a couple of hundred miles farther north, you would be on rolling plains about midway between Columbus and Cincinnati, Ohio.

Actually, this journey, which takes in nearly the full length of the Cumberland Gap National Historical Park, runs almost directly on top of the Virginia/Kentucky border, so there are some places where you may have a foot in each state and others where you are definitely in Kentucky. The trail follows a woods road along the crest of Cumberland Mountain, providing access to a multitude of rock outcrops for grandstand views, designated campsites, a reconstructed mountain community, and a walk through an oak-hickory forest populated by white-tailed deer, squirrels, rattlesnakes, and a surprise animal you would not expect to find in the commonwealth.

Despite the fact that the route has only minor ups and downs, use of the trail is rather light; there is a good possibility that you will not see another hiker. Water is very scarce, so be sure to carry plenty with you and fill up whenever the opportunity presents itself.

Because this is not a circuit or round-trip hike, you will need to do a car shuttle. From the US 58/US Alternate 58 intersection at Jonesville (about 65.0 miles west of Bristol via US 58), drive US 58 west for approximately 23.0 miles to Ewing. Turn right onto VA 725, and leave one car next to the

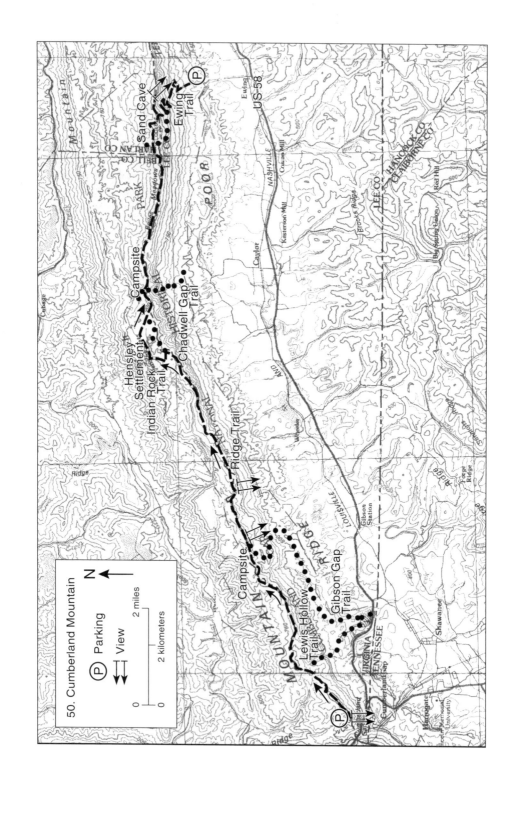

50. Cumberland Mountain

(P) Parking

View

0   2 miles

0   2 kilometers

N

entrance of a local community park in another 0.9 mile.

Return to US 58 and turn right, driving through the Cumberland Mountain Tunnel and into Kentucky in 14.0 more miles. Just about 1.0 mile later, take the exit to the visitors center to obtain the required camping permit. From here, it is a simple matter of driving up the twisting 4.0-mile Pinnacle Road to leave your car in the overlook parking area.

First Day

Total distance: 12.6 miles
Hiking time: 7 hours
Vertical rise: 1,500 feet

Begin the hike by taking the Overlook Trail at the far right end of the parking lot—not the section of the pathway next to the pavilion. The reason you do this is so that you don't miss the superb viewpoint within a few hundred yards that looks onto Fern Lake and Middlesboro, Kentucky, US 58 in Virginia, the small towns of Cumberland Gap, and Harrogate in Tennessee, and the southern portion of Cumberland Mountain stretching to the southwest.

Pass by a Civil War cannon at 0.3 mile; there will be another overlook a short distance to the right at 0.4 mile. Leaving behind the throngs of tourists you may encounter here, gradually rise on the Ridge Trail to a short path on the right at 1.0 mile that would take you to a rock outcrop for the best view yet of the US 25E/US 58 cloverleaf and Harrogate.

Attain a small knob at 1.1 miles and descend into a gap where false Solomon's seal arches over the pathway. The Sugar Run Trail descends to the left into Kentucky at 2.1 miles; stay right and arrive at another intersection only 150 feet later. The Lewis Hollow Trail (see Hike 49) descends to the right and arrives at the Wilderness Road

Campground in 1.1 miles. Stay left on the Ridge Trail and, as you ascend beside false foxglove, be sure to turn around and look back at the Pinnacle. The aptly named Table Rock, covered in lichens, is to your left at 4.7 miles.

The Gibson Gap Trail descends to the right at 5.6 miles. Directly across from it, and located on sloping ground, is the Gibson Gap Campsite. A small outcrop to the right at 8.1 miles provides a view to the east of US 58 winding through Indian Creek Valley. Continue along the small ups and downs, sometimes passing though open areas with ox-eye daisies, other times within the deep shadows of intertwining rhododendron branches. There are so many acorns and hickory nuts scattered upon the ground that you may feel like you are roller skating past the small overhanging rock at 10.1 miles.

Be alert at 10.8 miles! You want to leave the Ridge Trail, turn left, and rise along the Indian Rock Trail at 10.8 miles, passing by some cliffs, a small cave, and two somewhat reliable streams.

Break out into the openness of the Hensley Settlement (potable water available from late spring to early fall) and walk by an outhouse and other buildings. Established by Sherman Hensley in 1904, this isolated mountain community flourished for the first half of the 20th century, reaching a peak population of close to 100 people during the Great Depression. Nearly self-sufficient, members of the settlement obtained what necessities they could not produce by walking or riding horses down the narrow mountain trails to towns in Kentucky. Matching the rest of America's migration from farm to city after World War II, the settlement began to lose its citizens. It was totally abandoned in the 1950s.

The buildings quickly began to deteriorate, but since 1965, the park service has

From the Pinnacle Overlook

restored all of the structures you see today. Work continues so that the houses, barns, fences, and fields of three of the farmsteads will survive the harsh weather they have always faced perched here on the ridgeline of a 3,000-foot-tall mountain. Hopefully, you will meet and strike up a conversation with one of the farmer-interpreters who are employed by the park service and who live here during the usual tourist months, farming the land by using many of the techniques used by the original inhabitants.

Come to an intersection with the blacksmith shop on one corner at 11.4 miles and turn right along the grassy roadway that is bordered by split-rail fences. The Brush Mountain Schoolhouse is to the right at 11.7 miles; be sure to wander around the cemetery on your left to find Sherman Hensley's grave. The first to live on the mountain, he was also the last to leave. Keep to the right at 11.9 miles, but almost immediately swing to the left beside a cabin and reenter the woods (do not make the mistake of staying on what appears to be the main route). Although nothing remains but a sign identifying it, pass by the site of Sherman Hensley's home at 12.1 miles.

Bear left onto the Ridge Trail at 12.2 miles, passing by the Hensley Horse Campsite (with outhouse) at 12.4 miles and arriving at your destination for the night, the Chadwell Gap Campsite, at 12.6 miles. Even in the height of summer, the 3,385-foot elevation of your temporary home should ensure fairly pleasant and cool sleeping temperatures.

Second Day

Total distance: 8.0 miles
Hiking time: 4 hours
Vertical rise: 540 feet
After packing up and leaving no trace of your having been here, continue your jour-

ney along the Ridge Trail, passing by the Martins Fork Campsite trail to the left at 0.4 mile and rising into a forest of rhododendron, hemlock, and ferns. Descend to a low knob at 0.5 mile, on which the Chadwell Gap Trail descends to the right for 2.1 miles to VA 688. Stay to the left, noting how, interestingly, rhododendron is predominant on the hillside above you, yet mountain laurel is the more prominent bush on the downhill side of the trail.

Cross a small water run, which may be dry in summer, at 1.6 miles, and pass by a large leaning and overhanging rock at 2.5 miles. The western terminus of the Ewing Trail (a horse route) comes in from the right at 3.5 miles; stay left on the Ridge Trail, marked as leading to White Rocks.

The trail to the left at 3.7 miles goes to the Sand Cave. Although the round-trip journey of less than a mile is very steep in places, you should consider taking this side trail. With an entrance 75 feet high, the cave is so large that entire congregations used to gather inside it for Sunday morning services. Of particular interest and beauty is the floor of the cave, made up of at least seven different colors of deep sand.

As you continue along the Ridge Trail, a flat stretch of the pathway will take you through Bailes Meadow at 4.1 miles. The large hoofprints you may have been seeing in the dust are not those of some mutant, Godzilla-sized deer, nor from any escaped cattle from the Hensley Settlement; they were made by elk. Right about now you are probably saying, "What? Elk in Virginia?" You bet!

In one of the most successful wildlife restoration projects ever undertaken in the East, several hundred elk were relocated from the western U.S. and released on old surface-mined land in eastern Kentucky in 1997. As with any animal relocation, the

In the Hensley Settlement

mortality rate was high for the first year, but it has since dropped to a rate comparable to their more established western relatives. Spending much of their time on the strip mines' artificially created grasslands, the elk, roaming creatures by nature, move to the shade of deep woodlands in the summertime, and some have now made their way to the forested slopes of the park. There is nothing more thrilling than to be hiking in the fall and hear the bugling call of these magnificent creatures once again echo across the hills and valleys of far southwest Virginia after an absence of more than a century.

For the moment, bypass the eastern terminus of the Ewing Trail coming in from the right at 4.5 miles and continue along the Ridge Trail to the sign for White Rocks. It takes a little bit of scrambling to reach them, but once you are on the large outcrop at 4.75 miles, your can see for many miles. Just in front of you, US 58 makes its final push to the western edge of Virginia, while farther away, the jumbled crests of Forge Ridge, Simmons Ridge, Wallen Ridge, and Powell Mountain rise up to the southern horizon in Tennessee. Soaring upon thermals, turkey vultures may circle just a few feet above your head, giving you a chance to make out the individual feathers at the ends of their large wings. The hike is almost over, so take a break, or maybe even a well-deserved nap, on the sun-warmed rocks.

After loitering as long as possible, retrace your steps, turn left, and descend along the stinging nettle-lined Ewing Trail. The horse trail portion of the Ewing Trail comes in from the right at 5.3 miles; stay left and continue to descend on long switchbacks, going by redbud blossoms in the spring and ox-eye daisies later in the summer.

The trail splits at 7.25 miles; stay to the right as the horse route goes off to the left. Pass by a picnic shelter in a grassy area of Civic Park at 7.8 miles and follow a gravel road to the park's entrance. Your shuttled car sits next to the end of VA 788 at 8.0 miles, ready to whisk you away to your next exploration of the outdoor world. Happy trails.

Index